ISBN 978-1-330-61055-8
PIBN 10082160

This book is a reproduction of an important historical work. Forgotten Books uses state-of-the-art technology to digitally reconstruct the work, preserving the original format whilst repairing imperfections present in the aged copy. In rare cases, an imperfection in the original, such as a blemish or missing page, may be replicated in our edition. We do, however, repair the vast majority of imperfections successfully; any imperfections that remain are intentionally left to preserve the state of such historical works.

1 MONTH OF
FREE
READING

at

www.ForgottenBooks.com

By purchasing this book you are eligible for one month membership to ForgottenBooks.com, giving you unlimited access to our entire collection of over 1,000,000 titles via our web site and mobile apps.

To claim your free month visit:
www.forgottenbooks.com/free82160

English
Français
Deutsche
Italiano
Español
Português

www.forgottenbooks.com

Mythology Photography **Fiction**
Fishing Christianity **Art** Cooking
Essays Buddhism Freemasonry
Medicine **Biology** Music **Ancient**
Egypt Evolution Carpentry Physics
Dance Geology **Mathematics** Fitness
Shakespeare **Folklore** Yoga Marketing
Confidence Immortality Biographies
Poetry **Psychology** Witchcraft
Electronics Chemistry History **Law**
Accounting **Philosophy** Anthropology
Alchemy Drama Quantum Mechanics
Atheism Sexual Health **Ancient History**
Entrepreneurship Languages Sport
Paleontology Needlework Islam
Metaphysics Investment Archaeology
Parenting Statistics Criminology
Motivational

THE BOOK OF EDINBURGH ANECDOTE

BY FRANCIS WATT

T. N. FOULIS
LONDON & EDINBURGH
1912

Published November 1912

Printed by MORRISON & GIBB LIMITED, *Edinburgh*

TO

CHARLES BAXTER, Writer to the Signet

Sienna

In Faithful Memory

of the Old Days and the

Old Friends

THE LIST OF CHAPTERS

THE LIST OF ILLUSTRATIONS

THE LIST OF ILLUSTRATIONS

THE LIST OF ILLUSTRATIONS

CHAPTER ONE
THE PARLIAMENT HOUSE AND THE LAWYERS

CHAPTER ONE
PARLIAMENT HOUSE & LAWYERS

THE PARLIAMENT HOUSE HAS ALWAYS had a reputation for good anecdote. There are solid reasons for this. It is the haunt of men, clever, highly educated, well off, and the majority of them with an all too abundant leisure. The tyranny of custom forces them to pace day after day that ancient hall, remarkable even in Edinburgh for august memories, as their predecessors have done for generations. There are statues such as those of Blair of Avontoun and Forbes of Culloden, and portraits like those of "Bluidy Mackenzie" and Braxfield,—all men who lived and laboured in the precincts,—to recall and revivify the past, while there is also the Athenian desire to hear some new thing, to retail the last good story about Lord this or Sheriff that.

So there is a great mass of material. Let me present some morsels for amusement or edification. Most are stories of judges, though it may be of them before they were judges. A successful counsel usually ends on the bench, and at the Scots bar the exceptions are rare indeed. The two most prominent that occur to one are Sir George Mackenzie and Henry Erskine. Now, Scots law lords at one time invariably, and still frequently, take a title from landed estate. This was natural. A judge was a person with some landed property, which was in early times the only property considered as such, and in Scotland, as everybody knows, the man was called after his estate. Monkbarns of the *Antiquary* is a classic instance, and it was only giving legal confirmation to this, to make the title a fixed one in the case of the judges. They never signed their names this way, and were sometimes sneered at as paper lords. To-day, when the relative value of things is altered, they would probably prefer their paper title. According to tradition their wives laid claim to a corresponding dignity, but James v., the founder of the College of Justice, sternly repelled the presumptuous dames, with a remark out of keeping with his traditional reputation for gallantry. "He had made the carles lords, but wha the deil made the carlines leddies?" Popular custom was kinder than the King, and they got to be called ladies, till a newer fashion deprived them of the honour. It was sometimes awkward. A judge and his wife went furth of Scotland, and the exact relations between Lord A. and Mrs. B. gravelled the wits of many an honest landlord. The gentleman and lady were evidently on the most intimate terms, yet how to explain their different names? Of late the powers that be have intervened in the lady's favour, and she has now her title assured her by royal mandate.

Once or twice the territorial designation bore an ugly purport. Jeffrey kept, it is said, his own name, for Lord Craigcrook would never have done. Craig is Scots for neck, and why should a man name himself a hanging judge to start with? This was perhaps too great a concession to the cheap wits of the Parliament

House, and perhaps it is not true, for in Jeffrey's days territorial titles for paper lords were at a discount, so that Lord Cockburn thought they would never revive, but the same thing is said of a much earlier judge. Fountainhall's *Decisions* is one of those books that every Scots advocate knows in name, and surely no Scots practising advocate knows in fact. Its author, Sir John Lauder, was a highly successful lawyer of the Restoration, and when his time came to go up there was one fly in the ointment of success. His compact little estate in East Lothian was called Woodhead. Lauder feared not unduly the easy sarcasms of fools, or the evil tongues of an evil time. Territorial title he must have, and he rather neatly solved the difficulty by changing Woodhead to Fountainhall, a euphonious name, which the place still retains.

When James VI. and I. came to his great estate in England, he was much impressed by the splendid robes of the English judges. His mighty Lord Chancellor would have told him that such things were but "toys," though even he would have admitted, they influenced the vulgar. At any rate Solomon presently sent word to his old kingdom, that his judges and advocates there were to attire themselves in decent fashion. If you stroll into the Parliament House to-day and view the twin groups of the Inner House, you will say they went one better than their English brothers.

A Scots judge in those times had not seldom a plurality of offices: thus the first Earl of Haddington was both President of the Court of Session and Secretary of State. He played many parts in his time, and he played them all well, for Tam o' the Coogate was nothing if not acute. There are various stories of this old-time statesman. This shows forth the man and the age. A highland chief was at law, and had led his men into the witness-box just as he would have led them to the tented field. The Lord President had taken one of them in hand, and sternly kept him to the point, and so wrung the facts out of him. When Donald escaped he was asked by his fellow-clansman whose turn was to follow, how he had done? With every mark of sincere contrition and remorse, Donald groaned out, that he was afraid he had spoken the truth, and "Oh," he said, "beware of the man with the partridge eye!" How the phrase brings the old judge, alert, keen, searching, before us! By the time of the Restoration things were more specialised, and the lawyers of the day could give more attention to their own subject They were very talented, quite unscrupulous, terribly cruel; Court of Justice and Privy Council alike are as the house of death. We shudder rather than laugh at the anecdotes. Warriston, Dirleton, Mackenzie, Lockhart, the great Stair himself, were remarkable men who at once attract and repel. Nisbet of Dirleton, like Lauder of Fountainhall, took his title from East Lothian—in both cases so tenacious is the legal grip, the properties are still in their families— and Dirleton's *Doubts* are still better known, and are less read, if that be possible, than Fountainhall's *Decisions*. You can even to-day look on Dirleton's big house on the south side of the Canongate, and Dirleton, if not "the pleasantest dwelling in Scotland," is a very delightful place, and within easy reach of the capital. But the original Nisbet was, I fear, a worse rascal than any of his fellows, a treacherous, greedy knave. You might bribe his predecessor to spare blood, it was said, " but Nisbet was always so sore afraid of losing his own great estate, he could never in his own opinion be officious enough to serve his cruel masters." Here is *the* Nisbet story. In July 1668, Mitchell shot at Archbishop Sharp in the High Street, but, missing him, wounded Honeyman, Bishop of Orkney, who sat in the coach beside him. With an almost humorous cynicism some one remarked, it is only a bishop, and the crowd immediately discovered a complete lack of interest in the matter and in the track of the would-be assassin. Not so the Privy Council, which proceeded to a searching inquiry in the course whereof one Gray was examined, but for some time to little purpose. Nisbet as Lord Advocate took an active part, and bethought him of a trick worthy of a private inquiry agent. He pretended to admire a ring on the man's finger, and asked to look at it; the prisoner was only too pleased. Nisbet sent it off by a messenger to Gray's wife with a feigned message from her husband. She stopped not to reflect, but at once told all she knew! this led to further arrests and further examinations during which Nisbet suggested torture as a means of extracting information from some taciturn ladies! Even his colleagues were abashed. " Thow rotten old devil," said Primrose, the Lord Clerk Register, " thow wilt get thyself stabbed some day." Even in friendly talk and counsel these old Scots, you will observe, were given to plain language. Fate was kinder to Dirleton than he deserved, he died in quiet, rich, if not honoured, for his conduct in office was scandalous even for those times, yet his name is not remembered with the especial detestation allotted to that of "the bluidy advocate Mackenzie," really a much higher type of man. Why the unsavoury epithet has stuck so closely to him is a curious caprice of fate or history. Perhaps it is that ponderous tomb in Old Greyfriars, insolently flaunting within a stone-throw of the Martyrs' Monument, perhaps it is that jingle which (you suspect half mythical) Edinburgh callants used to occupy their spare time in shouting in at the keyhole, that made the thing stick. However, the dead-and-gone advocate preserves the stony silence of the tomb, and is still the most baffling and elusive personality in Scots history. The anecdotes of him are not of much account. One tells how the Marquis of Tweeddale, anxious for his opinion, rode over to his country house at Shank at an hour so unconscionably early that Sir George was still abed. The case admitted of no delay, and the Marquis was taken to his room. The matter was stated and the opinion given from behind the curtains, and then a *woman's hand* was stretched forth to receive the fee! The advocate was not the most careful of men, so Lady Mackenzie deemed it advisable to take control of the financial department. Of this dame the gossips hinted too intimate relations with Claverhouse, but there was no open scandal. Another brings us nearer the man. Sir George, by his famous entail act, tied up the whole land of the country in a settlement so strict that various measures through the succeeding centuries only gradually and partially released it. Now the Earl of Bute was the favoured lover of his only daughter, but Macken-

SIR THOMAS HAMILTON, FIRST EARL OF HADDINGTON

From the Portrait at Tynninghame

zie did not approve of the proposed union. The wooer, however ardent, was prudent; he speculated how the estate would go if they made a runaway match of it. Who so fit to advise him as the expert on the law of entail? Having disguised himself—in those old Edinburgh houses the light was never of the clearest—he sought my lord's opinion on a feigned case, which was in truth his own. The opinion was quite plain, and fell pat with his wishes; the marriage was duly celebrated, and Sir George needs must submit. All his professional life Mackenzie was in the front of the battle, he was counsel for one side or the other in every great trial, and not seldom these were marked by most dramatic incidents. When he defended Argyll in 1661 before the Estates, on a charge of treason, the judges were already pondering their verdict when "one who came fast from London knocked most rudely at the Parliament door." He gave his name as Campbell, and produced what he said were important papers. Mackenzie and his fellows possibly thought his testimony might turn the wavering balance in their favour—alas! they were letters from Argyll proving that he had actively supported the Protectorate, and so sealed the fate of the accused. Again, at Baillie of Jerviswood's trial in 1684 one intensely dramatic incident was an account given by the accused with bitter emphasis of a private interview between him and Mackenzie some time before. The advocate was prosecuting with all his usual bluster, but here he was taken completely aback, and stammered out some lame excuse. This did not affect the verdict, however, and Jerviswood went speedily to his death. The most remarkable story about Mackenzie is that after the Estates had declared for the revolutionary cause in April 1689, and his public life was over, ere he fled southward, he spent great part of his last night in Edinburgh in the Greyfriars Churchyard. The meditations among the tombs of the ruined statesmen were, you easily divine, of a very bitter and piercing character. Sir George Lockhart, his great rival at the bar and late Lord President of the Court of Session, had a few days before been buried in the very spot selected by Mackenzie for his own resting-place, where now rises that famous mausoleum. Sir George was shot dead on the afternoon of Sunday 31st March in that year by Chiesly of Dalry in revenge for some judicial decision, apparently a perfectly just one, which he had given against him. Even in that time of excessive violence and passion Chiesly was noted as a man of extreme and ungovernable temper. He made little secret of his intention; he was told the very imagination of it was a sin before God. "Let God and me alone; we have many things to reckon betwixt us, and we will reckon this too." He did the deed as his victim was returning from church; he said he "existed to learn the President to do justice," and received with open satisfaction the news that Lockhart was dead. "He was not used to do things by halves." He was tortured and executed with no delay, his friends removed the body in the darkness of night and buried it at Dalry, so it was rumoured, and the discovery of some remains there a century afterwards was supposed to confirm the story. The house at Dalry was reported to be haunted by the ghost of the murderer; it was the fashion of the time to people every remarkable spot with gruesome phantoms.

An anecdote, complimentary to both, connects the name of Lockhart with that of Sir James Stewart of Goodtrees (pronounced Gutters, Moredun is the modern name), who was Lord Advocate both to William III. and Queen Anne. An imposing figure this, and a man of most adventurous life. In his absence he was sentenced to death by the High Court of Justiciary. This was in 1684. The Lord Advocate (Bluidy Mackenzie to wit), after sentence, electrified the court by shouting out, that the whole family was sailing under false colours, "these forefault Stewarts are damned Macgregors" (the clan name was proscribed). And yet Mackenzie ought to have felt kindly to Stewart, as perhaps he did, and possibly gave him a hint when to make himself scarce. One curious story tells of Mackenzie employing him in London with great success in a debate about the position of the Scots Episcopal Church. Both Lockhart and Mackenzie confessed him their master in the profound intricacies of the Scots law. A W.S. once had to lay a case before Lockhart on some very difficult question. Stewart was in hiding, but the agent tracked him out, and got him to prepare the memorial. Sir George pondered the paper for some time, then he started up and looked the W.S. broad in the face, "by God, if James Stewart is in Scotland or alive, this is his draft ; and why did you not make him solve your difficulty?" The agent muttered that he wanted both opinions. He then showed him what Stewart had prepared; this Lockhart emphatically accepted as the deliverance of the oracle. Stewart had a poor opinion of contemporary lawyers. Show me the man and I'll show you the law, quoth he. Decisions, he said, went by favour and not by right. Stewart made his peace with James's government, near the end, and though he did so without any sacrifice of principle, men nicknamed him Jamie Wilie. It seemed a little odd that through it all he managed to keep his head on his shoulders. A staunch Presbyterian, he was yet for the time a liberal and enlightened jurist, and introduced many important reforms in Scots criminal law. That it fell to him to prosecute Thomas Aikenhead for blasphemy was one of fate's little ironies; Aikenhead went to his death on the 8th January 1697. The Advocate's Close, where Stewart lived, and which is called after him, still reminds us of this learned citizen of old Edinburgh.

In the eighteenth century we are in a different atmosphere; those in high place did not go in constant fear of their life, they were not so savage, so suspicious, so revengful, they were witty and playful. On the other hand, their ways were strangely different from the monotonous propriety of to-day. Kames and Monboddo are prominent instances, they were both literary lawyers and constant rivals. Once Kames asked Monboddo if he had read his last book; the other saw his chance and took it, " No, my lord, you write a great deal faster than I am able to read." Kames presently got *his* chance. Monboddo had in some sense anticipated the Darwinian theory, he was certain at any rate that everybody was born with a tail. He believed that the sisterhood of midwives were pledged to remove it, and it is said he watched many a birth as near as decency permitted but always with disappointing results. At a party he politely invited Kames to enter the room before him. "By no means," said Kames, "go first, my lord, that I may get a look at your tail." Kames had a grin between a sneer and a smile, probably here the sneer predominated. But perhaps it was taken as a compliment. "Mony is as proud of his tail as a squirrel," said Dr. Johnson. He died when eighty-seven. He used to ride to London every year, to the express admiration and delight of George III. One wonders if he ever heard of the tradition that at Strood, in Kent, all children are born with tails—a mediæval jape from the legend of an insult to St. Thomas of Canterbury : he might have found this some support to his theory ! On the bench he was like a stuffed monkey, but for years he sat at the clerks' table. He had a lawsuit about a horse, argued it in person before his colleagues and came hopelessly to grief. You are bound to assume the decision was right, though those old Scots worthies dearly loved a slap at one another, and thus he would not sit with Lord President Dundas again; more likely, being somewhat deaf, he wished to hear better. He was a great classical scholar, and said that no man could write English who did not know Greek, a very palpable hit at Lord Kames, who knew everything but Greek. The suppers he gave at St. John Street, off the Canongate, are still fragrant in the memory, "light and choice, of Attic taste," no doubt; but the basis you believe was Scots, solid and substantial. And they had native dishes worth eating in quaint eighteenth-century Edinburgh ! The grotesque old man had a beautiful daughter, Elizabeth Burnet, whose memory lives for ever in the pathetic lines of Burns. She died of consumption in 1790, and to blunt, if possible, the father's sorrow, his son-in-law covered up her portrait. Monboddo's look sought the place when he entered the room. "Quite right, quite right," he muttered, "and now let us get on with our Herodotus." For that day, perhaps, his beloved Greek failed to charm. Kames was at least like Monboddo in one thing—oddity. On the bench he had "the obstinacy of a mule and the levity of a harlequin," said a counsel; but his broad jokes with his broad dialect found favour in an age when everything was forgiven to pungency. He wrote much on many themes. If you want to know a subject write a book on it, said he, a precept which may be excellent from the author's point of view, but what about the reader?—but who reads him now? Yet it was his to be praised, or, at any rate, criticised. Adam Smith said, we must all acknowledge him as our master. And Pitt and his circle told this same Adam Smith that they were all his scholars. Boswell once urged his merits on Johnson. "We have at least Lord Kames," he ruefully pleaded. The leviathan frame shook with ponderous mirth, "Keep him, ha, ha, ha, we don't envy you him." In far-off Ferney, Voltaire read the *Elements of Criticism*, and was mighty wroth over some cutting remarks on the *Henriade*. He sneered at those rules of taste from the far north "By Lord Mackames, a Justice of the Peace in Scotland." You suspect that "master of scoffing" had spelt name and office right enough had he been so minded. Kames bid farewell to his colleagues in December 1782 with, if the story be right, a quaintly coarse expression. He died eight days after in a worthier frame of mind—he wrote and studied to his last hour. "What," he said, "am I to sit idle with my tongue in my cheek till death comes for me?" He expressed a stern satisfaction that he was not to survive his mental powers, and he wished to be away. He was curious as to the next world, and the tasks that he would have yet to do. There is something heroic about this strange old man.

We come a little later down, and in Braxfield we are in a narrower field, more local, more restricted, purely legal. Such as survive of the Braxfield stories are excellent. The *locus classicus* for the men of that time is Lord Cockburn's *Memorials*. Cockburn, as we have yet to see, was himself a wit of the first water, and the anecdotes lost nothing by the telling. Braxfield was brutal and vernacular. One of "The Fifteen" had rambled on to little purpose, concluding, "Such is my opinion." "*Your* opeenion," was Braxfield's *sotto voce* bitter comment, better and briefer even than the hit of the English judge at his brother, "what he calls his mind." Two noted advocates (Charles Hay, afterwards Lord Newton, was one of them) were pleading before him —they had tarried at the wine cup the previous night, and they showed it. Braxfield gave them but little rope. "Ye may just pack up your papers and gang hame ; the tane o' ye's riftin' punch and the ither belchin' claret" (a quaint and subtle distinction!) "and there'll be nae guid got out o' ye the day." As Lord Justice-Clerk, Braxfield was supreme criminal judge ; his maxims were thoroughgoing. "Hang a thief when he is young, and he'll no' steal when he is auld." He said of the political reformers: "They would a' be muckle the better o' being hangit," which is probably the truer form of his alleged address to a prisoner: "Ye're a vera clever chiel, man, but ye wad be nane the waur o' a hanging." "The mob would be the better for losing a little blood." But his most famous remark, or rather aside, was at the trial of the reformer Gerrald. The prisoner had urged that the Author of Christianity himself was a reformer. "Muckle He made o' that," growled Braxfield, "He was hangit." I suspect this was an after-dinner story, at any rate it is not in the report; but how could it be? It is really a philosophic argument in the form of a blasphemous jest. He had not always his own way with the reformers. He asked Margarot if he wished a counsel to defend him. "No, I only wish an interpreter to make me understand what your Lordship says." The prisoner was convicted and, as Braxfield sentenced him to fourteen years' transportation, he may have reflected, that he had secured the last and most emphatic word. Margarot had defended himself very badly, but as conviction was a practical certainty it made no difference. Of Braxfield's private life there are various stories, which you can accept or not as you please, for such things you cannot prove or disprove. His butler gave him notice, he could not stand Mrs. Macqueen's temper; it was almost playing up to his master. "Man, ye've little to complain o'; ye may be thankfu' ye're no married upon her." As we all know, R. L. Stevenson professedly drew his Weir of Hermiston from this original. One of the stories he tells is how Mrs. Weir praised an incompetent cook for her Christian char-

JOHN CLERK, LORD ELDIN

From a Mezzotint after Sir Henry Raeburn, R. A.

acter, when her husband burst out, " I want Christian broth! Get me a lass that can plain-boil a potato, if she was a whüre off the streets." That story is more in the true Braxfield manner than any of the authentic utterances recorded of the judge himself, but now we look at Braxfield through Stevenson's spectacles. To this strong judge succeeded Sir David Rae, Lord Eskgrove. The anecdotes about him are really farcical. He was grotesque, and though alleged very learned was certainly very silly, but there was something irresistibly comical about his silliness. Bell initiated a careful series of law reports in his time. " He taks doun ma very words," said the judge in well-founded alarm. Here is his exhortation to a female witness: "Lift up your veil, throw off all modesty and look me in the face"; and here his formula in sentencing a prisoner to death: " Whatever your religi–ous persua–sion may be, or even if, as I suppose, you be of no persuasion at all, there are plenty of rever–end gentlemen who will be most happy for to show you the way to yeternal life." Or best of all, in sentencing certain rascals who had broken into Sir James Colquhoun's house at Luss, he elaborately explained their crimes; assault, robbery and hamesucken, of which last he gave them the etymology; and then came this climax—"All this you did; and God preserve us! joost when they were sitten doon to their denner."

The two most remarkable figures at the Scots bar in their own or any time were the Hon. Henry Erskine and John Clerk, afterwards Lord Eldin. Erskine was a consistent whig, and, though twice Lord Advocate, was never raised to the bench; yet he was the leading practising lawyer of his time, and the records of him that remain show him worthy of his reputation. He was Dean of the Faculty of Advocates, but he presided at a public meeting to protest against the war, and on the 12th January 1796 was turned out of office by a considerable majority. A personal friend of Erskine, and supposed to be of his party, yielded to the storm and voted against him. The clock just then struck three. "Ah," murmured John Clerk, in an intense whisper which echoed through the quiet room, "when the cock crew thrice Peter denied his Master." But most Erskine stories are of a lighter touch. When Boswell trotted with Johnson round Edinburgh, they met Erskine. He was too independent to adulate the sage, but before he passed on with a bow, he shoved a shilling into the astonished Boswell's hand, "for a sight of your bear," he whispered. George III. at Windsor once bluntly told him, that his income was small compared with that of his brother, the Lord Chancellor. "Ah, your Majesty," said the wit, "he plays at the guinea table, and I only at the shilling one." In a brief interval of office he succeeded Henry Dundas, afterwards Lord Melville. He told Dundas he was about to order the silk gown. "For all the time you may want it," said the other, "you had better borrow mine." "No doubt," said Harry, "your gown is made to fit any party, but it will never be said of Henry Erskine that he put on the abandoned habits of his predecessor." But he had soon to go, and this time Ilay Campbell, afterwards Lord President, had the post, and again the gown was tossed about in verbal pleasantries. "You must take nothing off it, for I will soon need it again," said the outgoer.

PARLIAMENT HOUSE & LAWYERS

"It will be bare enough, Henry, before you get it," was the neat reply. Rather tall, a handsome man, a powerful voice, a graceful manner, and more than all, a kindly, courteous gentleman, what figure so well known on that ancient Edinburgh street, walking or driving his conspicuous yellow chariot with its black horses? Everybody loved and praised Harry Erskine, friends and foes, rich and poor alike. You remember Burns's tribute: "Collected, Harry stood awee." Even the bench listened with delight. "I shall be brief, my Lords," he once began. "Hoots, man, Harry, dinna be brief—dinna be brief," said an all too complacent senator—a compliment surely unique in the annals of legal oratory. And if this be unique, almost as rare was the tribute of a humble nobody to his generous courage. "There's no a puir man in a' Scotland need to want a friend or fear an enemy, sae long as Harry Erskine's to the fore." Not every judge was well disposed to the genial advocate. Commissary Balfour was a pompous official who spoke always *ore rotundo*: he had occasion to examine Erskine one day in his court, he did so with more than his usual verbosity. Erskine in his answers parodied the style of the questions to the great amusement of the audience; the commissary was beside himself with anger. "The intimacy of the friend," he thundered, "must yield to the severity of the judge. Macer, forthwith conduct Mr. Erskine to the Tolbooth." "Hoots! Mr. Balfour," was the crushing retort of the macer. On another occasion the same judge said with great pomposity that he had tripped over a stile on his brother's property and hurt himself. "Had it been your own style," said

19

Erskine, "you certainly would have broken your neck."

Alas! Harry was an incorrigible punster. When urged that it was the lowest form of wit, he had the ready retort that therefore it must be the foundation of all other kinds. Yet, frankly, some of those puns are atrocious, and even a century's keeping in Kay and other records has not made them passable. Gross and palpable, they were yet too subtle for one senator. Lord Balmuto, or tradition does him wrong, received them with perplexed air and forthwith took them to *Avizandum*. Hours, or as some aver, days after, a broad smile relieved those heavy features. " I hae ye noo, Harry, I hae ye noo," he gleefully shouted ; he had seen the joke! All were not so dull. A friend pretended to be in fits of laughter. "Only one of your jokes, Harry," he said. "Where did you get it ?" said the wit. "Oh, I have just bought 'The New Complete Jester, or every man his own Harry Erskine.'" The other looked grave. He felt that pleasantries of the place or the moment might not wear well in print. They don't, and I refrain for the present from further record. When Lord President Blair died suddenly on 27th November 1811, a meeting of the Faculty of Advocates was hastily called. Blair was an ideal judge, learned, patient, dignified, courteous. He is the subject of one of those wonderful Raeburn portraits (it hangs in the library of the Writers to the Signet), and as you gaze you understand how those who knew him felt when they heard that he was gone for ever. Erskine, as Dean, rose to propose a resolution, but for once the eloquent tongue was mute : after some broken sentences he sat down, but his hearers understood and judged it "as good a speech as he ever made." It was his last. He was neither made Lord President nor Lord Justice-Clerk, though both offices were open. He did not murmur or show ill-feeling, but withdrew to the little estate of Almondell, where he spent six happy and contented years ere the end.

Clerk was another type of man. In his last years Carlyle, then in his early career, noted that "grim strong countenance, with its black, far projecting brows." He fought his way slowly into fame. His father had half humorously complained, " I remember the time when people seeing John limping on the street were told, that's the son of Clerk of Eldin; but now I hear them saying, 'What auld grey-headed man is that?' and the answer is, 'That is the father of John Clerk.'" He was a plain man, badly dressed, with a lame leg. "There goes Johnny Clerk, the lame lawyer." "No, madam," said Clerk, "the lame *man*, not the lame *lawyer*." Cockburn says that he gave his client his temper, his perspiration, his nights, his reason, his whole body and soul, and very often the whole fee to boot. He was known for his incessant quarrels with the bench, and yet his practice was enormous. He lavished his fees on anything from bric-à-brac to charity, and died almost a poor man. In consultation at Picardy Place he sat in a room crowded with curiosities, himself the oddest figure of all, his lame foot resting on a stool, a huge cat perched at ease on his shoulder. When the oracle spoke, it was in a few weighty Scots words, that went right to the root of the matter, and admitted neither continuation

nor reply. His Scots was the powerful direct Scots
of the able, highly-educated man, a speech faded
now from human memory. Perhaps Clerk was *prin-
ceps* but not *facile*, for there was Braxfield to reckon
with. On one famous occasion, to wit, the trial of Deacon Brodie, they went at it, hammer and tongs, and
Clerk more than held his own, though Braxfield as
usual got the verdict. They took Clerk to the bench
as Lord Eldin, when he was sixty-five, which is not
very old for a judge. But perhaps he was worn out
by his life of incessant strife, or perhaps he had not
the judicial temperament. At any rate his record is as
an advocate, and not as a senator. He had also some
renown as a toper. There is a ridiculous story of his
inquiring early one morning, as he staggered along
the street, "Where is John Clerk's house?" of a servant girl, a-"cawming" her doorstep betimes. "Why,
you're John Clerk," said the astonished lass. "Yes, yes,
but it's his house I want," was the strange answer. I
have neither space nor inclination to repeat well-
known stories of judicial topers. How this one was
seen by his friend coming from his house at what seemed an early hour. "Done with dinner already?" queried the one. "Ay, but we sat down yesterday," retorted the other. How this luminary awakened in a
cellar among bags of soot, and that other in the guard-
house; how this set drank the whole night, claret, it
is true, and sat bravely on the bench the whole of
next day; how most could not leave the bottle alone
even there; and biscuits and wine as regularly attended the judges on the bench as did their clerks and
macers. The pick of this form is Lord Hermand's

reply to the exculpatory plea of intoxication: "Good Gad, my Laards, if he did this when he was drunk, what would he not do when he's sober?" but imagination boggles at it all, and I pass to a more decorous generation.

The names of two distinguished men serve to bridge the two periods. The early days of Jeffrey and Cockburn have a delightful flavour of old Edinburgh. The last years are within living memory. Jeffrey's accent was peculiar. It was rather the mode in old Edinburgh to despise the south, the last kick, as it were, at the "auld enemy"; Jeffrey declared, "The only part of a Scotsman I mean to abandon is the language, and language is all I expect to learn in England." The authorities affirm his linguistic experience unfortunate. Lord Holland said that "though he had lost the broad Scots at Oxford, he had only gained the narrow English." Braxfield put it briefer and stronger. "He had clean tint his Scots, and found nae English." Thus his accent was emphatically his own; he spoke with great rapidity, with great distinctness. In an action for libel, the object of his rhetoric was in perplexed astonishment at the endless flow of vituperation. "He has spoken the whole English language thrice over in two hours." This eloquence was inconvenient in a judge. He forgot Bacon's rule against anticipating counsel. Lord Moncreiff wittily said of him, that the usual introductory phrase "the Lord Ordinary having heard parties' procurators" ought to be, in his judgment, "parties' procurators having heard the Lord Ordinary." Jeffrey, on the other hand, called Moncreiff "the whole duty of man," from his conscientious zeal. All the same, Jeffrey was an able and useful judge, though his renown is greater as advocate and editor. Even he, though justly considerate, did not quite free himself from the traditions of his youth. He "kept a prisoner waiting twenty minutes after the jury returned from the consideration of their verdict, whilst he and a lady who had been accommodated with a seat on the bench discussed together a glass of sherry." Cockburn, his friend and biographer, the keenest of wits, and a patron of progress, stuck to the accent. "When I was a boy no Englishman could have addressed the Edinburgh populace without making them stare and probably laugh; we looked upon an English boy at the High School as a ludicrous and incomprehensible monster:" and then he goes on to say that Burns is already a sealed book, and he would have it taught in the school as a classic. " In losing it we lose ourselves," says the old judge emphatically. He writes this in 1844, nearly seventy years ago. We do not teach the only Robin in the school. Looked at from the dead-level of to-day his time seems picturesque and romantic : were he to come here again he would have some very pointed utterances for us and our ways, for he was given to pointed sayings. For instance, "Edinburgh is as quiet as the grave, or even Peebles." A tedious counsel had bored him out of all reason. " He has taken up far too much of your Lordship's time," sympathised a friend. "Time," said Cockburn with bitter emphasis, "Time! long ago he has exhaustit *Time*, and has encrotch'd upon—Eternity." A touch of Scots adds force to such remarks. This is a good example.

PARLIAMENT HOUSE & LAWYERS

One day the judge, whilst rummaging in an old book shop, discovered some penny treasure, but he found himself without the penny! He looked up and there was the clerk of court staring at him through the window. "Lend me a bawbee," he screamed eagerly. He got the loan, and in the midst of a judgment of the full court he recollected his debt; he scrambled across the intervening senators, and pushed the coin over: "There's your bawbee, Maister M., with many thanks."

At one time the possession of the correct "burr" was a positive hold on the nation. Lord Melville, the friend and colleague of Pitt, ruled Scotland under what was called the Dundas despotism for thirty years. He filled all the places from his own side, for such is the method of party government, and he can scarce be blamed, yet his rule was protracted and endured, because he had something more than brute force behind him. For one thing, he spoke a broad dialect, and so came home to the very hearts of his countrymen. When he visited Scotland he went climbing the interminable High Street stairs, visiting poor old ladies that he had known in the days of his youth. Those returns of famous Scotsmen have furnished a host of anecdotes. I will only give one for its dramatic contrasts. Wedderburn was not thought a tender-hearted or high-principled man, yet when he returned old, ill and famous he was carried in a sedan chair to a dingy nook in old Edinburgh, the haunt of early years, and there he picked out some holes in the paved court that he had used in his childish sports, and was moved well-nigh to tears. He first left Edinburgh in quite a different mood. He began as a Scots advocate, and one day was reproved by Lockhart (afterwards Lord Covington), the leader of the bar, for some pert remark. A terrible row ensued, at which the President confessed "he felt his flesh creep on his bones." It was Wedderburn's *Sturm und Drang* period. He had all the presumption of eager and gifted youth, he tore the gown from his back declaring he would never wear it again in that court. We know that he was presently off by the mail coach for London, where he began to climb, climb, climb, till he became the first Scots Lord High Chancellor of Great Britain.

And now a word as to modern times. One or two names call for notice. A. S. Logan, Sheriff Logan, as he was popularly called, died early in 1862, and with him, it was said, disappeared the only man able in wit and laughter to rival the giants of an earlier epoch. He still remains the centre of a mass of anecdote, much of it apocryphal. His enemies sneered at him as a laboured wit, and averred a single joke cost him a solitary walk round the Queen's Drive. Once when pleading for a widow he spoke eloquently of the cruelty of the relative whom she was suing. The judge suggested a compromise. "Feel the pulse of the other side, Mr. Logan," said he, humorously. "Oh, my Lord," was the answer, "there can be no pulse where there is no heart." This seems to me an example of the best form of legal witticism, it is an argument conveyed as a jest. Of his contemporary Robert Thomson (1790–1857), Sheriff of Caithness, there are some droll memories. Here is one. He was a constant though a bad rider, and as a bad rider will, he fell from his horse. Even in falling practice makes perfect. The worthy sheriff did not fall on his head —very much the opposite, in fact. As he remained sitting on the ground, a witness of the scene asked if he had sustained any injury. " Injury !" was the answer; "no injury at all I assure you! Indeed, sir, quite the reverse, quite the reverse." Inglis, like Blair, impressed his contemporaries as a great judge; how far the reputation will subsist one need not discuss, nor need we complain that the stories about him are rather tame. This may be given. Once he ridiculed with evident sincerity the argument of an opposite counsel, when that one retorted by producing an opinion which Inglis had written in that very case, and which the other had in fact paraphrased. Inglis looked at it. " I see, my lord, that this opinion is dated from Blair Athol, and anybody that chooses to follow me to Blair Athol for an opinion deserves what he gets." The moral apparently is, don't disturb a lawyer in his vacation, when he is away from his books and is " off the fang," as the Scots phrase has it. But this is a confession of weakness, and is only passable as a way of escaping from a rather awkward position. In the same case counsel proceeded to read a letter, and probably had not the presence of mind to stop where he ought. It was from the country to the town agent, and discussed the merits of various pleaders with the utmost frankness, and then, "You may get old——for half the money, but for God's sake don't take him at any price." In a limited society like the Parliament House, such a letter has an effect like the bursting of a bombshell, and I note the incident, though the humour be accidental. This other has a truer tang of the place. No prisoner goes undefended at the High Court; young counsel perform the duty without fee or reward. The system has called forth the admiration of the greedier Southern, though an English judge has declared that the worst service you can do your criminal is to assign him an inexperienced counsel. One Scots convict, at least, agreed. He had been accused and thus defended and convicted. As he was being removed, he shook his fist in the face of his advocate: " Its a' through you, you d—d ass." The epithet was never forgotten. The unfortunate orator was known ever afterwards as the " d—d ass." Sir George Deas was the last judge who talked anything like broad Scots on the bench. Once he and Inglis took different sides on a point of law which was being argued before them. Counsel urged that Inglis's opinion was contrary to a previous decision of his own. " I did not mean," said the President, " that the words should be taken in the sense in which you are now taking them." " Ah," said Lord Deas, " your lordship sails vera near the wind there." This is quite in the early manner; Kames might have said it to Monboddo.

CHAPTER TWO
THE CHURCH

CHAPTER TWO   THE CHURCH

THERE ARE MANY PICTURESQUE INCID-
ents in the history of the old Scots Church in Edinburgh; chief of them are the legends that cling round
the memory of St. Margaret. Her husband, Malcolm
Canmore, could not himself read, but he took up the
pious missals in which his wife delighted and kissed
them in a passion of homage and devotion. There
is the dramatic account of her last days, when the
news was brought her of the defeat and death of her
husband and son at Alnwick, and she expired hold-
ing the black rood of Scotland in her hand, whilst the
wild yells of Donald Bane's kerns rent the air, as they
pressed round the castle to destroy her and hers. Then
follows the story of the removal of her body to Dun-
fermline in that miraculous mist in which modern
criticism has seen nothing but an easterly haar. Then
we have her son King David's hunting in wild Drum-
sheugh forest on Holy-rood day, and the beast that
nearly killed him, his miraculous preservation, and the
legend of the foundation of Holyrood. In the dim
centuries that slipped away there was much else of
quaint and homely and amusing and interesting in
mediæval church life in Edinburgh, but the monkish
chroniclers never thought it worth the telling, and it
has long vanished beyond recall. This one story is a
gem of its kind. Scott, who never allowed such fruit
to go ungathered, has made it well known. It is one
of the incidents in the fight between the Douglases
and the Hamiltons at Edinburgh on 30th April 1520,
known to all time as *Cleanse the Causeway*, because the
Hamiltons were swept from the streets. Beaton, Arch-

31

bishop of Glasgow, was a supporter of Arran and the Hamiltons, who proposed to attack the Douglases and seize Angus, their leader. Angus sent his uncle, Gawin Douglas, Bishop of Dunkeld, whose "meek and thoughtful eye" Scott has commemorated in one of his best known lines, to remonstrate with his fellow-prelate. He found him sitting in episcopal state, and who was to tell that this was but the husk of a coat of mail? His words were honied, but Gawin let it be seen that he was far from convinced; whereat the other in a fit of righteous indignation protested on his conscience that he was innocent of evil intent, and for emphasis he lustily smote his reverend breast, too lustily, alas! for the armour rang under the blow. "I perceive, my lord, your conscience clatters," was Gawin's quick comment, to appreciate which you must remember that "clatter" signifies in Scots to tell tales as well as to rattle. Old Scotland was chary of its speech, being given rather to deeds than words, but it had a few like gems. Was it not another Douglas who said that he loved better to hear the lark sing than the mouse cheep? Or one might quote that delightful "I'll mak' siccar" of Kirkpatrick in the matter of the slaughter of the Red Comyn at Dumfries in 1306; but this is a little away from our subject.

At the Reformation, for good or for ill, the womb of time brought forth a form of faith distinctively Scots. Here, at any rate, we have Knox's *History of the Reformation of Religion within the Realme of Scotland* to borrow from. It is usually the writer, not the reader, who consults such books, yet Knox was a master of the picturesque and the graphic. He was great in scornful humour; now and again he has almost a Rabelaisian touch. Take, for instance, his account of the riot on St. Giles' Day, the 1st September 1558. For centuries an image of St. Giles was carried through the streets of Edinburgh and adored by succeeding generations of the faithful, but when the fierce Edinburgh mob had the vigour of the new faith to direct and stimulate their old-time recklessness, trouble speedily ensued. The huge idol was raped from the hands of its keepers and ducked in the Nor' Loch. This was a punishment peculiarly reserved for evil livers, and the crowd found a bitter pleasure in the insult. Then there was a bonfire in the High Street in which the great image vanished for ever amid a general saturnalia of good and evil passions.

The old church fell swiftly and surely, but some stubborn Scots were also on that side, and Mary of Guise, widow of James V. and Queen Regent, was a foe to be reckoned with. She had the preachers up before her (Knox reproduces her broken Scots with quite comic effect), but nothing came of the matter. The procession did not cease at once with the destruction of the image. In 1558 a " marmouset idole was borrowed fra the Greyfreires," so Knox tells us, and he adds with a genuine satirical touch, "A silver peise of James Carmichaell was laid in pledge"—evidently the priests could not trust one another, so he suggests. The image was nailed down upon a litter and the procession began. " Thare assembled Preastis, Freeris, Chamonis and rottin Papistes with tabornes and trumpettis, banneris, and bage-pypes, and who was thare to led the ring but the Queen Regent hir self with all hir schavelings for honor of that feast." The thing went orderly enough as long as Mary was present, but she had an appointment to dinner, in a burgher's house betwixt " the Bowes," and when she left the fun began. Shouts of " Down with the idol! Down with it!" rent the air, and down it went. "Some brag maid the Preastis patrons at the first, but when thei saw the febilness of thare god (for one took him by the heillis, and dadding his head to the calsey, left Dagon without head or hands, and said: ' Fie upon thee, thow young Sanct Geile, thy father wold haif taryad four such ') this considered (we say) the Preastis and Freiris fled faster than thei did at Pynckey Clewcht. Thare might have bein sein so suddane a fray as seildome has been sein amonges that sorte of men within this realme, for down goes the croses, of goes the surpleise, round cappes cornar with the crounes. The Gray Freiris gapped, the Black Freiris blew, the Preastis panted and fled, and happy was he that first gate the house, for such ane suddan fray came never amonges the generation of Antichrist within this realme befoir. By chance thare lay upoun a stare a meary Englissman, and seeing the discomfiture to be without blood, thought he wold add some meary-nes to the mater, and so cryed he ower a stayr and said : ' Fy upoun you, hoorsones, why have ye brokin ordour? Down the street ye passed in array and with great myrthe, why flie ye, vilanes, now without ordour? Turne and stryk everie one a strok for the honour of his God. Fy, cowardis, fy, ye shall never be judged worthy of your wages agane!' But exhortations war then unprofitable, for after that Bell had brokin his neck thare was no comfort to his confused army." I pass over Knox's interviews with Mary, well known and for ever memorable, for they express the collision of the deepest passions of human nature set in romantic and exciting surroundings; but one little incident is here within my scope. It was the fourth interview, when Mary fairly broke down. She wept so that Knox, with what seems to us at any rate ungenerous and cruel glee, notes, "skarslie could Marnock, hir secreat chalmerboy gett neapkynes to hold hys eyes dry for the tearis: and the owling besydes womanlie weaping, stayed hir speiche." Then he is bidden to withdraw to the outer chamber and wait her Majesty's pleasure. No one will speak to him, except the Lord Ochiltree, and he is there an hour. The Queen's Maries and the other court ladies are sitting in all their gorgeous apparel talking, laughing, singing, flirting, what not? and all at once a strange stern figure, the representative of everything that was new and hostile, addresses them, nay, unbends as he does so, for he merrily said: "O fayre Ladyes, how pleasing war this lyeff of youris yf it should ever abyd, and then in the end that we myght passe to heavin with all this gay gear. But fye upoun that knave Death, that will come whither we will or not! And when he hes laid on his ariest, the foull worms wil be busye with this flesche, be it never so fayr and so tender; and the seally soull, I fear, shal be so feable that it can neather cary with it gold, garnassing, targatting, pearle, nor pretious stanes."

Were they awed, frightened, angry, scornful, contemptuous? Who can tell? Knox takes care that no-body has the say but himself. You may believe him honest—but impartial! We have no account on the other side. Mary did not write memoirs; if she had, it is just possible that Knox had therein occupied the smallest possible place, and the beautiful Queen's Maries vanished even as smoke. There *were* writers on the other side, but they mostly invented or retailed stupid vulgar calumnies. We have one picture by Nicol Burne—not without point—of Knox and his second wife, Margaret Stuart, the daughter of Lord Ochiltree and of the royal blood, whom he married when he was sixty and she was sixteen. It tells how he went a-wooing "with ane great court on ane trim geld-ing nocht lyke ane prophet or ane auld decrepit priest as he was, bot lyke as he had bene ane of the blud royal with his bendis of taffetie feschnit with golden ringis and precious stanes."

All that Knox did was characteristic. This, how-ever, is amusing. On Sunday 19th August 1565, a month after his marriage to Mary, Darnley attended church at St. Giles'. Knox was, as usual, the preacher. He made pointed references to Ahab and Jezebel, and indulged in a piquant commentary upon pass-ing events. The situation must have had in it, for him, something fascinating. There was the unwilling and enraged Darnley, and the excited and gratified congregation. Knox improved the occasion to the very utmost. He preached an hour beyond the or-dinary time. Perhaps that additional hour was his chief offence in Darnley's eyes. He " was so moved at this sermon and being troubled with great fury he

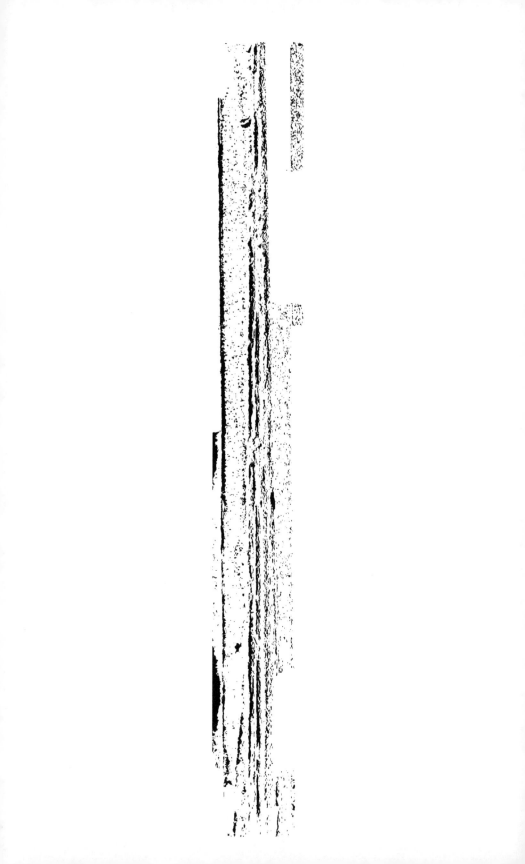

THE CHURCH IN EDINBURGH

passed in the afternoon to the Hawking." You excuse the poor foolish boy!

I hurry over the other picturesque incidents of the man and the time; the last sermon with a voice that once shook the mighty church, now scarce heard in the immediate circle; the moving account of his last days; the elegy of Morton, or the brief epitaph that Morton set over his grave. He was scarce in accord even with his own age; his best schemes were sneered at as devout imagination. Secretary Maitland's was the one tongue whose pungent speech he could never tolerate or forgive, and he had voiced with bitter irony the reply of the nobles to Knox's demand for material help for the church. "We mon now forget our selfis and beir the barrow to buyld the housses of God." And yet he never lost heart. In 1559, when the affairs of the congregation were at a low ebb, he spoke words of courage and conviction. "Yea, whatsoever shall become of us and of our mortall carcasses, I dowt not but that this caus (in dyspyte of Sathan) shall prevail in the realme of Scotland. For as it is the eternall trewth of the eternall God, so shall it ones prevaill howsoever for a time it be impugned." And so the strong, resolute man vanishes from the stage of time, a figure as important, interesting, and fateful as that of Mary herself.

I pass to the annals of the Covenant. It was signed on 1st March 1638, in the Greyfriars Church. It is said, though this has been questioned, that when the building could not hold the multitude, copies were laid on two flat gravestones which are shown you today, and all ranks and ages pressed round in the fervour of excitement; many added "till death" after their names, others drew blood from their bodies wherewith to fill their pens. The place was assuredly not chosen with a view to effect, yet the theatre had a fitness which often marks the sacred spots of Scots history. The graveyard was the resting-place of the most famous of their ancestors; the Castle, the great centrepiece of the national annals, rose in their view. The aged Earl of Sutherland signed first, Henderson prayed, the Earl of Loudoun spoke to his fellow-countrymen, and Johnston of Warriston read the scroll, which he had done so much to frame. Endless sufferings were in store for those who adhered to the national cause. After Bothwell Brig in 1679 a number were confined in the south-west corner of the churchyard in the open air in the rigour of the Scots climate, and just below in the Grassmarket a long succession of sufferers glorified God in the mocking words of their oppressors. Strange, gloomy figures those Covenanters appear to us, with their narrow views and narrow creeds, lives lived under the shadow of the gibbet and the scaffold: yet who would deny them the virtues of perfect courage and unalterable determination? Let me gather one or two anecdotes that still, as a garland, encircle "famous Guthrie's head," as it is phrased on the Martyrs' Monument. He journeyed to Edinburgh to subscribe the Covenant, encountering the hangman as he was entering in at the West Port; he accepted the omen as a clear intimation of his fate if he signed. And then he went and signed! He was tried before the Scots Parliament for treason. By an odd accident he had "Bluidy Mackenzie" as one of his defending counsel.

38

THE CHURCH IN EDINBURGH

These admired his skill and law, and at the end seemed more disturbed at the inevitable result than did the condemned man himself. He suffered on the 1st June 1661 at the Cross. One lighter touch strikes a strange gleam of humour. His physicians had forbidden him to eat cheese, but at his last meal he freely partook of it. " The Doctors may allow me a little cheese this night, for I think there is no fear of the gravel now," he said with grim cynicism. He spoke for an hour to a surely attentive audience. These were the early days of the persecution; a few years later and the drums had drowned his voice. At the last moment he caused the face cloth to be lifted that he might with his very last breath declare his adherence to the Covenants: the loving nickname of Siccarfoot given him by his own party was well deserved! His head was stuck on the Netherbow, his body was carried into St. Giles', where it was dressed for the grave by some Presbyterian ladies who dipped their handkerchiefs in his blood. One of the other side condemned this as a piece of superstition and idolatry of the Romish church. "No," said one of them, " but to hold up the bloody napkin to heaven in their addresses that the Lord might remember the innocent blood that was spilt." So Wodrow tells the story, and he goes on:" In the time that the body was a-dressing there came in a pleasant young gentleman and poured out a bottle of rich oyntment on the body, which filled the whole church with a noble perfume. One of the ladys says, ' God bless you, sir, for this labour of love which you have shown to the slain body of a servant of Jesus Christ.' He, without speaking to any, giving them a bow, removed, not loving to be discovered." A strange legend presently went the round of Edinburgh and was accepted as certain fact by the true-blue party. Commissioner the Earl of Middleton, an old enemy of Guthrie's, presided at his trial. Afterwards, as his coach was passing under the Netherbow arch some drops of blood from the severed head fell on the vehicle. All the art of man could not wash them out, and a new leather covering had to be provided. Guthrie left a little son who ran with his fellows about the streets of Edinburgh. He would often come back and tell his mother that he had been looking at his father's head. This last may seem a very trivial anecdote, but to me, at least, it always brings home with a certain direct force the horrors of the time. The years rolled on and brought the Revolution of 1688. A divinity student called Hamilton took down the head and gave it decent burial.

Richard Cameron fell desperately fighting on the 20th July 1680 at Airds Moss, a desolate place near Auchinleck. Bruce of Earlshall marched to Edinburgh with Cameron's head and hands in a sack, while the prisoners who were taken alive were also brought there. At Edinburgh the limbs were put upon a halbert, and carried to the Council. I must let Patrick Walker tell the rest of the story. "Robert Murray said, 'There's the Head and Hands that lived praying and preaching and died praying and fighting.' The Council ordered the Hangman to fix them upon the Netherbow Port. Mr. Cameron's father being in the Tolbooth of Edinburgh for his Principles, they carried them to him to add Grief to his Sorrow and enquired if he knew them. He took his son's Head and

SIR ARCHIBALD JOHNSTON, LORD WARRISTON

From a Painting bv George Jamesone

Hands and kissed them. 'They are my Son's, my dear Son's,' and said: 'It is the Lord, good is the Will of the Lord who cannot wrong me nor mine, but has made Goodness and Mercy to follow us all our Days.' Mr. Cameron's Head was fixed upon the Port and his Hands close by his Head with his Fingers upward."

Of Sir Archibald Johnston of Warriston, Bishop Gilbert Burnet, his relative, says: "Presbytery was to him more than all the world." At the Restoration he knew his case was hopeless and effected his escape to France, but was brought back and suffered at the Cross. You would fancy life was so risky and exciting in those days that study and meditation were out of the question, but, on the contrary, Warriston was a great student (it was an age of ponderous folios and spiritual reflection), could seldom sleep above three hours out of the twenty-four, knew a great deal of Scots Law, and many other things besides; and with it all he and his fellows—Stewart of Goodtrees, for instance—spent untold hours in meditation. Once he went to the fields or his garden in the Sheens (now Sciennes) to spend a short time in prayer. He so remained from six in the morning till six or eight at night, when he was awakened, as it were, by the bells of the not distant city. He thought they were the eight hours bells in the morning; in fact, they were those of the evening.

Another class of stories deals with the stormy lives and unfortunate ends of the persecutors, and there is no name among those more prominent than that of the Archbishop of St. Andrews, him whom Presbyterian Scotland held in horror as Sharp, the Judas, the Apostate. Years before his life closed at Magus Muir he went in continual danger; he was believed to be in direct league with the devil. Once he accused a certain Janet Douglas before the Privy Council of sorcery and witchcraft, and suggested that she should be packed off to the King's plantations in the West Indies. "My Lord," said Janet, "who was you with in your closet on Saturday night last betwixt twelve and one o'clock?" The councillors pricked up their ears in delighted anticipation of a peculiarly piquant piece of scandal about a Reverend Father in God. Sharp turned all colours and put the question by. The Duke of Rothes called Janet aside and, by promise of pardon and safety, unloosed Janet's probably not very reluctant lips. "My lord, it was the muckle black Devil."

Here is a strange episode of this troubled time. Patrick Walker in his record of the life and death of Mr. Donald Cargill tells of a sect called the sweet singers, "from their frequently meeting together and singing those tearful Psalms over the mournful case of the Church." To many of the persecuted it seemed incredible that heaven should not declare in some terrible manner vengeance on a community that was guilty of the blood of the Saints, and as this little band sang and mused it seemed ever clearer to them that the fate of Sodom and Gomorrah must fall on the wicked city of Edinburgh. They needs must flee from the wrath to come, and so with one accord "they left their Houses, warm soft Beds, covered Tables, some of them their Husbands and Children weeping upon them to stay with them, some women taking the sucking Children in their arms" (to leave *these* behind were a counsel of perfection too high even for a saint!) "to

THE CHURCH IN EDINBURGH

Desert places to be free of all Snares and Sins and communion with others and mourn for their own sins, the Land's Tyranny and Defections, and there be safe from the Land's utter ruin and Desolations by Judgments. Some of them going to Pentland hills with a Resolution to sit there to see the smoke and utter ruin of the sinful, bloody City of Edinburgh." The heavens made no sign; Edinburgh remained unconsumed. A troop of dragoons were sent to seize the sweet singers; the men were put in the Canongate Tolbooth, the women into the House of Correction where they were soundly scourged. Their zeal thus being quenched they were allowed to depart one by one, the matter settled. And so let us pass on to a less tragic and heroic, a more peaceful and prosaic time.

After the revolution reaction almost inevitably set in. Religious zeal—fanaticism if you will—died rapidly down, and there came in Edinburgh, of all places, the reign of the moderates, or as we should now say, broad churchmen, learned, witty, not zealous or passionate, "the just and tranquil age of Dr. Robertson." Principal William Robertson was a type of his class. We come across him in the University, for he was Principal, and we meet him again as man of letters, for the currents of our narrative are of necessity cross-currents. Here the Robertson anecdotes are trivial. Young Cullen, son of the famous doctor, was the bane of the Principal's life; he was an excellent mimic, could not merely imitate the reverend figure but could follow exactly his train of thought. In 1765, some debate or other occupied Robertson in the General Assembly; Cullen mimicked the doctor in a few remarks on the

43

occasion to some assembled wits. Presently in walks the Principal and makes the very speech, a little astonished at the unaccountable hilarity which presently prevailed. Soon the orator smelt a rat. "I perceive somebody has been ploughing with my heifer before I came in," so he rather neatly turned the matter off. Certain young Englishmen of good family were boarded with Robertson: one of them lay in bed recovering from a youthful escapade, when a familiar step approached, for that too could be imitated, and a familiar voice read the erring youth a solemn lecture on the iniquities of his walk, talk, and conversation. He promised amendment and addressed himself again to rest, when again the step approached. Again the reproving voice was heard. He pulled aside the curtain and protested that it was too bad to have the whole thing twice over—it was Robertson this time, however, and not Cullen. The Principal once went to the father of this remarkable young man for medical advice. He was duly prescribed for, and as he was leaving the doctor remarked that he had just been giving the same advice for the same complaint to his own son. "What," said Robertson, "has the young rascal been imitating me here again?" The young rascal lived to sit on the bench as Lord Cullen, a grave and courteous but not particularly distinguished senator. The Principal was also minister of Old Greyfriars'. His colleague here was Dr. John Erskine. The evangelical school was not by any means dead in Scotland, and Erskine, a man of good family and connections, was a devoted adherent. It is pleasant to think that strong bonds of friendship united the colleagues whose habits of thought were so different. You remember the charming account of Erskine in *Guy Mannering* where the colonel goes to hear him preach one Sunday. He was noted for extraordinary absence of mind. Once he knocked up against a cow in the meadows; in a moment his hat was off his head and he humbly begged the lady's pardon. The next she he came across was his own wife, "Get off, you brute!" was the result of a conceivable but ludicrous confusion of thought. His spouse observed that he invariably returned from church without his handkerchief; she suspected one of the old women who sat on the pulpit stairs that they might hear better, or from the oddity of the thing, or from some other reason, and the handkerchief was firmly sewed on. As the doctor mounted the stairs he felt a tug at his pocket. "No the day, honest woman, no the day," said Erskine gently. Dr. Johnson was intimate with Robertson when he was in Edinburgh and was tempted to go and hear him preach. He refrained. "He could not give a sanction by his presence to a Presbyterian Assembly."

Dr. Hugh Blair (1718–1800), Professor of Rhetoric in the University, was another of the eminent moderates. Dr. Johnson said : " I have read over Dr. Blair's first sermon with more than approbation ; to say it is good is to say too little." The King and indeed everybody else agreed with Johnson, the after time did not, and surely no human being now-a-days reads the once famous *Rhetoric* and the once famous *Sermons*. Blair was vain about everything. Finical about his dress, he was quite a sight as he walked to service in the

BOOK OF EDINBURGH ANECDOTE

High Kirk. "His wig frizzed and powdered so nicely, his gown so scrupulously arranged on his shoulders, his hands so pure and clean, and everything about him in such exquisite taste and neatness." Once he had his portrait painted ; he desired a pleasing smile to mantle his expressive countenance. The model did *his* best and the artist did *his* best ; the resulting paint was hideous. Blair destroyed the picture in a fit of passion. A new one followed, in which less sublime results were aimed at, and the achievement did not sink below the commonplace. An English visitor told him in company that his sermons were not popular amongst the southern divines : Blair's piteous expression was reflected in the faces of those present. Because, said the stranger, who was plainly a master in compliment, "they are so well known that none dare preach them." The flattered Doctor beamed with pleasure. Blair's colleague was the Rev. Robert Walker, and it was said by the beadle that it took twenty-four of Walker's hearers to equal one of Blair's, but then the beadle was measuring everything by the heap on the plate. An old student of Blair's with Aberdeen accent, boundless confidence and nothing else, asked to be allowed to preach for him on the depravity of man. Blair possibly thought that a rough discourse would throw into sharp contrast his polished orations ; at any rate he consented, and the most cultured audience in Edinburgh were treated to this gem : " It is well known that a sou has a' the puddins o' a man except ane ; and if *that* doesna proove that man is fa'an there's naething will."

Dr. Alexander Webster, on the other hand, was of

the evangelical school, though an odd specimen, since he preached and prayed, drank and feasted, with the same whole-hearted fervour. The Edinburgh wits called him Doctor Magnum Bonum, and swore that he had drunk as much claret at the town's expense as would float a 74-ton-gun ship. He died somewhat suddenly, and just before the end spent one night in prayer at the house of Lady Maxwell of Monreith, and on the next he supped in the tavern with some of his old companions who found him very pleasant. He was returning home one night in a very unsteady condition. "What would the kirk-session say if they saw you noo?" said a horrified acquaintance. "Deed, they wadna believe their een" was the gleeful and witty answer. This bibulous divine was the founder of the Widows Fund of the Church of Scotland, and you must accept him as a strange product of the strange conditions of strange old Edinburgh.

The material prosperity of the Church, such as it was, did not meet with universal favour. Lord Auchinleck, Boswell's father, a zealous Presbyterian of the old stamp, declared that a poor clergy was ever a pure clergy. In former times, he said, they had timmer communion cups and silver ministers, but now we were getting silver cups and timmer ministers.

It is alleged of one of the city ministers, though I know not of what epoch, that he performed his pastoral ministrations in the most wholesale fashion. He would go to the foot of each crowded close in his district, raise his gloved right hand and pray unctuously if vaguely for "all the inhabitants of this close."

Some divines honestly recognise their own imperfections. Dr. Robert Henry was minister of the Old Kirk: his colleague was Dr. James M'Knight. Both were able and even distinguished men, but not as preachers. Dr. Henry wittily said, "fortunately they were incumbents of the same church, or there would be twa toom kirks instead of one." One very wet Sunday M'Knight arrived late and drenched. "Oh, I wish I was dry, I wish I was dry," he exclaimed; and then after some perfunctory brushing, "Do you think I'm dry noo?" "Never mind, Doctor," said the other consolingly, "when ye get to the pulpit you'll be dry enough."

As the last century rolled on the moderate cause weakened and the evangelical cause became stronger. The Rev. Sir Henry Moncreiff was one of the great figures of that movement. Referring to his power in the Assembly a country minister said: "It puts you in mind of Jupiter among the lesser Gods." Another was Dr. Andrew Thomson, minister of St. George's, who died in 1831. An easy-going divine once said to him that "he wondered he took so much time with his discourses; for himself, many's the time he had written a sermon and killed a salmon before breakfast." "Sir," was the emphatic answer, "I had rather have eaten your salmon, than listened to your sermon."

The evangelical party were much against pluralities. The others upheld them on the ground that only thus could the higher intellects of the church be fostered and rewarded. Dr. Walker had been presented to Colinton in the teeth of much popular opposition. He had obtained a professorship at the same time, and this was urged in his favour. "Ah," said an old country-

REV. SIR HENRY MONCRIEFF-WELLWOOD

man, "that makes the thing far waur; he will just make a bye job of our souls."

Dr. Chalmers is the great figure of the Disruption controversy, but most of his work lay away from Edinburgh. Well known as he was, there existed a submerged mass to whom he was but a name. In 1845 he began social and evangelical work in the West Port. An old woman of the locality, being asked if she went to hear any one, said, "Ou ay, there's a body Chalmers preaches in the West Port, and I whiles gang to keep him in countenance, honest man!"

Chalmers was the founder of the Free Church; its great popular preacher for years afterwards was Thomas Guthrie. His fame might almost be described as world-wide; his oratory was marked by a certain vivid impressiveness that brought the scenes he described in actual fact before his hearers. A naval officer hearing him picture the wreck of a vessel, and the launching of the lifeboat to save the perishing crew, sprang from one of the front seats of the gallery and began to tear off his coat that he might rush to render aid. He was hardly pulled down by his mother who sat next him. Guthrie had other than oratorical gifts, he was genial and open-hearted. A servant from the country, amazed at the coming and going and the hospitality of the manse, said to her mistress: "Eh, mem, this house is just like a 'public,' only there's nae siller comes in!"

Another leader, second only to Chalmers, was Dr. Candlish, much larger in mind than in body. "Ay," said an Arran porter to one who was watching the Doctor, "tak' a gude look, there's no muckle o' him, but there's a deal in him!" Lord Cockburn's words are to the like effect. "It requires the bright eye and the capacious brow of Candlish to get the better of the smallness of his person, which makes us sometimes wonder how it contains its inward fire." The eager spirit of this divine chafed and fretted over many matters; his oratory aroused a feeling of sympathetic indignation in its hearers, afterwards they had some difficulty in finding adequate cause for their indignation. When the Prince Consort died his sorrowing widow raised a monument to him on Deeside, whereon a text from the Apocrypha was inscribed. Candlish declaimed against the quotation with all the force of his eloquence. "I say this with the deepest sorrow if it is the Queen who is responsible, I say it with the deepest indignation whoever else it may be." These words bring vividly before us an almost extinct type of thought. And this, again, spoken eight days before his death and in mortal sickness, has a touch of the age of Knox: "If you were to set me up in the pulpit I still could make you all hear on the deafest side of your heads."

Times again change, the leaders of religious thought in Scotland are again broad church, if I may use a non-committal term. They have often moved in advance of their flocks. At a meeting in Professor Blackie's house in 1882 a number of Liberal divines were present. Among them Dr. Macgregor and Dr. Walter C. Smith. They were discussing the personality of the Evil One in what seemed to an old lady a very rationalistic spirit. "What," she said in pious horror, "would you deprive us of the Devil?"

With this trivial anecdote may go that of another

THE CHURCH IN EDINBURGH

conservative old woman more than a century earlier. The Rev. David Johnson, who died in 1824, was minister of North Leith. In his time a new church was built, which was crowned with a cross wherein lurked, to some, a suggestion of prelacy if not popery. "But what are we to do?" said the minister to a knot of objecting pious dames. "Do!" replied one of them, "what wad ye do, but just put up the auld cock again!" (no doubt the weather-cock). This cock, or one of its predecessors, crows in history centuries before. On the 21st March 1567 the Castle of Edinburgh was given in charge to Cockburn of Skirling. That day there was a great storm which, among greater feats, blew the tail from the cock on the steeple at Leith. An ancient prophecy ran the round of the town as miraculously fulfilled:

"When Skirling sall be capitaine
The Cock sall want his tail."

Thus the diary of Robert Birrell, at any rate.

The strictness of old-time Sabbath observance is well known. Lord George Campbell, afterwards Duke of Argyll, was in command of a corps of Fencibles in Edinburgh in the early years of last century. He was skilled in whistling. He sat one Sunday morning at the open window of his hotel in Princes Street, and exercised his favourite art. An old woman passing by to church viewed him with holy horror and shook her fist at him, "Eh! ye reprobate! ye reprobate!" she shouted.

It were easy to accumulate anecdotes of the church officers of Edinburgh. I find space for two. In old days Mungo Watson was beadle of Lady Yester's Church under Dr. Davidson. His pastime was to

51

mount the pulpit and thunder forth what he believed to be a most excellent discourse to an imaginary audience. Whilst thus engaged he was surprised by Dr. Davidson, who shut him up very quickly: "Come down, Mungo, come down, toom barrels mak' most sound." In *Jeems the Doorkeeper, a Lay Sermon*, Dr. John Brown has drawn a charming picture of the officer of his father's church in Broughton Place. The building was crowded, and part of the congregation consisted of servant girls, "husseys" as Jeems contemptuously described them. Some were laced to the point of suffocation, and were not rarely carried out fainting to the vestry. Jeems stood over the patient with a sharp knife in his hand. "Will oo rip her up noo?" he said as he looked at the young doctor; the signal was given, the knife descended and a cracking as of canvas under a gale followed, the girl opened her eyes, and closed them again in horror at the sight of the ruined finery. But we are chronicling very small beer indeed, and here must be an end of these strangely assorted scenes and pictures.

CHAPTER THREE

THE TOWN'S COLLEGE AND SCHOOLS

CHAPTER THREE
TOWN'S COLLEGE AND SCHOOLS

THE OFFICIAL TITLE OF THE UNIVER-
sity of Edinburgh is *Academia Jacobi Sexti.* So "our
James," as Ben Jonson calls him, gave a name to this
great seat of learning, and in the form of a charter he
gave it his blessing, and there he stopped! Bishop
Reid, the last Roman Catholic Bishop of Orkney, left
eight thousand merks for a college in Edinburgh, and
though that sum sinks considerably when put into
current coin of the realm, it is not to be neglected. It
was obtained and applied, but the real patrons, authors, managers and supporters for centuries of the University was the good town of Edinburgh through its
Town Council. It was *Oure Tounis Colledge.* They
appointed its professors and ruled its destinies until
almost our own time. The Scottish University Act
of 1858 greatly lessened, though it by no means destroyed, their influence.

In a country so much under ecclesiastical influence
as Scotland of the Reformation, the union between the
College and the Kirk was close and intimate; still it
was a corporation of tradesmen that managed the
University, and though the professors kicked, there is
no doubt they managed it very well. There has ever
been something homely and unconventional about
the college. It was opened on the 14th October 1583;
the students were to wear gowns, they were to speak
Latin, none was to soil his mouth with common Scots,
and none was to go to taverns, or (it was later ordain-
ed) to funerals—a serious form of entertainment for
which old Scotland evinced a peculiar zest.

55

Ah, those counsels of perfection! how the years set them at naught! Why they alone of all men in Edinburgh should not go to taverns or funerals was not a question wherewith they troubled themselves; they simply went. Gowns they never wore, and though half-hearted attempts were now and again made to introduce them, these never succeeded. Sir Alexander Grant, the late Principal, tells us that a working man, whose son was a student, wrote to him, pointing out the advantage of gowns in covering up a shabby dress. Sir Alexander seemed rather struck with this point of view, though after all, the gown must cost something, which might have been better applied to the cloak. The students, as now, lived anywhere.

The histories give many quaint details as to the manners of other days. The classes began at five in summer and six in winter; the bursars rung the bell and swept the rooms; the janitor was a student or even a graduate. His it was to lock the door at eleven at night. The early professors, who did not confine themselves to one subject but carried their class right through, were called regents. One of them, James Reid, had taken up the office in 1603; he was popular in the council, in the town, and in the whole city, but after more than twenty years' service he came to grief on a quarrel with the all-powerful Kirk. In 1626, William Struthers, Moderator of the Presbytery, spoke of philosophy as the dish-clout of divinity. At a graduation ceremony, Reid quoted Aristippus to the effect that he would rather be an unchristian philosopher than an unphilosophical divine! for which innocent retort the regent was forced to throw up his office.

TOWN'S COLLEGE AND SCHOOLS

One wonders what would have happened if Town Council and Kirk had come to loggerheads, but they never did, and through a college committee and a college bailie they directed the affairs of the University. Creech, best known to fame as Burns's publisher, and the subject of some kindly or some unkindly half-humorous verse, was in his time college bailie; but Creech was a great many things in his time, though the world has pretty well forgotten him. The Lord Provost was the important figure in University as well as City life. In 1665 he was declared by the council Rector of the College, yet in the years that followed he did nothing in his office. Long afterwards, in 1838, there was a trial of students before the Sheriff, for the part these had taken in a great snowball bicker with the citizens. Witty Patrick Robertson was their counsel, and was clever enough to throw a farcical air over the whole proceedings. "You are Rector of the University, are you not?" he asked the then Lord Provost. "No! I may be, but I am not aware of it," was the rather foolish answer. A caricature was immediately circulated of the man who does not know he is Rector! This office was not the present Lord Rectorship, which only dates from the Act of 1858.

Edinburgh has never been a rich town. In the old days, it was as poor as poor might be, and so was its college; they had nothing in the way of plate to show visitors, or to parade on great occasions. Their only exhibits were the college mace and George Buchanan's skull! There was a legend about the mace. In 1683 the tomb of Bishop Kennedy at St. Andrews was opened: it contained five silver maces—quite a providential arrangement, one for each of the Scots Universities, and one to spare! But there was a mace in Edinburgh before this. We have note of it in 1640, and in 1651 the Town Council had it on loan for the use of the public. In 1660 the macer of the Parliament needs must borrow it till his masters get one of their own. There is a quaint, homely touch about this passing on of the mace from one body to another. It had been a valuable and interesting relic, but in the night between 29th and 30th October 1787 the library was forced, and the mace stolen from the press wherein it lay, and was never seen more. Ten guineas reward was offered, but in vain. Every one presently suspected Deacon Brodie, himself a member of the Council, and perhaps the most captivating and romantic burglar on record. Ere a year was over, he was lying in the Tolbooth a condemned felon, but he uttered no word as to the precious bauble. The year after that, very shame induced the Council to procure an elegant silver mace, with a fine Latin inscription, and the arms of James VI., the arms of the City, and the arms of the University itself, invented for the special purpose. It was just in time to be used on the laying of the foundation-stone of the new university buildings in 1789, and it has been used ever since on great occasions only. The loan of it is not asked for any more! every body corporate now has a mace of its own!

The Buchanan skull is still held by the college. That eminent scholar died on the 28th September 1582, and was buried in the Greyfriars Churchyard. John Adamson, Principal of the University between 1623 and 1651, got the skull by bribing the sexton, and bequeathed it to the college. The story rather revolts the taste of to-day, but grim old Scotland had a strange hankering after those elements of mortality. Its remarkable thinness was noted, in fact the light could be seen through it, and anatomists of later years dwelt on the fine breadth of forehead, and remarkable contours. It was judged, moreover, a skull of a Celtic type—Celtic was possibly enough Buchanan's race. Long afterwards Sir William Hamilton, at the Royal Society in Edinburgh, compared it with the skull of a Malay robber and cut-throat, and showed that, according to the principles of the phrenologists, the Malay had the finer head. This was meant as a *reductio ad absurdum* of phrenology, though, after all, the evidence of identification could not be satisfactory. If the sexton consented to be bribed he was not likely, in old Greyfriars, to be at a loss for a skull, but it seems irreverent to pursue the subject further.

Robert Leighton, Principal between 1653 and 1662, was afterwards Bishop of Dunblane, and then Archbishop of Glasgow. In 1672 he was still living in his rooms in the college, and was there waited upon one day by Chorley, an English student studying divinity at Glasgow. He brought the compliments of his college and tutor, and invited the prelate to his approaching laureation. He next presented him with the laureation thesis, which was gratefully received, but when the visitor produced a pair of "fine fringed gloves" "he started back and with all demonstrations of humility excused himself as unworthy of such a present." Chorley, however, whilst humble was persistent, and though the Archbishop refused again and again and retreated backwards, Chorley followed, and at the end fairly pinned Leighton against the wall! His Grace needs must yield, "but it was amazing to see with what humble gratitude, bowing to the very ground, this great man accepted them." So much for the author of the classic *Commentary on the 1st Epistle of St. Peter.* Is it not a picture of the time when men were extreme in all things, though Leighton alone was extreme in humility? Was there not (you ask) something ironic in the self-depreciation? I do not think so, for you look as "through a lattice on the soul" and recognise a spirit ill at ease in an evil day, one who might have uttered Lord Bacon's pathetic complaint *multum incola fuit anima mea* with far more point and fitness than ever Bacon did.

Of a later Principal, Gilbert Rule (1690–1701), a less conspicuous but very pleasing memory remains. His window was opposite that of Campbell, Professor of Divinity. Now Dr. Rule was ever late at his books, whilst Campbell was eager over them ere the late northern dawn was astir; so the one candle was not out before the other was lighted. They were called the evening and the morning star. Rule died first, and when Campbell missed the familiar light, he said, "the evening star was now gone down, and the morning star would soon disappear," and ere long it was noted that both windows were dark. Among his other gifts, Gilbert Rule was a powerful preacher. In some ministerial wandering it was his lot to pass a night in a solitary house in a nook of the wild Grampians. At midnight enter a ghost, who would take no denial; Gilbert must out through the night till a certain spot was reached; then the ghost vanished and the Doctor got him back to bed, with, you imagine, chattering teeth and dismal foreboding. Next day the ground was opened, and the skeleton of a murdered man discovered. Gilbert preached on the following Sunday from the parish pulpit, and reasoned so powerfully of judgment and the wrath to come that an old man got up and confessed himself the murderer. In due course he was executed and the ghost walked no more.

William Carstares, Principal between 1703 and 1715, was a great figure in Church and State. "Cardinal" Carstares they nicknamed him at Dutch William's Court, and both that astute monarch and Queen Anne, Stuart as she was, gave him almost unbounded confidence. In tact and diplomacy he excelled his contemporaries and in the valuable art of knowing what to conceal even when forced to speak. He was put to it, for the most famous anecdote about him tells of his suffering under the thumbikins in 1684. They were applied for an hour with such savage force that the King's smith had to go for his tools to reverse the screws before it was possible to set free the maimed and bruised thumbs. In Carstares' picture the thumbs are very prominent, in fact or flattery they show forth quite untouched. At the King's special request he tried them on the royal digits; His Majesty vowed he had confessed anything to be rid of them. We have a pleasing picture of an annual fish dinner at Leith whereat the Principal was entertained by his colleagues. Calamy the English nonconformist was a guest, and was much delighted with the talk and the fare, and especially "the freedom and harmony between the Principal and the masters of the college," they expressing a veneration for him as a common father, and he a tenderness for them as if they had all been his children.

Principal Robertson (1762–1793) is still a distinguished figure, but he belongs to Letters in the first place, and the Church in the second; yet even here he was eminent. A charming anecdote tells how as Principal he visited the logic class where John Stevenson, his own old teacher, was still prelecting. He addressed the students in Latin, urging them to profit, as he hoped he had himself profited, by the teaching of Stevenson, whereat "the aged Professor, unable any longer to suppress his emotion, dissolved in tears of grateful affection, and fell on the neck of his favourite pupil, his Principal."

George Husband Baird (1793–1840) was a much more commonplace figure. His middle name was thought felicitous; he was husband to the Lord Provost's daughter and there seemed no other sufficient reason to account for his elevation. This play upon names, by the way, has always been a favourite though puerile form of Edinburgh wit. The better part of a century afterwards we had one of our little wars on the Gold Coast, and some local jester asked for the difference between the folk of Ashantee and those of Edinburgh. The first, it was said, took their law from Coffee and the second their coffee from Law! The Ashantee war of the 'seventies is already rather dim and ancient history, but Coffee, it may be remembered, was the name of their king, and the other term referred to a well-known Edinburgh house still to the fore. However, we return to our Baird for a moment.

He was Minister of the High Church as well as Principal. Discoursing of the illness of George III., he wept copiously and unreasonably; "from George Husband Baird to George III. *greeting*," said one of his hearers.

There is a mass of legendary stories about the ordinary professors, but the figures are dim, and the notes of their lives mostly trivial. For instance, there is Dr. John Meiklejohn, who was Professor of Church History, 1739–1781: "He had a smooth round face, that never bore any expression but good-humour and contentment," he droned monotonously through his lectures, glad to get away to his glebe at Abercorn, eight miles off. He delighted to regale the students at his rural manse, and pressed on them the produce of the soil, with a heartiness which he never showed in inviting their attention to the fathers of the church. "Take an egg, Mr. Smith," he would genially insist, "*they are my own* eggs, for the eggs of Edinburgh are not to be depended on." Of like kidney was David Ritchie, who was Professor of Logic and Metaphysics and Minister of St. Andrew's Church, but "was more illustrious on the curling pond, than in the Professor's chair." But, then, to him in 1836 succeeded Sir William Hamilton, and for twenty years the chair was *the* philosophical chair of Britain. The records of his fame are not for this page; his passionate devotion to study, his vast learning, are not material for the anecdotist. He was fond of long walks with a friend into the surrounding country, and in his day it was still very easy to leave the town behind you. Though he started with a companion, he was presently away in advance or on the other side of the road, muttering to himself in Greek or

Latin or English, forgetful of that external world which occupied no small place in his philosophy. "Dear me, what did you quarrel about?" asked a lady, to his no small amusement. The Council did not always select the most eminent men. About a century before, in 1745 to wit, they had preferred for the chair of Moral Philosophy William Cleghorn to David Hume. There was no other choice, it was said. A Deist might possibly become a Christian, but a Jacobite could not become a Whig. Ruddiman's amanuensis, Adam Walker, was a student at this class, where he had listened to a lecture on the doctrine of necessity. "Well, does your Professor make us free agents or not?" said his employer. "He gives us arguments on both sides and leaves us to judge," was the reply. "Indeed," was Ruddiman's caustic comment, "the fool hath said in his heart, there is no God, and the Professor will not tell you whether the fool is right or wrong."

Many of us remember Dunbar's *Greek Lexicon*, so much in use till superseded by Liddell and Scott's. Its author was Professor of Greek in the University from 1806 to 1852. He fell from a tree, it was said, into the Greek chair. In fact, he commenced life as gardener; confined by an accident he betook himself to study, with highly satisfactory results. His predecessor in the chair had been Andrew Dalzel, an important figure in his time, perhaps best remembered by the ineptitude of his criticism of Scott, whom he entertained unawares in his class. Scott sent him in an essay, "cracking up" Ariosto above Homer. Dalzel was naturally furious: "Dunce he was and dunce he would remain." You cannot blame the professor, but *dis*

aliter visum! Dunbar's successor was John Stuart
Blackie (1852–1882), one of the best known Edinburgh figures of his time. He had a creed of his own,
ways of his own, and a humour of his own. Even
the orthodox loved and tolerated the genial individ-
ualist who was never malicious. "Blackie's neyther
orthodox, heterodox, nor any ither dox; he's juist
himsel'!" An ardent body of abstainers under some
mistaken idea asked him to preside at one of their
meetings. He thus addressed them: "I cannot understand why I am asked to be here, I am not a teeto-
taler—far from it. If a man asks me to dine with
him and does not give me a good glass of wine, I say
he is neither a Christian nor a gentleman. Germans
drink beer, Englishmen drink wine, ladies tea, and
fools water." Blackie was an advocate as well as a
professor. Possibly he had in his mind a certain Act
of 1716, to wit, the 3rd of Geo. I. chap. 5, whereby
a duty was imposed "of two pennies Scots, or one-
sixth of a penny sterling on every pint of ale and beer
that shall be vended and sold within the City of Edinburgh." Among the objects to which the duty was
to be applied was the settling of a salary upon the
Professor of Law in the University of Edinburgh and
his successor in office not exceeding £100 per annum.
Here is a portrait by himself which brings vividly back,
true to the life, that once familiar figure of the Edinburgh pavement: "When I walk along Princes Street
I go with a kingly air, my head erect, my chest expan-
ded, my hair flowing, my plaid flying, my stick swing-
ing. Do you know what makes me do that? Well, I'll
tell you—just con-ceit." Even those who knew him

not will understand that the Edinburgh ways never quite seemed the same when that picturesque figure was seen no longer there. And yet the Blackie anecdotes are disappointing. There is a futile story that he once put up a notice he would meet his *classes* at such an hour. A student with a very elementary sense of humour cut off the *c*, and he retorted by deleting the *l*. All this is poor enough. Alas! he was only of the silver or, shall we say, of the iron age of Auld Reekie?

Aytoun in an address at the graduation of 1863, spoke of the professors of his time as the instructors, and almost idols, of the rising generation. He himself filled the chair of Rhetoric between 1845 and 1865. A quaint though scarcely characteristic story is preserved of his early years. One night he was, or was believed to be, absent from home, " late at een birling the wine." An irate parent stood grimly behind the door the while a hesitating hand fumbled at the latch, the dim light of morn presently revealed a cloaked figure, upon whom swift blows descended without stint or measure. It was not young Aytoun at all, but a mighty Senator of the College of Justice who had mistaken the door for his own, which was a little farther along the street!

One of the idols to whom Aytoun referred was no doubt his father-in-law, John Wilson (1820–1853), the well-known Christopher North, described by Sir R. Christison as "the grandest specimen I have ever seen of the human form, tall, perfectly symmetrical, massive and majestic, yet agile." Even in old age he had many of his early characteristics. He noted a coal carter brutally driving a heavily-laden horse up the steep streets of Edinburgh; he remonstrated with the fellow, who raised his whip in a threatening manner as if to strike. The spirit of the old man swelled in righteous anger, he tore away the whip as if it had been straw, loosened the harness, threw the coals into the street, then clutching the whip in one hand and leading the horse by the other, he marched through Moray Place, to deposit the unfortunate animal in more kindly keeping.

There are stories of the library that merit attention. I will give the name of Robert Henderson, appointed librarian in 1685, where he so continued till 1747—sixty-two years altogether, the longest record of University service extant. Physically of a lean and emaciated figure, he had a very high opinion of his own erudition. Now in the old college there was a certain ruinous wall to which was attached the legend, that it would topple over on some great scholar. The librarian affected an extreme anxiety when in the vicinity of the wall. At length it was taken down. Boswell told the story to Johnson. The sage did not lose the chance for a very palpable hit at Scots learning. "They were afraid it never would fall!" he growled. There was a like tradition regarding that precipitous part of Arthur's Seat quaintly named Samson's Ribs. An old witch prophesied they would be sure to fall on the greatest philosopher in Scotland. Sir John Leslie was afraid to pass that way.

The relations between the Town Council and the professors in the first half of the nineteenth century were sometimes far from harmonious. The days were past when the Academy of James VI. was merely the

"Tounes Colledge," it was more and more a University with a European reputation. A cultured scholar of the type of Sir William Hamilton, "spectator of all time and of all existence," in Plato's striking phrase, was not like to rest contented under the sway of the Town Council. Possibly the Council sneered at him and his likes, as visionary, unpractical, eccentric; possibly there was truth on both sides, so much *does* depend on your point of view. The University, somewhat unwisely, went to law with the Council, and came down rather heavily ; nor were the Council generous victors. The Lord Provost of the time met Professor Dunbar one day at dinner—" We have got you Professors under our thumb, and by —— we will make you feel it," said he rather coarsely. The professors consoled each other with anecdotes of Town Council oddities in college affairs. One councillor gave as a reason why he voted for a professorial candidate that, " He was asked by a leddy who had lately given him a good job." " I don't care that," said another, snapping his fingers, "for the chair of ——, but whoever the Provost votes for, I'll vote for somebody else." An English scholar had come to Edinburgh as candidate for a chair. He called on a worthy member of the Council to whom his very accent suggested black prelacy, or worse. " Are ye a jined member ? " The stranger stared in hopeless bewilderment. " Are ye a jined member o' onie boadie ? " was the far from lucid explanation. However, the Act of 1858 has changed all this, and town and gown in Edinburgh fight no more. Well, there is no gown, and the University has always been a good part of the good town of Edinburgh, as much now as ever. Take a broad view from first to last, and how to deny that the Council did their duty well! Principal Sir Alexander Grant in his *Story of the University of Edinburgh* bears generous and emphatic testimony as to this, and here we may well leave the matter.

I must now desert the groves of the Academy of James VI. to say a word on a lesser school and its schoolmasters. Here we have the memorable and illustrative story of the great barring out of September 1595 at the old High School. The scholars had gone on the 15th of that month to ask the Council for the week's holiday of privilege as was usual. It was curtly refused, whereupon some "gentlemen's bairns" collected firearms and swords, and in dead of night seized the schoolhouse, which they fortified in some sort. Their Rector, Master Pollock, was refused admittance next morning, and complained to the magistrates. Bailie John Macmorran came to the spot with a posse of officers, but William Sinclair, son of the Chancellor of Caithness, took his stand at a window and threatened to pistol the first who approached. Bailie Macmorran was a big man in his day—his house, now restored as University Hall, still rises stately and impressive in Riddle's Close, on the south side of the Lawnmarket—and he was not to be put down by a schoolboy; he ordered his satellites to crash in the door with the beam they were bringing forward. It is not hard to reconstitute the scene: the bailie, full of civic importance and wrath, the angry boy at the window, the pride of youth and blood in his set, determined face. Presently the pistol shot
69

rang out, and Macmorran fell dead on the pavement with a bullet through his brain. The whole town rushed to the spot, seized the frightened boys and thrust them into the Tolbooth, but finally they were liberated without hurt, after, it would seem, some form of a trial.

There are many quaint details as to the scholars. They used to go to the fields in the summer to cut rushes or bent for the floor of the school, but, you see, fighting was the work or the game of nearly every male in Scotland, and even the children must needs have their share. On these expeditions the boys fell to slashing one another with their hooks, and they were stopped. The winter of 1716 was distinguished by furious riots, though not of the same deadly nature. The pupils demolished every window of the school and of the adjacent parish church of Lady Yester, also the wall which fenced the playground.

I will not gather records of the various Rectors, not even of Dr. Alexander Adam, the most famous of them all. You can see to-day his portrait by Raeburn, and one of Raeburn's best in the Gallery on the Mound, and think of his striking utterance in the last hours of his life, " Boys, it is growing dark, you may go home." In his prime he had a profound conviction of his own qualities and those of his school. "Come away, sir,"—thus he would address a new scholar,— " you will see more here in an hour than you will in any other school in Europe." He had a long series of eminent pupils, among them Scott, Horner, and Jeffrey, and the manner in which they have spoken of him justifies his words and his reputation.

CHAPTER FOUR

SURGEONS AND DOCTORS

CHAPTER FOUR
THE SURGEONS & THE DOCTORS

THE PHYSICIANS, THE SURGEONS, THE medical schools of Edinburgh have long and famous histories. A few facts may assist the reader to understand the anecdotes which fill this chapter. The Guild of Surgeons and Barbers received a charter of Incorporation from the Town Council on the 1st July 1505, and to this in 1506 the sanction of James IV. was obtained. On 26th February 1567 the surgeons and apothecaries were made into one body; henceforth they ceased to act as barbers and, after 1722, save that the surgeons kept a register of barbers' apprentices, there was no connection whatever between the profession and the trade. In 1778 a charter was obtained from George III., and the corporation became the Royal College of Surgeons of the City of Edinburgh. In early days they had a place of meeting in Dixon's Close, but in 1656 they acquired and occupied Curriehill House, once the property of the Black Friars. In May 1775 the foundation-stone of a new hall was laid in Surgeons Square, hard by the old High School. Here the Incorporation met till the opening of the new Surgeons Hall in 1832 on the east side of Nicolson Street, a little way south of the old University buildings. Just as the barbers became separated from the surgeons, so in time a distinction was drawn between these last and the physicians. In 1617, James VI. in the High Court of Parliament decreed the establishment of a College of Physicians for Edinburgh. In poverty-stricken Scotland a scheme often remained a mere scheme for many long years.

BOOK OF EDINBURGH ANECDOTE

In 1656, Cromwell issued a patent establishing a College of Physicians on the lines laid down by James VI., but he passed away and his scheme with him, and it was not till 1681 that the charter was finally obtained. Their ancient place of meeting was near the Cowgate Port, but in 1775 the foundation of a splendid building was laid by Professor Cullen, their most eminent member. It stood opposite St. Andrew's Church, George Street, but in 1843 this was sold to the Commercial Bank for £20,000, and in 1844 the foundation-stone was laid of the present hall in Queen Street.

The first botanical garden in Edinburgh was founded by Sir Andrew Balfour (1630–1694), who commenced practice in the capital in 1670. He obtained from the Town Council a small piece of land between the east end of the Nor' Loch and Trinity College, which had formed part of the Trinity Garden. Here were the old Physic Gardens. About 1770 this was completely abandoned in favour of new land on the west side of Leith Walk, and in less than a hundred years, namely, in 1824, the new and splendid Royal Botanical Gardens were established in Inverleith Row; to this all the "plant" of the old gardens was transferred.

As to the medical faculty in the University, I note that the chair of anatomy was founded in 1705, and that its most famous occupants were the three Alexander Monro's, known as *primus*, *secundus*, and *tertius*, who held the professorship between them for 126 years, namely, from 1720 to 1846. The first Monro distinguished himself at the battle of Prestonpans, not by slaying but by healing. He attended diligently to the wounded on both sides and got them conveyed to Edinburgh. The second was professor from 1754 to 1808, a remarkable period of fifty-four years. His father made an odd bargain with the Town Council. If they would appoint his son to succeed him he would carefully train him for the post in the best schools both at home and abroad. They agreed, and the experiment turned out a complete success. He had studied at London, Leyden, Paris, and Berlin, and when he returned his father asked the city notabilities to hear his first lecture. Monro had got it up by heart, but he lost his presence of mind and forgot every word; he had to speak extempore, yet he knew his subject and soon found his feet. He lectured without notes ever after. The most popular Scots divines have always done the same. Monro *tertius* was not equal to his father or grandfather. The memory of his great predecessors was too much for him, "froze the genial current of his soul," made him listless and apathetic. He had as rival the famous Dr. John Barclay, extramural lecturer on anatomy, 1797–1825. This last was very ready and self-possessed. Once he had to lecture on some part of the human frame; the subject lay before him covered with a sheet. He lifted the sheet, laid it down again, and proceeded to give an excellent discourse on anatomy, but not quite according to the programme; in fact, a mistake had been made, and there was nothing under the sheet; but, again, the feat does not seem altogether surprising. However, the mistake was not so dire as that of one of his assistants, who after dinner one night hurried to the dissecting room to prepare the subject for next day. He pulled off the cloth, but it was at once pulled back again; he pulled it off again, the same thing happened : the farthing dip that faintly illumined the room almost fell from his nerveless hand, a low growl revealed the unexpected presence of a dog whose teeth had supplied the opposing force! Barclay's lectures were flavoured with pungent doses of caustic old Edinburgh wit. He warned his students to beware of discoveries of anatomy. " In a field so well wrought, what remained to discover? As at harvest, first come the reapers to the uncut grain and then the gleaners, and finally the geese, idly poking among the rubbish. Gentlemen, *we are the geese*!" It was not rarely the habit of professors in former times to give free tickets for their courses. The kindness was sometimes abused. Barclay applied a humorous but sufficient corrective. Once he had a note from Mr. Laing, bookseller, father of Dr. David Laing the well-known antiquary, requesting a free ticket for some sucking sawbones. Barclay professed himself delighted to confer the favour, but invited his proposed pupil to accompany him to Mr. Laing's shop, where he selected books on anatomy to the exact value of his ticket, and sagely remarking that without text-books his lectures were useless, presented them to the astonished youth as a gift from Mr. Laing! Taking no denial he bundled the youth and the books out of the place. He did not again find it necessary to repeat the lesson. In Sir Robert Christison's *Life* some remarkable instances are given of this curious form of benevolence at somebody else's expense, but the subject need not be pursued. Barclay had collected a considerable museum, of which a fine elephant, an early Jumbo in fact, was the gem. His friends, who were numerous and powerful, tried to get a chair of comparative anatomy founded for him in the University. Various members of the medical faculty opposed it tooth and nail, as poaching on their preserves. One of Kay's most famous caricatures represents Barclay seated on an elephant charging the college gate, which is barred against him by a learned crowd. The opposition succeeded and Barclay was never elected professor.

Barclay had been brought up for the church, and in his early days had, during the absence of the Rev. Mr. Baird of Bo'ness, wagged his head in the pulpit of that divine. "How did they like him?" asked Baird of Sandy, the village sage or the village idiot or, perhaps, both. "Gey weel, minister, gey weel, but everybody thought him daft." "Why, Sandy?" "Oh, for gude reasons, minister; Mr. Barclay was aye skinning puddocks" (frogs). It was reported that dogs fled in terror at the sight of him; the sagacious animals feared capture and dissection; he had incautiously cut up a dog in the presence of its kind and thus had an ill name in the canine world! Not that this implied any ill-will to dogs; quite the contrary, as witness a story of John Goodsir (1814–1867), who succeeded Monro *tertius* as professor of anatomy in 1846. He had carefully studied the anatomy of the horse. " I love the horse, I love the horse," he said with genuine fervour, " I have dissected him twice!"

Barclay possessed an uncle, a full-blown divine,

and the founder of a sect by some called after him. Nephew and uncle argued theological points. The young man was so hard to convince that the elder sent a heavy folio flying at his head; he dodged the missile, but if not confuted, was at any rate silenced.

Many of the anecdotes of the surgeon's life in old Edinburgh turn on this question of anatomy. Until the Anatomy Act of 1832, that science was terribly hampered by the want of subjects. The charter of 1505 provided an allowance of one body annually, which was almost ludicrously insufficient, hence body snatching became almost a necessity, perhaps among the surgeons themselves it was counted a virtue, but they dared not say it openly. On 20th May 1711, the college solemnly protested against body snatching. On the 24th of January 1721 a clause was ordered to be inserted in indentures binding apprentices not to violate graves, but the populace, rightly or wrongly, thought those rascal surgeons had tongue in cheek all the time, and were ever inclined to put the worst possible construction on every circumstance that seemed to point that way. Lauder of Fountainhall commemorates an early case. On the 6th February 1678 four gipsies, a father and three sons, were hanged together at Edinburgh, for killing another gipsy called Faa at Romanno. To the Edinburgh burghers of the day the gipsy and the cateran were mere wild beasts of prey, and these four wretches were hung in haste, cut down in haste, and forthwith huddled together with their clothes on—it was not worth while to strip them of their rags—into a shallow hole in Greyfriars Churchyard. Next morning the grave lay open, and the body of the youngest son, aged six-teen, was missing. It was remembered he had been the last thrown over, and the first cut down, and the last buried. Perhaps he had revived, thrown aside a scanty covering of earth, and fled to Highland hill or Border waste. Others opined that the body had been stolen by some chirurgeon or his servant for the purpose of dis-section, on which possibility Fountainhall takes occa-sion to utter some grave legal maxims; solemnly locks the door, as it were, in the absence of the steed. In 1742 a rifled grave was noted in the West Kirkyard, and a body, presumably its former tenant, was presently discovered near the shop of one Martin Eccles, surg-eon. Forthwith the Portsburgh drum was beating a mad tattoo through the Cowgate, and the mob pro-ceeded to smash the surgeon's shop. As for Martin, you may safely assume *non est inventus*, else had he been smashed likewise. Again, a sedan chair is discov-ered containing a dead body, apparently on its way to the dissecting room. The chairman and his assist-ant were banished, and the chair was burned by the common hangman. Again, one John Samuel, a gar-dener, moved thereto, you guess, by an all too consum-ing thirst, is taken at the Potterow Port trying to sell the dead body of a child, which was recognised as hav-ing been buried at Pentland the week before. He was soundly whipped through Edinburgh and banished Scotland for seven years.

A still more sordid and more terrible tragedy is a-mong the events of 1752. Two women, Ellen Torrence and Jean Waldy, meet in the street a mother with her little boy, they ask her to drink, an invitation, it seems, impossible to resist. Whilst one plied her with liquor, the other enticed the boy to her own den, where she promptly suffocated him. The body was sold for two shillings to the students, sixpence was given to the one who carried it, and it was only after long haggling that an additional tenpence was extorted "for a dram." They were presently discovered and executed. This almost incredible story, to which Gilbert Glossin in *Guy Mannering* makes a rather far-fetched reference in a discussion with Mr. Pleydell, proves at any rate one thing, there was a ready market for dead bodies in Edinburgh for purposes of dissection, and as the buyer was not too inquisitive, indeed he could scarcely afford to be, the bodies almost certainly were illegally procured; though, whatever the populace might think and suspect, there was never any case where there was the least evidence that the surgeon was a party to the murder. Any surgeon who was such must have been a criminal lunatic. The case of Dr. Knox, to be presently referred to, was the one that excited most notice and suspicion. It was carefully inquired into, and nothing was found against him. If there had been a *prima facie* case, the popular feeling was so strong that the Crown authorities needs must have taken action, but I anticipate a little.

From the latter half of the eighteenth century to the first part of the nineteenth, the resurrectionist and the pressgang were two subjects on which the popular imagination dwelt with a certain fascinated horror. The resurrectionist was so much in evidence that graves were protected with heavy iron frames (you still see one or two specimens in old Greyfriars and elsewhere), and churchyards were regularly watched. There is no need to set forth how the tenderest and deepest feelings of human nature were outraged by the desecration of the last resting-place. On the other hand, the doctors were mad for subjects. A certain enthusiasm for humanity possessed them, too. Were they not working to relieve suffering? There was something else: the love of daring adventure, the romance and mystery of the unholy midnight raid had their attraction; it was never difficult, you can believe, to collect a harum-scarum set of medical students for an expedition. Some men, afterwards very eminent, early distinguished themselves. Thus, the celebrated surgeon, Robert Liston (1794–1847), was engaged in more than one of the following adventures, the stories of which I here tell as samples of the bulk. One Henderson, an innkeeper, had died in Leven, in Fifeshire. Two students from Edinburgh had snatched the body and were conveying it away, when one of them suddenly felt ill. They took refuge with their burden, enclosed in a sack, in a convenient public-house. It happened to be the one formerly kept by Henderson, and now in charge of his widow and daughter. They were shown to an upper room, which contained a closed-in box bed, so frequent a feature in old Scots houses. The sick man was pulling himself together with brandy and what not, when a great hubbub arose downstairs. The town officers were searching the house for stolen property. The students were beside themselves with panic, though in fact the officers do not seem to have searched the upstairs room at all. However, "The thief doth fear each bush an officer." The two lads hastily took the body from the sack and put it in the bed, then they bolted through the window, and were seen no more. The room as it turned out was used by the widow as a bedroom, and it was only when she retired for the night—I need not follow the narrative further, save to note that the graveclothes had been made by herself!

When Liston was a student he heard from a country surgeon of an interesting case where a post-mortem seemed desirable in the interests of science. He and some others dressed as sailors and repaired to the place by boat, for it was on the shore of the Firth. The surgeon's apprentice met them as arranged, and everything went off well. The marauding party repaired for refreshment to a little change-house, leaving their sack under a near hedge. Here they spent a happy time in carousing and chaffing the country wench whom they found in charge. A loud shout of "Ship ahoy!" startled them. The girl said it was only her brother, and a drunken sailor presently staggered in with the sack on his shoulders. Pitching it to the ground, he said with an oath, "Now if that ain't something good, rot them chaps who stole it." Presently he produced a knife. "Let's see what it is," said he as he ripped the sack open. The sight of the contents worked a sudden change: the girl fled through the door with hysterical screams, the sailor on the instant dead sober followed, Liston seized the body, and all made for the boat, and they were soon safe back in Edinburgh. Liston is the chief figure of another adventure. He and his party had gone by boat to Rosyth to get the body of a drowned sailor. His sweetheart, nearly distracted at her recent loss, was scarce absent from the tomb night or day. They did manage to get the body lifted and on board the boat, when the woman discovered the violated grave. Her wild shrieks rang in their ears as they pulled for the opposite shore as hard as they could, but they kept secure hold of their prey. Another story tells of a party of tyros who had raised the body of a farmer's wife from Glencorse or some neighbouring churchyard. As they dragged along it seemed to their excited fancy that the body had recovered life and was hopping after them! They fled with loud yells of terror, and left their burden by the roadside. The widower was the first to discover it there next morning. He thought it was a case of premature burial and made some frantic efforts at resuscitation: the truth only gradually dawned upon him. This, I venture to think, was the story that suggested to R. L. Stevenson his gruesome tale of *The Body-snatcher*.

Yet another story tells of a certain Miss Wilson of Bruntsfield Links who was courted by two admirers. She showed a marked preference for one, and when he died she seemed heart-broken. The other, not content with having the field to himself, engaged the services of a professional body-snatcher and proceeded to Buccleuch burying-ground. Miss Wilson was mourning at the grave; they waited till she was gone and then set to work, and the surviving rival soon had the cruel satisfaction of knowing that the body of the other was on the anatomical table at the University!

I have mentioned the professional body-snatcher, and the class certainly existed. Obviously it was for-

BOOK OF EDINBURGH ANECDOTE

med of men of a low type, however afraid they might be to perpetrate actual murder. Among the best known was a certain Andrew Lees, called "Merry Andrew" by the students. He had been a carrier between a country town and Edinburgh, and his house was near the churchyard, which he despoiled at leisure. In after days he used to lament the times when he got subjects "as cheap as penny pies." It was said he drank sixteen glasses of raw whisky daily, and that on great occasions the glasses became pints. Various ruffians were associated with him, one nicknamed " Moudiewart," or mole, from his skill in the delving part of the operation. Perhaps a line from Shakespeare was in the mind of the nicknamer:

" Well said, old mole, can'st work i' the earth so fast?"
More probably it was all native wit. Another was a sham parson called "Praying Howard," who wept and supplicated with an unction hard to distinguish from the real article. There is no doubt these rascals thoroughly enjoyed their knavish pranks, and they were ever on the watch to hear of some one dying, friendless and alone; then one appeared among a household perplexed to know what to do with the remains of a person in whom they had no special interest. The stranger was a dear friend or near relative of the deceased, and was only anxious to bury him with all possible honour, and in due course a mock funeral was arranged, with parson, undertaker, and chief mourner. The procession started for some place in the country, but of course the real destination of the departed was one of the Edinburgh dissecting rooms. If things went well, Andrew and his fellows spent a night in

wild debauchery in some tavern of ill odour in every sense of the word.

At least those pranks were comparatively harmless. The dead were gone beyond the reach of hurt, and the feelings of the living were not outraged. As regards the rifling of graveyards, you wonder how it was so often successful. The watchers were, however, paid hirelings, they were frozen with superstitious terror, they were usually paralysed with drink, and they had watched hours and nights already, and nothing had happened. The assailants were infinitely more active in mind and body; they had full command of cash and of all necessary appliances, and they selected the time of their attack; more than all, they seemed absolutely free from superstitious feeling. Yet, with it all, it is curious that no Edinburgh doctor or student seems ever to have been put in actual peril.

I turn now to the Burke and Hare murders, which had important effects in various directions. The locus was Tanner's Close in the West Port, outside the city boundary. Here Burke kept a lodging-house, and here, on the 29th of November 1827, Donald, an old pensioner, died in debt to Burke. Thus a needy man found himself in possession of the body of his dead-and-gone debtor, and it seemed to him quite justifiable to fill up the coffin with rubbish, and sell the corpse to Dr. Knox of 10 Surgeon Square at £7, 10s., a sum which seemed for the moment a small fortune. Then the notion occurred to him or his associate, Hare, how easy to press the life out of some of the waifs and strays that floated about the Grassmarket and its adjacent quarters, the very lowest in Edinburgh! These were here to-day

85

and gone to-morrow, and if they never turned up again who was there to ask after them or mourn their loss? I shall not tell here the story of "Daft Jamie" and handsome Mary Paterson and the other victims, or of how the murderers were discovered, how Hare turned King's evidence, how Burke was convicted, whilst his associate, Helen Macdougal, escaped. Burke was executed amidst impressive and even terrible marks of popular indignation, and by a sort of poetic justice, which appealed to the popular imagination, he himself was dissected.

For us Dr. Knox is a more interesting and important figure. The thing cast a shadow over his brilliant career, and at last his life was lost in flats and shallows, yet he was one of the most striking figures of his time. Though a cruel attack of small-pox in his youth had left him blind in the left eye, and plain to the verge, or over the verge, of ugliness, he was a special favourite with women, by his talk, by his manner, by you know not what. According to Shakespeare, Richard Crookback, a more evil man, surely, in every way, had the same fatal gift. Knox was widely read and of wide culture. In a city of brilliant talkers he was, so his biographer would have us believe, among the very best, nay, he ranks him equal or superior to De Quincey. We are told that he was so tender-hearted that he hated to think of experiments on living animals; he did not believe that any real advantage was to be gained therefrom. He certainly was possessed of true enthusiasm for science; he was by no means a rich man, yet he spent £300 on a whale which he dissected, and whose skeleton he secured for the

museum. It was only an amiable weakness that he was
very careful in his dress and person. His friend, Dr.
Macdonald, afterwards professor of natural history
at St. Andrews, calling upon him one day, found him
with his sister Mary. She had a pair of curling-tongs
in her hand, with which she was touching up her brother's rather scanty locks. " Ah, ah ! I see," said Macdonald, " the modern Apollo attired by the Graces."
Knox was not unduly disturbed by remarks of this
sort. Monro's pupils considered themselves in the
opposite camp. One of them wagered that he would
put the anatomist out of countenance. He set himself
right before him in the street: " Well, by Jove, Dr.
Knox, you are the ugliest fellow I ever saw in my life!"
Knox quietly patted the impudent student on the
shoulder: " Ah! then you cannot have seen my brother
Fred!" As it happened, Fred was much the handsomer
of the two, but he had been rather a thorn in the side
of the anatomist, who had shown him much kindness,
and maybe Knox was not ill pleased at the chance
to give him a sly dig. His own students doted on him,
they called him Robert for short. " Yes," said an
enemy, "Robert le Diable"; as such the people regarded him. How he escaped death, or at least bodily
injury, is a little curious; even the students were af-
frighted at the yells and howls of the mob outside his
evening classroom. The lecturer pointed out that he
had never missed a single lecture, and that he was not
afraid. Once the rabble burned his effigy and attacked
his house. Knox escaped to his friend, Dr. Adams, in
St. Patrick Square. He was asked how he dare venture out. He said he preferred to meet his fate, what-

87

ever it was, outside than die like a rat in a hole, then he threw open the military cloak that he wore and revealed a sword, pistols, and a Highland dirk. The brutes might kill him, but he would account for at least twenty of them first. All sorts of legends were told about him. He had many Kaffir skulls in his museum, and he was alleged to have explained: "Why, sir, there was no difficulty in Kaffraria. I had but to walk out of my tent and shoot as many as I wanted for scientific and ethnological purposes." Knox *had* experiences in South Africa, but they were not of this kind. In chap books and popular ditties his name ever went with the West Port murderers—a verse may be given:

> " Burke an' Hare
> Fell doun the stair
> Wi' a leddy in a box
> Gaun tae Doctor Knox."

Once when walking in the Meadows with Dr. Adams, Knox gave a penny and said some pleasant words to a pretty little girl of six who was playing there. "Would she come and live with him," he said jestingly, " if he gave her a penny every day?" The child shook her head. " No; you'd maybe sell me to Dr. Knox." His biographer affirms he was more affected by this childish thrust than by all the hostility of the mob. He could give a shrewd thrust himself, however. Dr. John Reid, the physiologist, had dissected two sharks, in which he could discover no sign of a brain; he was much perplexed. " How on earth could the animals live without it ?" said he to Knox. " Not the least extraordinary," was the answer. " If you go over to the Parliament House any morning you will see a great number of

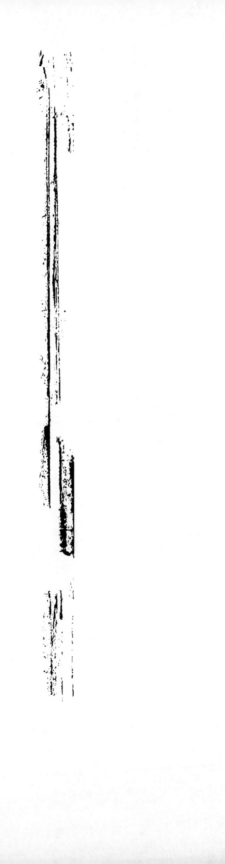

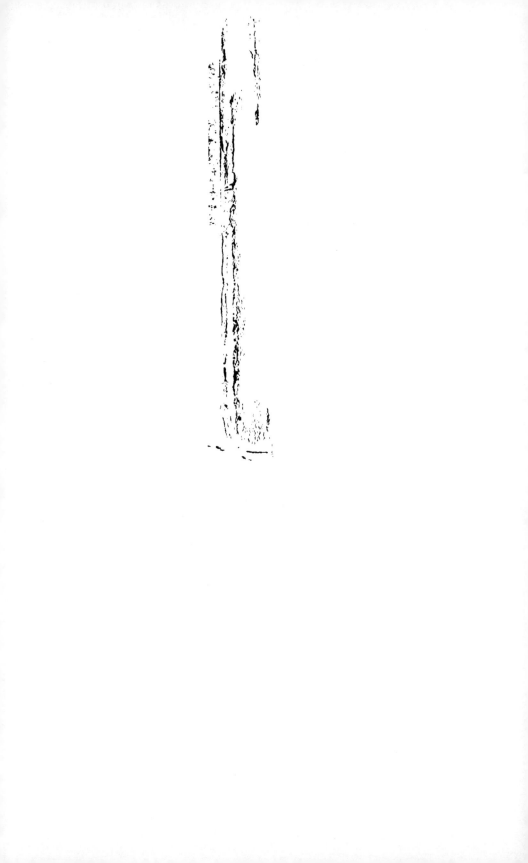

live sharks walking about without any brains whatever."

I have gone somewhat out of my way to complete
the story of the resurrectionist times. I return to an
earlier period with a note on the Royal Infirmary.
The great evil of the body-snatching incidents was
that it brought into disrepute and odium the profession towards which the public felt kindly and to which
they have been so greatly indebted for unpaid, un-
selfish, and devoted service. During nearly two hundred years the great Edinburgh hospital known as
" The Royal Infirmary " has borne witness to the
labours in the public cause of the Edinburgh doctors.
The story of its inception is creditable to the whole
community. It was opened in 1729 on a very humble scale in a small house. A charter was granted by
George II. in 1736, and on the 2nd August 1738 the
foundation-stone of a great building was laid to the east
of the college near the old High School. The whole
nation helped : the proprietors of stone quarries sent
stone and lime; timber merchants supplied wood; the
farmers carried materials; even day labourers gave the
contribution of their labour, all free of charge. Ladies
collected money in assemblies, and from every part
of the world help was obtained from Scotsmen settled
in foreign parts. Such is the old Royal Infirmary.
When it was unable further to supply the wants of
an ever-increasing population and the requirements
of modern science, the new Royal Infirmary was
founded in October 1870 and opened in October 1879
on the grounds of George Watson's Hospital, which
had been acquired for the purpose. The place is the

western side of the Meadow Walk, and the same devoted service to the cause of humanity has now been
given for more than thirty years in those newer walls.
But for the present we are concerned with incidents
in the lives of old eighteenth-century doctors. Dr.
Archibald Pitcairne (1652–1713), scholar and Jacobite, perhaps better known as that than as a physician,
was a well-known figure. He was buried in Greyfriars' Churchyard under a rectangular slab with four
pillars, on which there was an inscription by the
learned Ruddiman, himself a Jacobite scholar and
much in sympathy with the deceased. Pitcairne, like
the rest of Edinburgh, set great store on his wine;
with an almost sublime confidence he collected certain precious bottles and decreed in his will that
these should not be uncorked until the King should
enjoy his own again, but when the nineteenth century dawned it seemed hardly worth while to wait
any longer. Pious souls were found to restore the
tomb which, like so many other tombs in Greyfriars,
alas! had fallen into decay and disorder. They were
rewarded in a way which was surely after the master's
own heart. The 25th of December 1800 was the an-
niversary of the doctor's birth. The consent of Lady
Anne Erskine, his granddaughter, having been obtained, the bottles were solemnly uncorked, and they
were found to contain Malmsey in excellent preservation. Each contributor to the restoration received
a large glass quaintly called a jeroboam. This, you
do not doubt, they quaffed with solemn satisfaction
in memory of the deceased.

Pitcairne was far from " sound," according to the

standard of the time; he was deist or perhaps even atheist, it was opined, and one was as bad as the other, but he must have his joke at whatever price. At a sale of books a copy of Holy Writ could find no purchaser. "Was it not written," sniggered Pitcairne, "*Verbum Dei manet in æternum*?" The crowd had Latin enough to see the point. There was a mighty pother, strong remarks were freely interchanged, an action for defamation was the result, but it was compromised. I tell elsewhere of a trick played by Pitcairne on the tryers. Dr. Black, of the police establishment, played one even more mischievous on Archibald Campbell, the city officer. Black had a shop in the High Street, the taxes on which were much in arrear, and the irascible Highlander threatened to seize his "cattinary (ipecacuanha) pottles." Black connected the handle of his door with an electric battery and awaited developments. First came a clerk, who got nothing more than a good fright. He appeared before his master, who asked him what he meant by being "trunk like a peast" at that time of day? He set off for the doctor's himself, but when he seized the door handle he received a shock that sent him reeling into the gutter. "Ah," said one of the bystanders, who no doubt was in the secret, "you sometimes accuse me of liking a *glass*, but I think the doctor has given you a *tumbler*!" "No, sir," cried Archie as soon as he had recovered his speech. "He shot me through the shoulder with a horse-pistol. I heard the report by —— Laddie, do you see any plood?" An attempt was made to communicate with the doctor next day through the clerk, but the latter promptly refused.

"You and the doctor may paith go to the tevil; do you want me to be murdered, sir?"

Practical joking of the most pronounced description was much in favour in old Edinburgh. One Dempster, a jeweller in the Parliament Close, after a bout of hard drinking, was minded to cut his throat. A friend, described by Kay as "a gentleman of very convivial habits," remarked in jest that he would save him the trouble, and proceeded to stick a knife into him. It was at once seen that the joke—and the knife—if anything, had been pushed too far, and John Bennet, surgeon, was summoned in desperate haste; his treatment was so satisfactory that the wound was cured and the matter hushed up. The delighted Hamilton, relieved from dismal visions of the Tolbooth and worse, "presented Mr. Bennet with an elegant chariot," and from this time he was a made man. *His* ideas of humour were also a little peculiar. In payment of a bet he gave a dinner at Leith at which, as usual, everybody drank a great deal too much. They were to finish up the evening at the theatre, and there they were driven in mourning coaches at a funereal pace. All this you may consider mere tomfoolery, mad pranks of ridiculous schoolboys, but Bennet was a grave and reputable citizen; he was President of the Royal College of Surgeons in 1803, and died in 1805, and in the stories that I tell of him and others you have for good or ill eighteenth-century Edinburgh. He was a very thin man. He once asked a tailor if he could measure him for a suit of small clothes? "Oh," said the man of shears, "hold up your stick, it will serve the purpose well enough." You can only con-

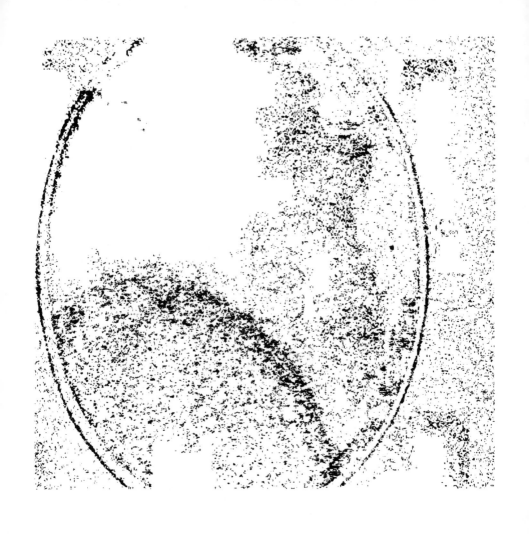

jecture whether the order was in fact given, for there the chronicle stops short. There are certain "large and comfortable words" in the *Rhyming Epistle to a Tailor* that would have served excellent well for a reply. Bennet had not the wit of Burns, and *his* reply is not preserved. You believe, however, it did not lack strength.

One of the best known surgeons of old Edinburgh was Alexander Wood (1725–1807), whose name still survives in a verse of Byron's. Once he "would a-wooing go," and was asked by his proposed father-in-law as to his means. He drew out his lancet case: "We have nothing but this," he said frankly. He got the lady, however. Sir James Stirling, the Provost, was unpopular on account of his opposition to a scheme for the reform of the Royal boroughs of Scotland. He was so like Wood that the one was not seldom mistaken for the other, and a tragedy of errors was well-nigh acted. An angry mob, under the mistaken impression that they had their Lord Provost, were dragging Wood to the edge of the North Bridge with the loudly expressed intention of throwing him over, but when he yelled above the din, " I'm lang Sandy Wood; tak' me to a lamp and ye'll see," the crowd dissolved in shouts of laughter.

When the great Mrs. Siddons was at the theatre it was a point of fashion with ladies to faint by the score. Wood's services were much in requisition, a good deal to his disgust. "This is glorious acting," said some one to him. "Yes, and a d—d deal o't too," growled Sandy, as he sweated from one unconscious fair to the other. Almost as well known as Sandy were his favourite sheep Willie and a raven, which followed him about whenever they could.

The most conspicuous figure of the eighteenth-century Edinburgh doctors was William Cullen (1710–1790), who in 1756 was made Professor of Chemistry in the University. One charming thing about those Edinburgh doctors is their breadth of culture: Cullen had the pleasure of reading *Don Quixote* in the original. When Dugald Stewart was a lad he fell ill, and was attended by Cullen, who recommended the great Spaniard to the ingenious youth. Doctor and patient had many a long talk over favourite passages. Dr. John Brown, afterwards author of the Brunonian system of medicine, was assistant to Cullen, but they quarrelled, and Brown applied for a mastership in the High School. Cullen could scarcely trust his ears. " Can this be oor Jock ? " quoth he.

Plain speaking was a note of those old Edinburgh medicals. Dr. John Clark was called in to consult as to the state of Lord Provost Drummond, who was ill of a fever. Bleeding seemed his only chance, but they thought him doomed, and it seemed useless to torture him. " None of your idle pity," said Clark, " but stick the lancet into him. I am sure he would be of that opinion were he able to decide upon his case." Drummond survived because, or in spite, of the operation. Lord Huntington died suddenly on the bench after having delivered an opinion. Clark was hurried in from the Parliament Close. " The man is as dead as a herring," said he brutally. Every one was shocked, for even in old Edinburgh plain speaking had its limits. He might have taken a lesson from

THE SURGEONS & THE DOCTORS

queer old Monboddo, who said to Dr. Gregory, " I
know it is not in the power of man to cure me; all I
wish is euthanasia, viz. a happy death." However, he
recovered. " Dr. Gregory, you have given me more
than I asked—a happy life." This was the younger
Gregory (1753–1821), Professor of Medicine in the
University, as his father had been earlier. He was an
eminent medical man, but a great deal more; his quick
temper, his caustic wit, his gift of style, made him a dan-
gerous opponent. The public laughed with him whether he was right or wrong. His *History of the Western Islands and Highlands of Scotland* showed that
he had other than medical interests. In 1793, when the
Royal Edinburgh volunteers were formed, he became
one of them, and he disturbed the temper of Sergeant
Gould, who said, " He might be a good physician, but
he was a very awkward soldier." He asked too many
questions. " Sir," said the instructor, "you are here to
obey orders and not to ask reasons; there is nothing
in the King's orders about reasons," and again, " Hold
your tongue, sir. I would rather drill ten clowns than
one philosopher."

He who professes universal knowledge is not in
favour with the specialist. Gregory visited Matthew
Baillie in London, and the two eminent medicos were
in after talk not entirely laudatory of one another.
" Baillie," said Gregory, " knows nothing but physic."
" Gregory," said the other, "seems to me to know everything but physic." This Matthew Baillie (1761–1823)
was a well-known physician of his time who had done
well in Edinburgh and gone south to do better still.
He worked sixteen hours a day, and no wonder he

was sometimes a little irritable. A fashionable lady once troubled him with a long account of imaginary ills, he managed to escape, but was recalled by an urgent message: " Might she eat some oysters on her return from the opera?" " Yes, ma'm," said Baillie, " shells and all."

Robert Liston (1794–1847) began as Barclay's assistant. Like other eminent surgeons stories are told of his presence of mind and fertility of resource during an operation. In an amputation of the thigh by Russell, Professor of Clinical Surgery at the University, an artery bled profusely. From its position it could not be tied up or even got at. Liston, with the amputating knife, chipped off a piece of wood from the operating table, formed it into a cone, and inserted it so as at once to stop the bleeding and so save the patient. In 1818 Liston left Barclay and lectured with James Syme (1799–1870) as his assistant, but in 1822 Syme withdrew and commenced to lecture for himself. His old master was jealous. "Don't support quackery and humbug," he wrote as late as 1830 in the subscription book of his rival's hospital. However, the two made it up before the end. This is not the place to speak of the skill of one of the greatest surgeons of his time; it was emphatically said of him " he never wasted a word, nor a drop of ink, nor a drop of blood."

A contemporary of Syme was Sir William Fergusson (1808–1877). He was one of that brilliant Edinburgh band who did so well in London; he began as a demonstrator to Knox. In London he became President of the Royal College of Surgeons, and the best known stories are of his later period. The speed and

PROFESSOR JAMES SYME
From a Drawing in the Scottish National Portrait Gallery

certainty of his work were remarkable. "Look out sharp," said a student, "for if you only even wink, you'll miss the operation altogether." Once when operating on a large deep-seated tumour in the neck, a severed artery gave forth an enormous quantity of blood; an assistant stopped the wound with his finger. "Just get your finger out of the way, and let's see what it is," and quick as lightning he had the artery tied up. There must have been something magical in the very touch of those great operators. A man afflicted with a tumour was perplexed as to the operation and the operator. But as he himself said: "When Fergusson put his hand upon me to examine my jaw, I felt that he was the man who should do the operation for me, the contrast between his examination and that of the others was so great."

A little earlier than these last were the famous family of Bells. Sir Charles Bell (1774–1842) is rather of London than of Edinburgh, though to him is ascribed the saying that "London is the place to live in, but not to die in." John Bell (1763–1820), his brother, was an Edinburgh surgeon of note, and a famous lecturer on surgery and anatomy. He had a violent controversy with Professor James Gregory, who attacked him in a *Review of the Writings of John Bell* by Jonathan Dawplucker. This malignant document was stuck up like a playbill on the door of the lecture room, on the gates of the college, and of the infirmary, where he operated; in short, everywhere, for such were the genial methods of Edinburgh controversy. Bell was much occupied and had large fees for his operations. A rich country laird once gave him a cheque

for £50, which the surgeon thought much below his
deserts. As the butler opened the door for him, he said
to that functionary: "You have had considerable trouble opening the door for me, here is a trifle for you,"
and he tossed him the bill. The laird took the hint
and immediately forwarded a cheque for £150. It is
worth while to note that Joseph Bell (1837–1911), who
sprang from the same family, has a place in literary
fiction as the original Sherlock Holmes.

The great name among modern Edinburgh doctors
is clearly that of Sir James Young Simpson (1811–
1870), an accomplished scholar and antiquarian, as
well as the discoverer of chloroform. His activity was
incessant. An apology was made to him because he
had been kept waiting for a ferry-boat. "Oh dear, no,"
said he, " I was all the time busy chloroforming the
eels in the pool." His pietistic tendencies by no means
quenched his sense of humour. Parting from a young
doctor who had started a carriage, " I have just been
telling him I will pray for his humility." Some one
propounded the not original view that the Bible and
Shakespeare were the greatest books in the world.
"Ah," said he, "the Bible and Shakespeare—and Oliver and Boyd's Edinburgh Almanac," this last huge
collection of facts he no doubt judged indispensable
for the citizen. The final and solemn trial of chloroform was made on the 28th November 1837. Simpson, Keith, and Duncan experimented on themselves.
Simpson went off, and was roused by the snores of Dr.
Duncan and the convulsive movements of Dr. Keith.
"He saw that the great discovery had been made, and
that his long labours had come to a successful end."

THE SURGEONS & THE DOCTORS

Some extreme clergymen protested. "It enabled women," one urged, "to escape part of the primeval curse; it was a scandalous interference with the laws of Providence." Simpson went on with his experiments. Once he became insensible under the influence of some drug. As he came to himself, he heard his butler, Clarke, shouting in anger and concern: "He'll kill himself yet wi' thae experiments, an' he's a big fule, for they'll never find onything better than clory." On another occasion, Simpson and some friends were taking chloral ether in aerated water. Clarke was much interested in the "new champagne chlory"; he took what was left downstairs and administered it to the cook, who presently became insensible. The butler in great alarm burst in upon the assembled men of science: "For God's sake, sir, come doun, I've pushioned the cook." Those personal experiments were indeed tricky things. Sir Robert Christison (1797–1882) once nearly killed himself with Calabar bean. He swallowed his shaving water, which acted promptly as an emetic, but he was very ill for some time. One of the most beautiful things in Simpson's story was the devotion of his own family to him, specially the care of his elder brother Alexander. "Oh, Sandie, Sandie," said Simpson again and again to the faithful brother, who stood by him even on his death-bed. To the outside world he seemed the one Edinburgh figure of first importance. A citizen was presented at the Court of Denmark to the King of that country. "You come from Edinburgh," said His Majesty. "Ah! Sir Simpson was of Edinburgh."

CHAPTER FIVE

ROYALTY

A DIFFICULTY MEETS YOU IN MAKING
Kings the subject of anecdote; the "fierce light" that
beats about a throne distorts the vision, your anecdote is perhaps grave history. Again, a monarch is
sure to be a centre of many untrustworthy myths.
What credit is to be placed, for instance, on engaging narratives like that of Howieson of Braehead and
James V.? Let us do the best we can. Here I pass
over the legends of Queen Margaret and her son David, but one story of the latter I may properly give.
Fergus, Prince of Galloway, was a timid if not repent-
ant rebel. He made friends with Abbot Alwyn of
Holyrood, who dressed him as a monk and presented
him with the brethren on the next visit of the King.
The kiss of peace, words of general pardon for all
past transgressions, were matters of form, not to be
omitted, but quite efficacious. Fergus presently revealed himself, and everybody accepted the dodge
as quite legitimate. You recall the trick by which
William of Normandy got Harold to swear on the
bones of the saints : the principle evidently was, get
your oath or your pardon by what dodge you choose,
but at all costs get it. Alexander, Lord of the Isles,
played a more seemly part in 1458 when he appeared
before James I. at the High Altar at Holyrood, and
held out in token of submission his naked sword with
the hilt towards the King. A quaint story is chronicled of James II. As a child he was held in Edinburgh
Castle by Crichton, the Lord Chancellor. The Queen
Mother was minded to abduct him; she announced a
pilgrimage to Whitekirk, a famous shrine or shrines,

for there was more than one of the name. Now a Queen, even on pilgrimage and even in old-time Scotland, must have a reasonable quantity of luggage, change of dresses, and what not. Thus no particular attention was given to a certain small box, though the Queen's servants, you believe, looked after it with considerable care. In fact it contained His Majesty *in propria persona*. By means of a number of airholes practised in the lid he managed to survive the journey. It is said his consent was obtained to his confinement, but those old Scots were used to carry their own lives and the lives of others in their hands, and he had little choice. This is the James who ended at Roxburgh by the bursting of a cannon. His son had peculiar relations with Edinburgh. In 1482 he gave the city its Golden Charter, exalting its civic rulers, and his Queen and her ladies knit with their own hands for the craftsmen the banner of the Holy Ghost, locally known for centuries as the "Blue Blanket," that famous ensign which it was ridiculously fabled the citizens carried with them to the Holy Land. At this, or rather against the proud spirit of its owners, James VI. girded in the *Basilicon Doron*. It made a last public appearance when it waved, a strange anachronism, in 1745 from the steeple of St. Giles to animate the spirits of the burghers against Prince Charles and his Highlanders, then pressing on the city. There it hung, limp, bedraggled, a mere hopeless rag! How unmeet, incongruous, improper, to use it against a Stuart! At any rate it was speedily pulled down, and stowed away for ever. James III. fell at Sauchieburn in 1488. It was rumoured he had surviv-

MARGARET TUDOR, QUEEN OF JAMES IV.

From the Painting by Mabuse

ed the battle and taken refuge on the *Yellow Carvel*
which Sir Andrew Wood, his Admiral, had brought
to the Forth. The rebel lords sent for Sir Andrew,
whom the Duke of Rothesay, afterwards James IV.,
mistook for his dead parent. "Sir, are you my father?"
said the boy. "I am not your father, but his faithful
servant," answered the brave sailor with angry tears.
The lords after many questions could make nothing
of him, so they let him go back to his ship, just in time
to save the lives of the hostages whom his brothers,
truculent and impatient, were about to string up at
the yard-arm.

The reign of James IV. is full of picturesque incident. There are stories of brilliant tournaments at
Edinburgh, where he sat on a ledge of the Castle rock
and presided over the sports of a glittering throng
gathered from far and near. There are the splendid
records of his marriage with Margaret, Henry VII.'s
daughter, the marriage that a hundred years afterwards was to unite the Crowns, the marriage whose
fateful import even then was clearly discerned; and
there is the tragic close at Flodden, of which, in the
scanty remnants of the Flodden Wall, Edinburgh
still bears the tangible memorials.

I prefer to note here quainter and humbler memorials. James had a curious, if fitful, interest in art
and letters. The picturesque Pitscottie boldly affirms
him "ane singular guid chirurgione." In the book of
the royal expenses we have some curious entries. A
fine pair of teeth had an unholy attraction for him.
He would have them out, on any or no pretext. "Item,
ane fellow because the King pullit furtht his teith,

xviii shillings." "Item, to Kynnard, ye barbour, for twa teith drawn furtht of his hed be the King, xviii sh." History does not record what the "fellow" or the "barbour" said on the subject, or whether they were contented with the valuation of their grinders, which was far from excessive since the computation is in Scots money, wherein a shilling only equalled an English penny. The barber, moreover, according to the practice of the time, was a rival artist, but—speculation is vain; though it will be observed that instead of the patients feeing the Royal physician, they were themselves feed to submit to treatment. This same Lindsay of Pitscottie is also our authority for another story to the full as quaint. James desired to know the original language of mankind. He procured him two children—human waifs and strays were plentiful in old Scotland; provided them with a dumb woman for nurse, and plumped the three down on Inchkeith, that tiny islet in the Forth a little way out from Leith. Our chronicler is dubious as to the result. "Some say they spak guid Hebrew, but I know not by authoris rehearse." The "guid Hebrew," if it ever existed, died with them. Nor is there any trace of a Scots Yiddish, a compound whereof you shudder at the bare conception.

Under James V. we have the popular legend of Howieson already referred to. James, or all tradition errs, was given to wandering in disguise through his kingdom to see how his subjects fared or to seek love adventures, or perhaps for both. The King of the Commons, as his folk called him, took things as they came and life as he found it. The story goes that he was courting some rustic damsel in Cramond village when he was set upon by a band of enraged rivals or relatives. He defended himself on the narrow bridge that then crossed the Almond, but spite his efficient swordplay was like to get the worst of it when a rustic, one Jock Howieson, who was working near at hand, came to his aid and laid about him so lustily with his flail that the assailants fled. There was some talk of a reward, and Jock confessed that his dearest wish was to own the land which he tilled. The stranger, without revealing his identity, or, rather, concealing it under the title of the Gudeman of Ballengiech (the traditional name adopted by James in his wanderings and derived from a road or pass at Stirling Castle), made an appointment with his preserver at Holyrood Palace. Jock turned up in due course, and was promised an interview with the King, whom he would recognise as the only man with his bonnet on. Jock, with rustic humour, replied that either he himself or his friend must be the King since they were the only two that were covered. A grant of the land, which conveniently turned out to be Crown property, speedily followed on the condition that when the King came that way Jock or his descendant should present him with a vessel of water wherein to wash his hands. "Accordingly in the year 1822 when George IV. came to Scotland the descendant of John Howieson of Braehead, who still possesses the estate, which was given to his ancestor, appeared at a solemn festival and offered His Majesty water from a silver ewer that he might perform the service by which he held his lands." Thus Sir Walter Scott in the *Tales of a Grandfather.*

BOOK OF EDINBURGH ANECDOTE

It seems that in 1822 the proprietor was William Howieson Crawford, Esq. of Braehead and Crawfordland. One fancies that the good Sir Walter jogged, if one may say so, Mr. Crawford's memory, and possibly arranged both "the solemn festival" and "the silver ewer." This entertaining legend has not escaped—how could it?—sceptical modern critics. It is shown that not for centuries after James did the story take coherent shape, and that as handed down it can scarce have happened. What can you say but that in some form or other it may have had a foundation in fact? That if it is not possible conclusively to prove, neither is it possible clearly to disprove, and finally it is at least *ben trovato*.

In setting down one or two anecdotes of James V.'s Queens I am on surer ground. In 1537, James was married to Magdalen, daughter of Francis I., in the Cathedral of Notre-Dame in Paris. They reached Scotland on the 27th of May. As the Queen landed she knelt down and kissed the soil, a pretty way of adopting her new fatherland that touched those hard Scots as it still touches us, but on the 10th of July the poor child, she was not complete seventeen, was lying dead at Holyrood. It was a cold spring: the Castle was high and bleak, Holyrood was damp and low. She was a fragile plant and she withered and faded away, for us the most elusive and shadowy of memories, yet still with a touch of old-world sweetness. All the land grieved for that perished blossom. It was the first general mourning known in Scotland, and there was in due time "the meed of some melodious tear" from George Buchanan and David Lindsay.

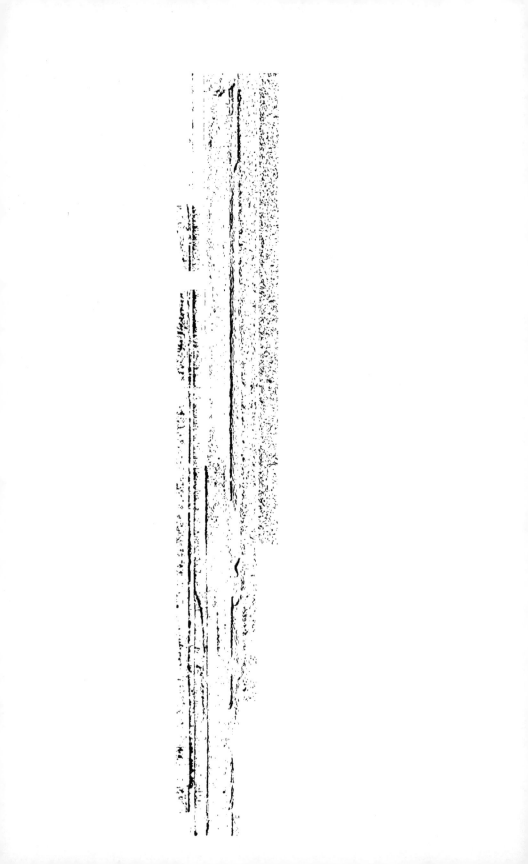

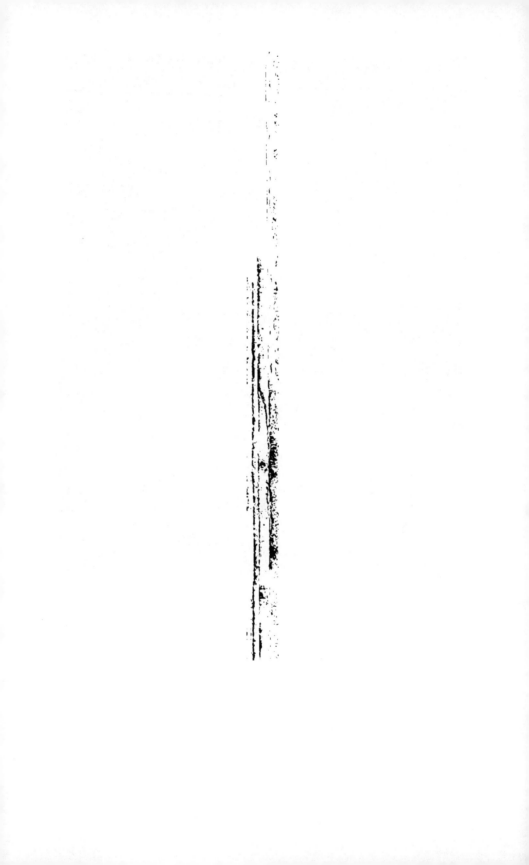

OF ROYALTY IN EDINBURGH

Before a year had passed away, to wit, in June 1538, James had brought another mate to Scotland, a very different character, known in our history as Mary of Guise, the famous mother of a still more famous daughter, Mary Queen of Scots. James V.'s widow was Queen Regent during most of the minority of her child, and she held her own with unfailing courage and ability. If she tricked and dodged she was like everybody else. In that bitter fight neither Catholic nor Protestant were over-scrupulous; she was on the unpopular and finally on the losing side, but she fought as steadfastly and stoutly for what gods she had as Knox himself, and she was not one of the royal authors. Her story is told for us mainly by her enemies, and chief of all by John Knox, the most deadly among them.

In 1556 he addressed a letter to her, by desire of the Congregation, exhorting her to renounce the errors of Rome; she handed this to Beaton, Bishop of Glasgow. "Please you, my Lord, to read a pasquil." Knox, a humorist himself, was peculiarly sensitive to scornful irony, and of that two of his contemporaries had a peculiar gift, the Queen Regent, Mary of Guise, and the Secretary, Maitland of Lethington. He never forgot nor forgave these thrusts, and he cordially hated both. This does not justify his vicious and one-sided account of the death-bed of this Royal lady in 1560: "God for his greit mercyis saik red us frome the rest of the Guysiane blude. Amen. Amen." Such were the folk of the time. In 1560 the Congregation made an attack on Leith, which was held by the French. They failed: the French, Knox tells us, stripped the slain and laid them along the wall. When the Regent looked across the valley at this strange decoration she could not contain herself for joy, and said, " Yonder are the fairest tapestrie that ever I saw. I wald that the haill feyldis that is betwix this place and yon war strowit with the same stuffe." I am quite ready to believe this story. On both sides death did not extinguish hatred, not even then was the enemy safe from insult. Does not Knox himself tell us with entire approval how his party refused the dead Regent the rights of her church, and how the body was " lappit in a cope of lead and keipit in the Castell" for long weary months till it could be sent to France, where the poor ashes were at length laid to rest in due form?

Whatever the creed of either side, both in practice firmly held that Providence was on the side of big battalions. Almost of necessity the Regent was continually scheming for troops and possession of castles and so forth. Some quaint anecdotes are told of her dealings with Archibald, sixth Earl of Angus, grandson of old " Bell the Cat," and gifted like him with power of emphatic utterance. Angus had married, in 1514, Margaret, the widow of James IV. For some time he was supreme in Scotland and was at the lowest a person to be reckoned with. In his passages of wit with the Regent she comes off second best, but then again the account is by Hume of Godscroft, historian and partisan of the house of Douglas. The time had not yet come for Kings to subsidise letters. Once Mary told Angus that she proposed to create the Earl of Huntly, his rival, a duke. " By the might of God "— his oath when angry—" then I will be a drake." He was punning on duke, which is Scots for duck, and meant to say that he would still be the greater, though possibly the Queen required a surgical operation before she understood. Once he came to pay his compliments to her in Edinburgh at the head of a thousand horsemen. She angrily reproved him for breach of the proclamation against noblemen being so attended ; but Angus had his answer ready. "The knaves will follow me. Gladly would I be rid of them, for they devour all my beef and my bread, and much, Madam, should I be beholden to you, if you could tell me how to get quit of them." Again, when she unfolded to him a plan for a standing army, he promptly said, "We will fight ourselves better than any hired fellows," she could hardly reply that it was against disturbing forces like his own that she longed for a defence. She proposed to garrison Tantallon, that strong fortress of the Douglas which still rises, mere shell though it be, in impressive ruin on the Lothian coast opposite the Bass Rock. Angus had his goshawk on his wrist, and was feeding it as he talked with the Queen, and one notes that it seemed quite proper for nobles to go about so accompanied. He made as if he addressed the bird, "Greedy gled, greedy gled, thou hast too much already, and yet desirest more": the Queen chose not to take the obvious hint, but persisted. Angus boldly faced the question. "Why not, Madam? Ah yes, all is yours, but, Madam, I must be captain of your muster and keeper of Tantallon." Not that these epigrams altered the situation, rather they expressed it. Even in the hostile narrative your sympathies are sometimes on the side of Mary of

Guise. In 1558 a calf with two heads was shown to her, apparently as a portent of calamity, like the *bos locutus est* of Livy, but what it exactly meant no one could say. "She scripped and said it was but a common thing," in which, at any rate, she has the entire approval of the modern world.

Her daughter Mary gave Edinburgh the most exciting, romantic, interesting, and important time in the city's annals. It was scarcely six years in all (19th August 1561–16th June 1567), but those were crowded years: the comparatively gay time at first; the marriage with Darnley; the assassination of Rizzio; the murder of Darnley; her seizure by Bothwell; her marriage to Bothwell; the surrender of Carberry, with her departure for Loch Leven. I scarce know what to select. On 15th April 1562 Randolph writes: "The Queen readeth daily after her dinner, instructed by a learned man, Mr. George Buchanan, somewhat of Livy." You wish it had been Virgil, because you are sure scholar and pupil had tried the *Sortes Virgilianæ* with results even more pregnant than happed to Mary's grandson Charles I., at Oxford, in the time of the civil wars, and the mere mention of George Buchanan is fateful. He, at any rate, was an earnest and high-minded man, and he employed all the grace of his Latin muse to say delightful things about her on more than one occasion, and he had, in after years, every term of invective to hurl at her also in Latin, but prose this time, and he felt himself justified in both. The modern point of view which would find her almost certainly guilty of being an accessary before the fact to the slaughter of Darnley, that would

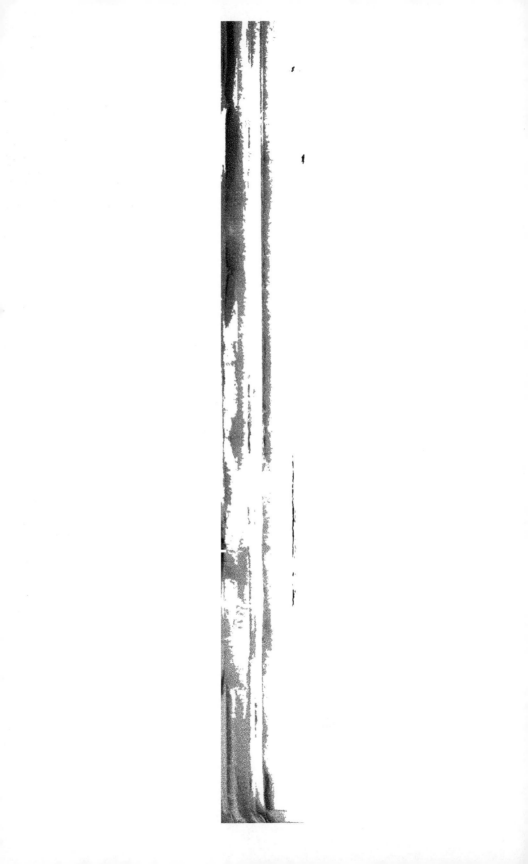

also find that the circumstances were so peculiar, that she was by no means altogether blameworthy, was not the conception of her own day. She was guilty, and therefore a monster of wickedness ; or she was innocent, and therefore a martyr : those are the sharply opposed views. It was not an age of compromise or judicial balance. Take another incident. Rizzio's murder was on 9th March 1566. Immediately after she won over Darnley, mixed up with the affair as he had been. The pair escaped from Holyrood in the midnight hours, through the burial vaults and tombs of the palace. Darnley made some sudden and half-involuntary reference to the freshly-turned grave of Rizzio that lay right in their path. Mary gripped his arm and vowed, in what must have been a terrible whisper, that ere a year had passed " a fatter than he should lie as low." Kirk-o'-field was on 10th February 1567.

I prefer here to deal with trivialities, not tragedies. How curiously from the first she occupied the thoughts of men : ere she was a month old grave statesmen were busy match-making ! In 1558 she married the Dauphin, afterwards Francis II. When the news came to Edinburgh it was felt that some celebration was necessary. " Mons Meg was raised forth from her lair " and fired once. The bullet was found on Wardie Muir, two miles off, and bought back by a careful Government to serve another occasion. We are told the cost of the whole affair was ten shillings and eightpence, no doubt Scots currency, and without any doubt at all the most frugal merry-making in history. I will relate this other comic interlude of the night of her arrival at

H

Holyrood. Knox tells the story of her landing with his never-failing graphic force: the thick and dark mist that covered the earth, a portent of the evil days to come, "the fyres of joy" that blazed through it all, "and a company of the most honest with instruments of musick and with musitians gave their salutationis at hir chamber wyndo. The melody (as she alledged) lyked hir weill and she willed the same to be contineued some nightis after." Knox is a little doubtful as to the sincerity of her thanks. Brantôme was of the Queen's company, and the gay Frenchman gives us a very different account of the proceedings. "There came under her window five or six hundred rascals of that town, who gave her a concert of the vilest fiddles and little rebecs, which are as bad as they can be in that country, and accompanied them with singing Psalms, but so miserably out of time and concert that nothing could be worse. Ah, what melody it was! What a lullaby for the night!" One of the Queen's Maries remembered and applied a favourite text of Montlin, Bishop of Valence, on which they had heard more than one sermon: "Is any merry, let him sing Psalms." If she showed herself a Scot by her Biblical quotation, you guess she revealed her French upbringing in an infinitely expressive shrug and grimace; but for that night even Mary's spirit was broken. She found no place for mirth and could scarce refrain from tears, yet she had the courage on that and other mornings gracefully to thank the musicians; only she shifted her bedroom to the floor above, and slept, you believe, none the worse for the change. The drop in material comfort, not to speak of anything else, must have been enormous, from gay, wealthy, joyous France to this austere, poverty-stricken land and people. Did not some mad scheme for instant return move through her brain? No, for after all she was a Queen and a Stuart, and it is mere commonplace to say that she never failed to confront her fate.

It were easy and useless to dwell on the glaring contrasts in character between Mary and her son James, between the most tragically unfortunate and the most prosaically fortunate of the Stuarts. Such contrasts between the character and fate of parent and child are not uncommon in daily life. The first day of James on earth was memorable for the dramatic meeting of his father and mother. He was born in Edinburgh Castle, in the little room that is shown you there, between nine and ten on the morning of Wednesday, 19th June 1566. About two in the afternoon Darnley came to see his child. Like everybody else in Edinburgh, he had known of the event for hours, since a few minutes after the birth heavy guns, almost at Mary's bedside and without a word of protest from the courageous woman, had roared out their signal to the capital that well-nigh went mad on the instant with joy and pride. The nurse put the child into Darnley's arms. "My Lord," said Mary simply and solemnly, "God has given you and me a son." Then she turned to Sir William Stanley: "This is the son who I hope shall first unite the two kingdoms of Scotland and England." The Englishman said something courteous about the prior rights of Mary and Darnley, and then Mary wandered off into the Rizzio business only three months before. What would have happened if they had then killed her? You fancy the colour went and came in Darnley's face. "These things are all past," he muttered. "Then," said the Queen, "let them go." As James grew up he became well-nigh the most eminent of royal and noble authors, and that strange mixture of erudition, folly, wisdom, and simplicity which marks him as one of the oddest characters in history. He was great in nicknames and phrases, and the nicknames stuck and the phrases are remembered. "Tam o' the Coogate" for the powerful Earl of Haddington; "Jock o' the Sclates" for the Earl of Mar, because he, when James's fellow-pupil, had been entrusted by George Buchanan with a slate thereon to note James's little peccadilloes in his tutor's absence; better than all, "Jingling Geordie" for George Heriot the goldsmith. What a word picture that gives you of the prosperous merchant prince who possibly hinted more than once that he could an he would buy up the whole Court! That well-known story of ostentatious benevolence can hardly be false. George visited James at Holyrood and found him over a fire of cedar wood, and the King had much to say of the costly fuel; and then the other invited him to visit his booth hard by St. Giles', where he was shown a still more costly fire of the Royal bonds or promissory notes, as we might call them in the language of to-day. We know that the relations between the banker and his Royal customer were of the very best; and how can we say anything but good of Heriot when we think of that splendid and beautiful foundation that to-day holds its own with anything that modern Edinburgh can show? As for his colloquial epigrams, there is the famous account of David I. as a " sair sanct " for the Crown ; his humorous and not altogether false statement, when the Presbyterian ministers came to interview him, " Set twal chairs, there be twal kings coming "; his description—at an earlier date, of course —of the service of the Episcopal Church as " an evil said mass in English wanting nothing but the liftings "; his happy simile apropos of his visit to Scotland in 1617 of his " salmon-lyke " instinct—a great and natural longing to see "our native soil and place of our birth and breeding." No wonder he got a reputation for wisdom ! A quaint anecdote dates his renown in that regard from a very early period indeed. On the day after his birth the General Assembly met, and were much concerned as to the religious education of the infant. They sent Spottiswoode, " Superintendant of Lothian," to interview the Queen on the subject. He urged a Protestant baptism and upbringing for the child. Mary gave no certain answer, but brought in her son to show to the churchmen, and probably also as the means of ending an embarrassing interview. Spottiswoode, however, repeated his demand, and with pedantic humour asked the infant to signify his consent. The child babbled something, which one of the hearers at least took for" Amen,"and " Master Amen " was the Court-name for Spottiswoode ever after.

James deserved to be called the British Solomon, but then how did it happen that the man had such a knack of making himself ridiculous ? On the night of the 23rd July 1593 the madcap Francis Earl of Bothwell made one of his wild raids on Holyrood. James came out of his chamber in terror and disorder, "with his breeks in his hand"; trembling, he implored the invaders to do him no harm. "No, my good bairn," said Bothwell with insolence (the King was twenty-seven at the time); and as a matter of fact no harm was done him. Fate tried the mother of James and the son of James far more severely than it ever tried James himself, and Mary Stuart and Charles the First managed things so ill that each in the end had to lay the head on the block, but no one ever spoke to them like that, and they never made themselves ridiculous. Mary was never less than Queen and Charles was never less than King, and each played the last scene so superbly as to turn defeat and ruin into victory and honour, and if you say it was birth and breeding and the heritage of their race how are you to account for the odd figure in between? Here is another trivial anecdote. On Tuesday, 5th April 1603, James set forth southward to take possession of his English throne. As Robert Chambers points out, here was the most remarkable illustration of Dr. Johnson's remark that the best prospect a Scotsman ever saw was the high road to England. Not very far from Holyrood stood splendid Seton Palace, and as James and his folk drew near they crossed another procession. It was the funeral train of the first Earl of Winton, who had been an attached adherent of James's mother. One of the Queen's Maries was a Seton, and James, as was right and proper, made way and halted till the procession of the mightier King Death had passed. He perched himself in the meantime on the garden wall, and you think of him hunched up there "glowering" at the proceedings. On his return to Scotland James spent at Seton Palace his second night after crossing the Tweed, and it was here he received Drummond of Hawthornden's poem of *Forth Feasting*. There was unbounded popular rejoicing, though not without an occasional discordant note; for the Presbyterian Scot was terribly suspicious. It happened that one of the royal guards died during the visit. He was buried with the service of the English Church, read by a surpliced clergyman; there was an unseemly riot, and the parson if he escaped hard knocks got the hardest of words. He was William Laud, afterwards Archbishop of Canterbury. Let me end those stories of James with one of a lighter character. I have spoken of James's schoolfellow, the Earl of Mar. He was left a widower, his wife Ann Drummond having died after giving birth to a son. An Italian magician had shown him, as in a glass darkly, the face of his second spouse. He identified the figure as that of Lady Mary Stuart of the Lennox family, who would have none of him; for the Drummond baby would be Earl of Mar, whilst hers would only be Mr. Erskine. Jock o' the Sclates was so mortified at the refusal that he took to his bed, and seemed like to make a mortal though ridiculous exit; but the King came to encourage him. " By God, ye shanna dee, Jock, for ony lass in a' the land! " In due course James brought about the marriage, which turned out well for all concerned.

The Kings after James had but a very remote and chance connection with Edinburgh. There are golfing anecdotes of Charles I. and James II., and there is not even that about Charles II. Charles I. when in Edin-

burgh was fond of the Royal game on the links at Leith,
then the favourite ground for the sport. It was whilst
so engaged he heard the news of the massacre in Ire-
land, and not unnaturally he threw down his club and
hastily quitted the links. The anecdote of James II. is
of a more detailed character, for Golfer's Land, grim
and battered, still stands in the Canongate. When
James held court at Holyrood as Duke of York, he
was given to golfing on the links. He had a match
with two English noblemen, his fellow-player in the
foursome being John Patterson, a poor shoemaker in
the Canongate, but a superb golfer. If you don't know
the story, at least you anticipate the result. The Englishmen were shamefully beaten, and the stake being
too small game for Royalty, Patterson netted the pro-
ceeds, with which he built Golfer's Land. The learned
Dr. Pitcairne adorned it with a Latin inscription, and
all you can say is you hope the legend is true. Another
story of James tells how one of the soldiers on duty at
Holyrood, mortal tired or perhaps mortal drunk, was
found asleep at his post. Grim old Tom Dalzell was
in charge, and he was not the man to overlook such
an offence, but marked out the culprit for instant execution. The Duke, however, intervened and saved the
man's life. I am glad to tell those stories of James, who
as a rule fares so ill at the hands of the historians.

Although I have said nothing of Charles II., his
statue perhaps deserves a word. It stands in Parliament Square, between St. Giles' and the Parliament
House. The local authorities were once minded to set
up the stone image of Cromwell in that same place,
indeed the stone had been got ready when the Restor-

ation changed the current of their thoughts, and after an interval of twenty-five years they put up one to Charles II. instead, the only statue that old Edinburgh for many a long day possessed.

Kings and Queens came and went for the better part of a century, but none of them came to Edinburgh, or even to Scotland, for you cannot count the fugitive visit of the Old Pretender as anything at all. It was not till Prince Charles Edward Stuart made the memorable descent on the capital in the '45 that I can again take up the easy thread of my narrative. Here anecdotes are abundant, but the most too well known for quotation: they tell of the cowardice of the citizens and the daring simplicity of the Highlanders. The capture of the city was without opposition. A burgher taking a walk saw a Highlander astride a gun, and said to him that surely he did not belong to the troops that were there yesterday. "Och no," quoth the Celt, "she pe relieved." According to all accounts, the invading army behaved well. An exception was the man who presented a musket at the head of a respectable shopkeeper, and when the trembling cit asked what he wanted, replied, "A bawbee." This modest request being instantly complied with, they parted the best of friends. The demands of others did not rise beyond a pinch of snuff, and one hopes it was not required in an equally heroic manner. The day of Charles's entry, his father as King and himself as Regent were proclaimed at the Cross by the heralds in their antique garb and with their antique rites, and conspicuous among the attendant throng was the beautiful Mrs. Murray of Broughton on horseback with a drawn sword, covered with white cockades, the conspicuous Stuart emblem. With her it was the one supreme moment of a life that was presently obscured in shadows. Her husband's reputation as traitor still lay in the future. You remember how Scott's father, Whig as he was, dashed to pieces the cup that Murray had touched, so that neither he nor any of his family might ever use it? At that same Cross, not many months after, the standards of the clans and of Charles were burnt by the hangman and Tron men or sweeps by the order of Cumberland, the least generous of foes. In the crowd there must have been many who had gazed on the other ceremonial. What a complete circuit fortune's wheel had made! Amidst the festivities of Holyrood those things were not foreseen. Then came Prestonpans, with many a legend grave or gay. I will not repeat in detail those almost threadbare stories of the Highland estimation of the plunder: how that chocolate was Johnny Cope's salve, and the watch that stopped was a beast that had died, and a pack-saddle was a fortune, and so forth. Here is perhaps the quaintest anecdote of misadventure. Two volunteers, one of them destined to the bench as Lord Gardenstone, were detailed to watch the precincts of Musselburgh. They were both convivial "cusses": they knew every tavern in Edinburgh and every change-house in the far and near suburbs: they remembered a little den noted for its oysters and its sherry—possibly an odd combination, but the stomachs of young Edinburgh were invincible. At any rate, they made themselves merry. But there were limbs of the law, active or "stickit," on the other side, and one as he prowled about espied the pair, and seized them without difficulty as they tried to negotiate that narrow bridge which still crosses the Esk at Musselburgh. They were dragged to the camp at Duddingston, and were about to be hanged as spies, but escaped through the intercession of still another lawyer, Colquhoun Grant, an adherent of the Prince. This same Colquhoun was a remarkable person, and distinguished himself greatly at Preston. He seized the horse of an English officer and pursued a great body of dragoons with awe-inspiring Gaelic curses. On, on went the panic-stricken mob, with Grant at their heels so close that he entered the Netherbow with them, and was just behind them at the Castle. He stuck his dirk into the gate, rode slowly down the High Street, ordered the Netherbow Port to be thrown open, and the frightened attendants were only too glad to see the back of him. In after years he beat his sword to a ploughshare, or rather a pen, and became a highly prosperous Writer to the Signet of Auld Reekie. It is related by Kay that Ross of Pitcarnie, a less fortunate Jacobite, used to extract " loans " from him by artful references to his exploits at Preston and Falkirk. The cowardice of the regular troops is difficult to account for, but there was more excuse for the volunteers, of whom many comical stories are told. The best is that of John Maclure the writing-master, who wound a quire of writing-paper round his manly bosom, on which he had written in his best hand, with all the appropriate flourishes, "This is the body of John Maclure, pray give it a Christian burial." However, when once the Prince was in, the citizens preserved a strict neutrality. Of sentimental Jacobites like Allan Ramsay we hear not a word : they lay low and said nothing. What could

they do but wait upon time? One clergyman was bold
enough, at any rate, namely, the Rev. Neil M'Vicar,
incumbent of St. Cuthbert's, who kept on praying for
King George during the whole time of the Jacobite occupation: " As for this young man who has come a-
mong us seeking an earthly crown, we beseech Thee
that he may obtain what is far better, a heavenly one."
Archibald Stewart was then Provost, and he was said
to have Jacobite leanings. His house was by the West
Bow, and here, it was rumoured, he gave a secret banquet to Charles and some of his chiefs. The folk in the
Castle heard of this, and sent down a party of soldiers to
seize the Prince. Just as they were entering the house
the guests disappeared into a cabinet, which was really
an entrance to a trap stair, and so got off. The story is
obviously false. Stewart was afterwards tried for neg-
lect of duty during the Rebellion, and the proceedings,
which lasted an inordinate time—the longest then on
record—resulted in his triumphant acquittal. The
Goverment had never omitted a damning piece of evidence like this—if the thing had happened. One comic
and instructive touch will pave my way to the next
episode. A certain Mrs. Irvine died in Edinburgh in the
year 1837 at the age of ninety-nine years or so, if the
story be true which makes her a young child in the '45.
She was with her nurse in front of the Palace, where
a Highlander was on guard: she was much attracted
by his kilt, she advanced and seized it, and even pulled
it up a little way. The nurse was in a state of terror,
but the soldier only smiled and said a few kind words
to the child. The moral of this story is that till the
Highlanders took the city the kilt was a practically

unknown garment to the folk in the capital. Six years before Mrs. Irvine died, to wit in 1831, she saw the setting up at the intersection of George Street and Hanover Street of the imposing statue by Chantrey which commemorates the visit of George IV. to Scotland. This visit was from 14th August to 29th August 1822. Sir Walter Scott stage-managed the business, and Lockhart has pointed out how odd the whole thing was. Scott was a Lowlander, and surely better read than any other in the history of his country, and who better knew that the history of Scotland is the history of the Lowlands, that Edinburgh was a Lowland capital, that the Highlands were of no account, save as disturbing forces? Yet, blinded by the picturesque effect, he ran the show as if the Highlands and the Highlands alone were Scotland. Chieftains were imported thence, Scott was dressed as a Highlander, George was dressed as a Highlander, Sir William Curtis, London alderman, was dressed as a Highlander: the whole thing trembled on the verge of burlesque. The silver St. Andrew's cross that Scott presented to the King when he landed had a Gaelic inscription! The King, not to be outdone, called for a bottle of Highland whisky and pledged Sir Walter there and then, and Sir Walter begged the glass that had touched the Royal lips, for an heirloom no doubt. He got it, thrust it into his coat-tail pocket, and presently reduced it to fragments in a moment of forgetfulness by sitting on it. There, fortunately, the thing was left: they did not try to reconstitute it, after the fashion of the Portland Vase in the British Museum. George IV. had a fine if somewhat corpulent figure (Leigh Hunt wrote to Archibald Constable at an earlier period that he had suffered imprisonment for not thinking the Prince Regent slender and laudable), and no doubt in the Highland garb he made a "very pretty man," but the knight from London was even more corpulent. Byron sings in *The Age of Bronze*:

> "He caught Sir William Curtis in a kilt,
> While thronged the Chiefs of every Highland clan
> To hail their brother Vich Ian an Alderman."

"Faar's yer speen?" (Where's your spoon?) said an envious and mocking Aberdeen bailie, to the no small discomfiture of the London knight, as he strutted to and fro, believing that his costume was accurate in every detail. Lockhart hints that possibly Scott invented the story to soothe the King's wounded feelings. On the 24th of August the Provost and Magistrates of Edinburgh entertained the King in Parliament House to a great banquet. The King gave one toast, "The Chieftains and Clans of Scotland, and prosperity to the Land of Cakes." He also attended a performance of *Rob Roy* at the theatre. Carlyle was in Edinburgh at the time, and fled in horror from what he called the "efflorescence of the flunkeyisms," but everybody else seemed pleased, and voted the thing a great success. No doubt it gave official stamp to what is perhaps still the ordinary English view of Scotland. The odd thing is that Scott himself never grasped the Highland character—at least, where has he drawn one for us? Rob Roy and Helen Macgregor and Fergus M'Ivor and Flora M'Ivor are mere creatures of melodrama, but the Bailie and Mattie and Jeanie Deans and Davie Deans and the Antiquary and

OF ROYALTY IN EDINBURGH

Edie Ochiltree and Andrew Fairservice and Mause and Cuddie Hedrigg are real beings of flesh and blood. We have met them or their likes on the muir or at the close fit, or on the High Street or in the kirk.

Twenty years passed, and a British Sovereign again comes to Scotland. On the 1st of September in 1842 Queen Victoria and Prince Albert arrived at Granton. They duly proceeded towards Edinburgh. The Lord Provost and Bailies ought to have met them at Canonmills to present the keys of the city, but they were "conspicuous by their absence," and the Royal party had to go to Dalkeith (like George the Fourth, they put up for the time in the Duke of Buccleuch's huge palace there). The local wits waxed merry; they swore that my Lord Provost and his fellows had overslept themselves, and a parody of a well-known song rang unpleasantly in civic ears:

> "Hey, Jamie Forrest,
> Are ye waukin' yet,
> Or are yer byles
> Snoring yet?"

However, the Royal party came specially from Dalkeith on a subsequent day, and received the keys at the Cross, and nobody even whispered "Anticlimax!"

CHAPTER SIX

MEN OF LETTERS. PART I

CHAPTER SIX   MEN OF LETTERS

GEORGE BUCHANAN IS THE FIRST IN time as he is one of the first in eminence of Scots men of letters. Many wrote before him; among the kings, James I. certainly, James V. possibly, and even yet they are worth reading by others than students. There is Gawin Douglas, the Bishop, there is Buchanan's contemporary, Knox, the Reformer, whose work is classic, but they are not men of letters in the modern sense of the term. Buchanan is. Literature was his aim in life, and he lived by it indirectly if not directly. He is always to me a perplexing figure. How deep was his reforming zeal, how deep his beliefs, I cannot tell. I have read, I trust not without profit, Mr. Hume Brown's two careful volumes upon this great Scot, but he has not solved my doubts. The old scholar was too learned, too travelled, too cultured to be in harmony with the Scotland of his day; a certain aloofness marks him, a stern and heroic rather than a human and sympathetic figure. You remember how consistently the British Solomon hated his sometime schoolmaster. Certain quaint anecdotes remain of their relations, but they have not to do with Edinburgh; yet he died in the capital, and in one or two memories that linger round those last hours you seem just at the end to get in real touch with the man, with the human figure under the cloak. In 1581 James Melville, the diarist, with certain friends, visited him in Edinburgh. They found him teaching the young man that served him : A, b, ab, and so forth. " I see you are not idle," said one of the visitors in ironical astonishment, but he said it was better than idleness. They mentioned his *magnum opus*, his History of Scotland, the literary

131

sensation of the day, if that day had literary sensa-tions. He stopped them. "I may da nae mair for thinking on another matter." "What is that?" says Mr. Andro. "To die," quoth he.

They went to the printer's to have a peep at the last sheets, just passing through the press, where they pres-ently spied some plain-spoken words like to be high-ly unpalatable at Court. Again they sought the old scholar and spoke to him about them. "Tell me, man," says he, "giff I have tould the truth." His visitors were of the same views as himself, and they could not shirk so plain an issue. "Yes, sir," says one of them, "I think sae." Then says the old man sternly: "Let it remain, I will byde it, whatever happen. Pray, pray to God for me and let Him direct all." A "Stoick" philosopher, says Melville, and so he proved to the end, which came on the 28th of September 1582, in Kennedy's Close, the second close to the west of the Tron Kirk, and long since vanished. The day before he died he found that he had not enough money to pay for his funeral, but even this, he said, must be given to the poor, his body could fare for itself. Wisely provident for its own renown Edinburgh gave him a public funeral in the Greyfriars Churchyard. Tradition marked the spot for some time, and then a blacksmith put up a tablet at his own cost, but that too vanished, and one is not certain that the learned Dr. David Laing succeeded in fixing the true place. As we have seen, the Univer-sity of Edinburgh possesses what is believed to be his skull. When Deacon Brodie stole the mace, this tro-phy did not come under his hand, or it had surely gone too.

WILLIAM DRUMMOND OF HAWTHORNDEN

From the Painting by Cornelius Jonson van Ceulen

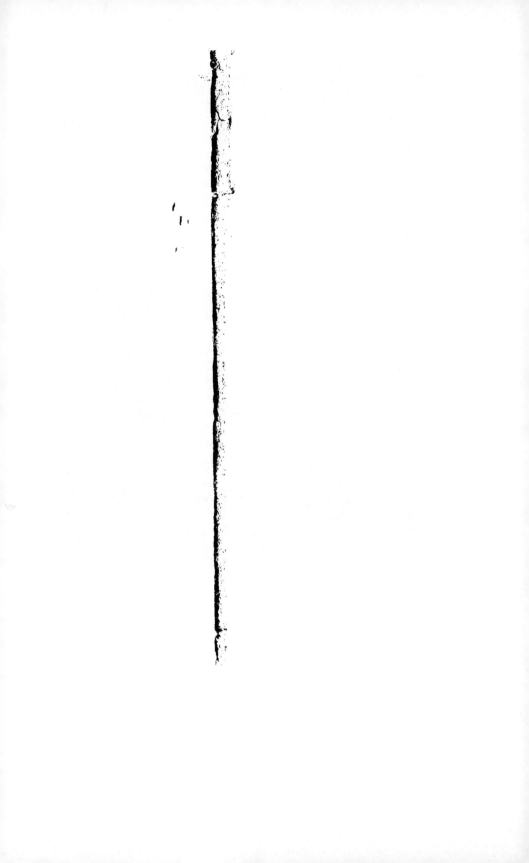

MEN OF LETTERS IN EDINBURGH

No one could be less like George Buchanan than William Drummond of Hawthornden, born three years after the death of the other, save that he also was a man of letters, and that he also had intimate connection with Edinburgh. Hawthornden is one of the beauty spots near the capital. Here Ben Jonson paid him, in 1618–19, one of the most famous visits in all the history of letters. The story is that Drummond was seated under a huge sycamore tree when Jonson's huge form hove in sight. The meeting of two poets needs must call forth a spark of poetry.

> " Welcome ! Welcome ! royal Ben !
> Thank ye kindly, Hawthornden ! "

A little suspicious, you may think ! Where did Ben Jonson learn to address a Scots laird in this peculiarly Scots fashion ? After all, Ben's forbears came from Annandale, and who that has seen Hawthornden will doubt here was the ideal spot for such an encounter? Drummond was a devoted cavalier ; his death was caused or hastened by that of Charles I. He was buried by his favourite river in the neighbouring churchyard of Lasswade. He has written his own epitaph :

> " Here Damon lies whose songs did sometime grace
> The wandering Esk—may roses shade the place."

The town of Edinburgh honoured itself and the two poets by a banquet, and in the next century Allan Ramsay honoured the pair in a more appropriate fashion. There was once a huge pile of buildings called the Luckenbooths, between St. Giles' Church and the north side of the High Street. The building at the east end, afterwards known as Creech's Land, from the bookseller who did business there, and who was locally famous as the Provost and is still remembered as Burns's publisher, was occupied by Ramsay, and here, in 1725, he established the first circulating library ever known in Scotland. It would have been the last if godly Mr. Robert Wodrow and his fellows could have had their way, on account of "the villainous, profane, and obscene books of plays" it contained. You see they neither weighed nor minced words at the time. As sign Allan stuck over the door the heads of Drummond of Hawthornden and Ben Jonson.

Scots literature was altogether on the side of the Crown, or one should rather say of the Stuarts. Who so stout a Jacobite as Allan, in words, at any rate? In deeds it was quite otherwise: you never hear of him in the '45. His copious muse that could throw off a popular ballad on the instant was silent during that romantic occupation of Edinburgh by the young Ascanius. It was prudence that saved him. He was a Jacobite and so against the powers that were, but he took no hurt; he was given to theatrical speculation and he did burn his fingers over an abortive business in that Carrubber's Close which has now a reputation far other, yet he came to no harm in the end, even if it be true that his prosperous painter son had finally to discharge some old debts. We have seen the view of the godly anent the books he sold or lent, and yet he dodged their wrath; but I wonder most of all how he escaped a drunkard's death. Who knew better that grimy, witty, sordidly attractive, vanished Edinburgh underworld of tavern and oyster-cellar—and worse? *The Gentle Shepherd* is all very well, and the *Tea-Table Miscellany*, with its senti-

mental faking up of old Scots songs, is often very ill,
though you cannot deny its service to Scots literature;
but not there is the real Allan to be found. He minces
and quibbles no longer when he sings the praises of
umquhile Maggie Johnson, who kept that famous
"howf" on Bruntsfield links.

> "There we got fou wi' little cost
>   And muckle speed.
> Now wae worth Death ! our sport's a' lost
>   Since Maggy's dead !"

Nor is his elegy on Luckie Wood of the Canongate
less hearty.

> "She ne'er gae in a lawin fause,
>   Nor stoups a' froath aboon the hause,
> Nor kept dow'd tip within her waws,
>   But reaming swats.
> She ne'er ran sour jute, because
>   It gees the batts."

Unfortunately I cannot follow him in his lamen-
tation over John Cowper or Luckie Spence, or dwell
on the part those worthies played in old Edinburgh
life. An' you be curious you must consult the original
—unexpurgated. Let us quote our Allan on at least
a quotable topic.

> "Then fling on coals and ripe the ribs,
>   And beek the house baith but and ben,
> That mutchkin stoup it hauds but dribs,
>   Then let's get in the tappit hen.
>
> Good claret best keeps out the cauld,
>   And drives away the winter sune ;
> It makes a man baith gash and bauld,
>   And heaves his saul beyond the mune."

Among drinking-songs it would be hard to beat
these lines for vigour. Did he quaff as heartily as he

sang? I think not, probably his comrades shouted "pike yer bane" to no purpose (he would have translated it to an English admirer as "no heel taps") to this little "black-a-vised" man with his nightcap for head-dress, and his humorous, contented, appreciative smile. The learned Thomas Ruddiman, his fellow-townsman and fellow-Jacobite, used to say "The liquor will not go down" when urged to yet deeper potations; perhaps Allan escaped with some such quip, at least there is no touch of dissipation about his life, nay, a well-founded reputation for honest, continuous, and prosperous industry. In the end he built that famous house on the Castle Hill, called, from its quaint shape, the "Goose Pie." "Indeed, Allan, now that I see you in it I think the term is very properly applied," said Lord Elibank. The joke was obvious and inevitable, but for all that rather pointless, unless it be that Ramsay affected a little folly now and then to escape envy or a too pressing hospitality. However, he lived reputably, died a prosperous citizen, and his is one of the statues you see to-day in the Princes Street Gardens.

Although Buchanan was one of the greatest scholars of his time in Europe, he was not the founder of a race in minute points of classical scholarship, especially in correct quantities of Latin syllables. Scotland was long lacking, perhaps the reason was the want of rich endowments, but Dr. Archibald Pitcairne (1652–1713), the physician, the Jacobite, and the scholar, had another reason: "If it had not been for the stupid Presbyterianism we should have been as good as the English at longs and shorts." Oddly enough, the same complaint was echoed within the national Zion itself. Dalzel, Professor of Greek and Clerk to the General Assembly, was, according to Sydney Smith, heard to declare, " If it had not been for that Solemn League and Covenant we should have made as good longs and shorts as they." Before I pass from Pitcairne I quote a ludicrous story of which he is the hero. His sceptical proclivities were well known in Edinburgh, and he was rarely seen inside a church. He was driven there, however, on one occasion by a shower of rain. The audience was thin, the sermon commonplace, but the preacher wept copiously and, as it seemed to Pitcairne, irrelevantly. He turned to the only other occupant of the pew, a stolid-visaged countryman, and whispered, " What the deevil gars the man greet ? " " You would maybe greet yoursel'," was the solemn answer, " if ye was up there and had as little to say."

I pass from one sceptic to another—one might say from one age to another. Edinburgh, in the latter part of the eighteenth century, according to Smollett's famous phrase, was a " hotbed of genius." When Amyot, the King's dentist, was in Edinburgh he said, as he stood at the Cross, that he could any minute take fifty men of genius by the hand. Of this distinguished company David Hume was the chief. To what extent this historian, philosopher, sceptic, is now read, we need not inquire; he profoundly influenced European thought, and gave a system of religious philosophy the deadliest blow it ever received. He was a prominent and interesting figure, and many and various are the legends about him. What were his real religious beliefs, if he had any, remains uncertain. He was hand in glove

with "Jupiter" Carlyle, Principal Robertson, Dr. Hugh
Blair, and other leading moderates. They thought
his scepticism was largely pretence, mere intellectual
bounce, so to speak ; they girded at his unreasonable
departure from the normal, and indeed Carlyle takes
every opportunity of thrusting at him on this account.
The Edinburgh folk regarded him with solemn horror. The mother of Adam, the architect, who was
also aunt to Principal Robertson, had much to say
against the 'atheist,' whom she had never seen. Her
son played her a trick. Hume was asked to the house
and set down beside her. She declared "the large
jolly man who sat next me was the most agreeable
of them all." "He was the very atheist, mother," said
the son, "that you were so much afraid of." "Oh," replied the lady, "bring him here as much as you please,
for he is the most innocent, agreeable, facetious man
I ever met with." His scepticism was subject for his
friends' wit and his own.. He heard Carlyle preach
in Athelstaneford Church. "I did not think that such
heathen morality would have passed in East Lothian."
One day when he sat in the Poker Club it was mentioned that a clerk of Sir William Forbes, the banker,
had bolted with £900. When he was taken, there was
found in one pocket Hume's *Treatise on Human Nature* and in the other Boston's *Fourfold State of Man*,
this latter being a work of evangelical theology. His
moderate friends presently suggested that no man's
morality could hold out against the combination. Dr.
Jardine of the Tron Kirk vigorously argued with him
on various points of theology, suggested by Hume's
Natural History of Religion. His friend, like most folk

in Edinburgh, lived in a flat off a steep turnpike stair, down which Hume fell one night in the darkness. Jardine got a candle and helped the panting philosopher to his feet. Your old Edinburgh citizen never could resist the chance of a cutting remark. The divine was no exception. "Davy, I have often tell't ye that 'natural licht' is no' sufficient." Like Socrates, he hid his wit under an appearance of simplicity. His own mother's opinion of him was: "Davy's a fine, good-natured crater, but uncommon wake-minded." He had his weaknesses, undoubtedly. Lord Saltoun said to him, referring to his credulity, "David, man, you'll believe onything except the Bible," but like other Scotsmen of his time he did not believe overmuch in Shakespeare. In 1757 he thus addresses the author of *Douglas*: "You possess the true theatrical genius of Shakespeare and Otway, refined from the barbarisms of the one, and the licentiousness of the other." Put beside this Burns's famous and fatuous line: "Here Douglas forms wild Shakespeare into plan," and what can you do but shudder? When young, he had paid his court to a lady of fashion, and had met with scant courtesy. He was told afterwards that she had changed her mind. "So have I," said the philosopher. On another occasion he was more gallant. Crossing the Firth in a gale he said to Lady Wallace, who was in the boat, that they would soon be food for the fishes. "Will they eat you or me?" said the lady. "Ah," was the answer, "those that are gluttons will undoubtedly fall foul of me, but the epicure will attack your ladyship." David, like the fishes he described, was a bit of an epicure of the simplest kind. He would sup with his moderate friends in Johnny Dowie's tavern in Libberton's Wynd. On the table lay his huge door-key, wherewith his servant, Peggy, had been careful to provide him that she might not have to rise to let him in. After all, the friends did not sit very late, and the supper was some simple Scots dish—haddock, or tripe, or fluke, or pies, or it might be trout from the Nor' Loch, for Dowie's was famous for these little dainties. But the talk! Would you match it in modern Edinburgh with all its pomp and wealth? I trow not—perhaps not even in mightier London.

The story is threadbare of how he was stuck in a bog under the Castle rock, and was only helped out by a passing Edinburgh dame on condition that he would say the Lord's Prayer and the Creed. More witty and more probable, though perhaps as well known, is the following: In the last years of his life he deserted the Old Town for the New. He had a house at the corner of St. Andrew Square, in a street as yet anonymous. "St. David Street" chalked up a witty young lady, Miss Nancy Ord, daughter of Chief Baron Ord, and St. David Street it is to this day. His servant, in a state of indignation, brought him the news. "Never mind, lassie, many a better man has been made a saint without knowing it," said the placid philosopher. A female member of a narrow sect called upon him near the end with an alleged message from Heaven. "This is an important matter. Madam, we must take it with deliberation. Perhaps you had better get a little temporal refreshment before you begin.—Lassie, bring this young lady a glass of wine." As she drank, he in his turn questioned, and found that the husband was a tallow-chandler. How fortunate, for he was out of candles! He gave an order, the woman forgot the message, and rushed off to fulfil it. Hume, you fancy, had a quiet chuckle at his happy release. He was a great friend of Mrs. Mure, wife of Baron Mure, and was a frequent visitor at their house at Abbeyhill, near Holyrood. On his death-bed he sent to bid her good-bye. He gave her his *History of England*. " O, Dauvid, that's a book ye may weel be proud o' ! but before ye dee ye should burn a' yer wee bookies," to which the philosopher, with difficulty raising himself on his arms, was only able to reply with some little show of vehemence, " *What for* should I burn a' my wee bookies?" But he was too weak to argue such points ; he pressed the hand of his old friend as she rose to depart. When his time came he went quietly, contentedly, even gladly, regretted by saint and sceptic alike. If Carlyle girded at him, his intimate friend, Adam Smith, who might almost dispute his claim to mental eminence, pictured him forth in those days as the perfectly wise man, so far as human imperfections allowed. The piety or caution of his friends made them watch the grave for some eight nights after the burial. The vigil began at eight o'clock, when a pistol was fired, and candles in a lanthorn were placed on the grave and tended from time to time. Some violation was feared, for a wild legend of Satanic agency had flashed on the instant through the town. Hume has no monument in Edinburgh, crowded as she is with statues of lesser folk; but the accident of position and architecture has in this, as in other cases, produced a striking if undesigned result. From one cause or another the valley

is deeper than of yore, and the simple round tower
that marks Hume's grave in the Calton burying-gro-
und crowns a half-natural, half-artificial precipice. It
is seen with effect from various points : thus you cannot miss it as you cross the North Bridge. Some memory of this great thinker still projects itself into the
trivial events of the modern Edinburgh day.

Of Hume's friend and companion, Adam Smith,
there are various anecdotes, more or less pointed,
bearing on his oblivious or maybe contemptuous indifference to the ordinary things of life. The best and
best known tells how, as he went with shuffling gait
and vacant look, a Musselburgh fishwife stared at him
in amazement. " Hech, and he is weel put on tae." It
seemed to her a pity that so well-dressed a simpleton
was not better looked after. No amount of learning
helps you in a crowded street.   The wisdom of the
ancients reports that Thales, wrapt in contemplation
of the stars, walked into a well and thus ended. Adam
Smith's grave is in a dark corner of the Canongate
Churchyard; it is by no means so prominent as
Hume's, nay, it takes some searching to discover.
When I saw it last I found it neglected and unvisited
alike by economic friends and foes.

Among Hume's intimate cronies was Dr. Carlyle
of Inveresk, whose *Autobiography* preserves for us the
best record of the men of his time. " The grandest
demigod I ever saw," says Sir Walter Scott, " commonly called Jupiter Carlyle, from having sat more
than once for the King of gods and men to Gavin
Hamilton, and a shrewd, clever old carle he was, no
doubt, but no more a poet than his precentor." This

last is apropos of some rhyming of Carlyle's as bad as rhymes can possibly be. In 1758 Carlyle and Principal Robertson and John Home were together in London; they went down to Portsmouth and aboard the *Ramilies*, the warship in the harbour, where was Lieut. Nelson, a cousin of Robertson's. The honest sailor expressed his astonishment in deliciously comical terms: "God preserve us! what has brought the Presbytery of Edinburgh here? for damme me if there is not Willy Robertson, Sandie Carlyle, and John Home come on board." He soon had them down in the cabin, however, and treated them to white wine and salt beef. A jolly meal, you believe, for divines or sceptics, philosophers or men of letters or business, those old Edinburgh folk had a common and keen enjoyment of life. Certainly Carlyle had. Dr. Lindsay Alexander of Augustine Church, Edinburgh, remembered as a child hearing one of the servants say of this divine, "There he gaed, dacent man, as steady as a wa' after his ain share o' five bottles o' port." Home by this time was no longer a minister of the Church. He had thrown up his living in the previous year on account of the famous row about the once famous tragedy of *Douglas*. He still had a hankering after the General Assembly, where, if he could no longer sit as teaching elder, he might as ruling elder, because he was Conservator of Scots privileges at Campvere, but he was something else; he was lieutenant in the Duke of Buccleuch's Fencibles, and as such had a right to attire himself in a gorgeous uniform, and it was so incongruously adorned that he took his seat in that reverend house. The country ministers stared with all their eyes, and one of them exclaimed, " Sure, that is John Home the poet! What is the meaning of that dress?" "Oh," said Mr. Robert Walker of Edinburgh, "it is only the farce after the play."

Eminent lawyers who are also industrious, and even eminent writers, were a feature of the time, but of them I have already spoken and there is little here to add. Monboddo had a remarkable experience in his youth; the very day, in 1736, he returned to Edinburgh from studying abroad he heard at nightfall a commotion in the street. In nightdress and slippers he stepped from the door and was borne along by a wild mob, not a few of whom were attired as strangely as himself. It was that famous affair of Captain Porteous, and, *nolens volens*, he needs must witness that sordid yet picturesque tragedy whose incidents, you are convinced, he never forgot, and often, as an old man, retailed to a newer generation.

Like many another Scots lawyer, Lord Kames had a keen love for the land, keener in his case because it had come to him from his forbears; but his zeal was not always according to knowledge. One of the "fads" of the time was a wonderful fertilising powder. He told one of his tenants that he would be able to carry the manure of an acre of land in his coat pocket, "And be able to bring back the crop in yer waistcoat pouch?" was the crushing reply. He would have his joke, cruel and wicked, at any cost. To him belongs the well-nigh incredible story of a murder trial at Ayr in 1780. He knew the accused and had played chess with him. "That's checkmate for you, Matthie," he chuckled in ungodly glee when the ver-

dict was recorded. This story, by the way, used to be told of Braxfield, to whom it clearly does not belong, and one wished it did not belong to Kames either. He spared himself as little as he did others. He lived in New Street, an early old-time improvement on the north side of the Canongate, and from there he went to the Parliament House in a sedan chair. One morning, near the end, he was being helped into it, for he was old and infirm, when James Boswell crossed his path. Jamie was always in one scrape or the other, but this time you fancy he had done something specially notorious. "I shall shortly be seeing your father," said Kames (old Auchinleck had died that year (1782), as on the 27th of December did Kames himself); "have you any message for him? Shall I tell him how you are getting on?" You imagine his diabolical grin and Bozzy's confused answer.

Beside these quaint figures Lord Hailes, with his ponderous learning, is a mere Dry-as-dust antiquary —the dust lies ever deeper over his many folios; of his finical exactness there still linger traditions in the Parliament House. It is said he dismissed a case because a word was wrongly spelt in one of the numbers of process. Thus he earned himself a couplet in the once famous *Court of Session Garland.*

" To judge of this matter I cannot pretend,
　For justice, my Lords, wants an ' e ' at the end."

So wrote Boswell, himself, though he only partly belongs to Edinburgh, not the least interesting figure of our period. There is more than one story of him and Kames. The judge had playfully suggested that Boswell should write his biography! How devoutly you wish he had. What an entertaining and famous book it had been! but perhaps he had only it in him to do one biography, and we know how splendid *that* was. Poor Bozzy once complained to the old judge that even he, Bozzy himself, was occasionally dull. "Homer sometimes nods," said Kames in a reassuring tone, but with a grin that promised mischief. The other looked as pleased as possible till the old cynic went on: "Indeed, sir, it is the only chance you have of resembling him." Old Auchinleck, his father, was horrified at his son's devotion to Johnson. "Jamie has gaen clean gyte. What do you think, man? He's done wi' Paoli—he's aff wi' the land-loupin' scoondrel o' a Corsican. Whae's tail do ye think he has preened himsel' tae noo? A dominie man—an auld dominie who keepit a schule and caa'ed it an Acaademy!" In fact, the great Samuel pleased none of the Boswell clan except Boswell and Boswell's baby daughter. Auchinleck had many caustic remarks even after he had seen the sage: "He was only a dominie, and the worst-mannered dominie I ever met." So much for the father. The wife was not more favourable: "She had often seen a bear led by a man, but never till now had she seen a man led by a bear." Afterwards, when the famous biography was published, the sons were horribly ashamed both of it and of him. Bozzy has given us so much amusement—we recognise his inimitable literary touch—that we are rather proud of and grateful to him; but then, we don't look at the matter with the eyes of his relatives.

Johnson was himself in Edinburgh. You remember how he arrived in February 1773 at Boyd's Whitehorse Inn off St. Mary's Wynd, not the more famous Inn of that name in the Whitehorse Close down the Canongate; how angry he was with the waiter for lifting with his dirty paw the sugar to put in his lemonade; how, in the malodorous High Street, he pleasantly remarked to Boswell, " I smell you in the dark "; how, as he listened at Holyrood to the story of the Rizzio murder, he muttered a line of the old ballad *Johnnie Armstrong's last good-night*—" And ran him through the fair bodie." They took him to the Royal Infirmary, and he noted the inscription "Clean your feet." " Ah," said he, " there is no occasion for putting this at the doors of your churches." The gibe was justified; he had just looked in at St. Giles', then used for every strange civic purpose, and plastered and twisted about to every strange shape. Most interesting to me is that Sunday morning, 15th August 1773, when Bozzy and Principal Robertson toiled with him up the College Wynd to see the University, and passed by Scott's birthplace. The Wizard of the North was then two years old, and who could guess that his fame in after years would be greater than that of those three eminent men of letters put together? In this strange remote way do epochs touch one another. No wonder Bozzy's relatives got tired of his last hobby, his very subject himself got tired. " Sir," said the sage, " you have but two topics, yourself and me. I am sick of both." Yet Bozzy knew what he was about when he stuck to his one topic. After his idol was gone, what was there for him but the bottle? It was one of the earliest recollections of Lord Jeffrey that he had assisted as a boy in putting the biographer to bed in a state of absolute unconsciousness. Next morning Boswell was told of the service rendered : he clapped the lad on the head, and complacently congratulated him. " If you go on as you've begun, you may live to be a Bozzy yourself yet." And so much bemused the greatest of biographers vanishes from our sight.

CHAPTER SEVEN
MEN OF LETTERS.   PART II

TO TURN TO SOME LESSER FIGURES.
Hugo Arnot, advocate, is still remembered as author
of one of the two standard histories of Edinburgh. No
man better known in the streets of the old capital: he
was all length and no breadth. That incorrigible joker,
Harry Erskine, found him one day gnawing a speldrin
—a species of cured fish chiefly used to remove the
trace of last night's debauch, and prepare the stomach
for another bout. It is vended in long thin strips.
"You are very like your meat," said the wit. The Edinburgh populace called a house which for some time
stood solitary on Moutries Hill, afterwards Bunkers
Hill, where is now the Register House, " Hugo Arnot," because the length was out of all proportion to
the breadth. One day he found a fishwife cheapen-
ing a Bible in Creech's shop; he had some semi-
jocular remarks, probably not in the best taste, at the
purchase and the purchaser. "Gude ha mercy on
us," said the old lady, " wha wad hae thocht that ony
human-like cratur wud hae spokan that way; but
you," she went on with withering scorn—"a perfect
atomy." He was known to entertain sceptical opinions, and he was pestered with chronic asthma, and
panted and wheezed all day long. "If I do not get
quit of this," he said, " it will carry me off like a roc-
ket." "Ah, Hugo, my man," said an orthodox but unkind friend, "but in a contrary direction." He could
joke at his own infirmities. A Gilmerton carter passed him bellowing " sand for sale " with a voice that
made the street echo. " The rascal," said the exasper-
ated author, " spends as much breath in a minute as

would serve me for a month." Like other Edinburgh
folk he migrated to the New Town, to Meuse Lane,
in fact, hard by St. Andrew Square. What with his
diseases and other natural infirmities, Hugo's temper
was of the shortest. He rang his bell in so violent a
manner that a lady on the floor above complained.
He took to summoning his servant by firing a pistol;
the remedy was worse than the disease. The caustic,
bitter old Edinburgh humour was in the very bones
of him. He was, as stated, an advocate by profession,
and his collection of criminal trials, by the way, is still
an authority. Once he was consulted in order that he
might help in some shady transaction. He listened
with the greatest attention. "What do you suppose
me to be?" said he to the client. "A lawyer, an advocate," stammered the other. "Oh, I thought you took
me for a scoundrel," sneered Arnot as he showed the
proposed client the door. A lady who said she was
of the same name asked how to get rid of an importunate suitor. "Why, marry him," said Hugo testily. "I
would see him hanged first," rejoined the lady. The
lawyer's face contorted to a grin. "Why, marry him,
and by the Lord Harry he will soon hang himself."
All very well, but not by such arts is British Themis
propitiated. Arnot died in November 1786 when he
was not yet complete thirty-seven. He had chosen
his burial-place in the churchyard at South Leith, and
was anxious to have it properly walled in ere the end,
which he clearly foresaw, arrived. It was finished just
in time, and with a certain stoical relief this strange
mortal departed to take possession.

Another well-known Edinburgh character was

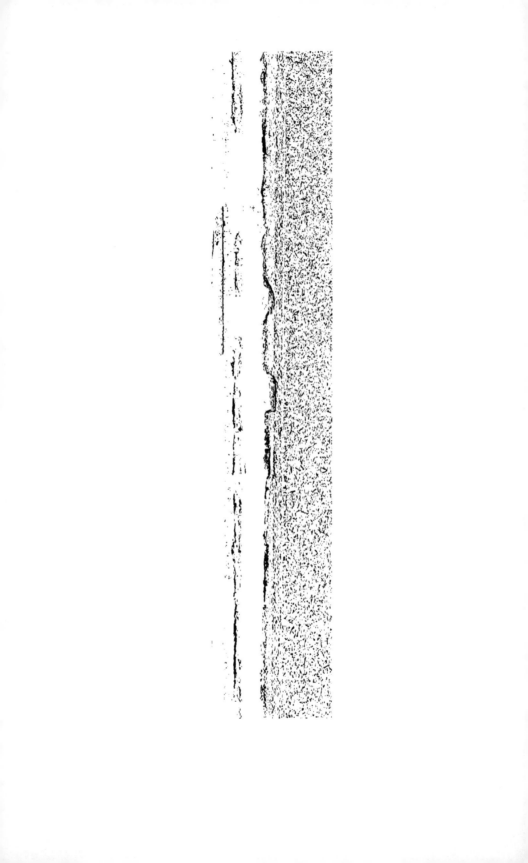

HENRY MACKENZIE, "THE MAN OF FEELING"

MEN OF LETTERS IN EDINBURGH

Henry Mackenzie. Born in 1745 he lived till 1831, and connects the different periods of Edinburgh literary splendour. His best service to literature was his early appreciation of Burns, but in his own time the *Man of Feeling* was one of the greatest works of the day, and the *Man of the World* and *Julia de Roubigné* followed not far behind. To this age all seems weak, stilted, sentimental to an impossible degree, but Scott and Lockhart, to name but these, read and admired with inexplicable admiration. In ordinary life Mackenzie was a hard-headed lawyer, and as keen an attendant at a cock main, it was whispered, as Deacon Brodie himself. He told his wife that he'd had a glorious night. "Where?" she queried. "Why, at a splendid fight." "Oh Harry, Harry," said the good lady, "you have only feeling on paper."

Tobias Smollett, though not an Edinburgh man, had some connection with the place. His sister, Mrs. Telfer, lived in the house yet shown in the Canongate, at the entrance to St. John Street. Here, after long absence, his mother recognised him by his smile. Ten years afterwards he again went north, and again saw his mother; he told her that he was very ill and that he was dying. "We'll no' be very lang pairted onie way. If you gang first, I'll be close on your heels. If I lead the way, you'll no' be far ahint me, I'm thinking," said this more than Spartan parent. But when you read the vivacious Mrs. Winifred Jenkins in the *Expedition of Humphrey Clinker*, you recognise how good a thing it was for letters that Smollett visited Edinburgh.

It is a little odd, but I have no anecdotes to tell

BOOK OF EDINBURGH ANECDOTE

(the alleged meeting between him and old John Brown
in Haddington Churchyard is a wild myth) of that
characteristic Edinburgh figure, Robert Fergusson,
the Edinburgh poet, the native and the lover. He
struck a deeper note than Allan Ramasy, has a more
intimate touch than Scott, is scarcely paralleled by
R. L. Stevenson, who half believed himself a reincar-
nation of " my unhappy predecessor on the causey
of old Edinburgh " . . . " him that went down—my
brother, Robert Fergusson."

> " Auld Reekie ! thou'rt the canty hole,
> A bield for mony a cauldrife soul
> Wha' snugly at thine ingle loll
> Baith warm and couth,
> While round they gar the bicker roll
> To weet their mouth."

There you see the side of Edinburgh that most
attracted him. He was no worse than his fellows perhaps, but perhaps he could not stand what they stood.
It is said that he once gave as an excuse, "Oh, sirs, anything to forget my poor mother and these aching
fingers." As Mr. H. G. Graham truly says : " It was a
poor enough excuse for forgetting himself." He used
to croon over that pleasing little trifle, *The Birks of
Invermay*, in Lucky Middlemist's or elsewhere, and
dream of trim rural fields he did not trouble to visit.
I have no heart to repeat the melancholy story of his
lonely death in the Schelles, hard by the old Darien
House at the Bristo Port in 1774, at the age of twenty-
four. His interest is as a ghost from the Edinburgh
underworld, you catch a glimpse of a more vicious
Grub Street. There must have been a circle of broken
professional men of all sorts, more or less clever, all

154

needy, all drunken and ready to do anything for a dram. What a crop of anecdotes there was! But no one gathered, and the memory of it passed away with the actors. Local history that chronicled the oddities of Kames or Monboddo refused to chronicle the pranks of lewd fellows of the baser sort. Only when the wastrel happened to be a genius do we piece together in some sort his career. Whatever one says about Fergusson, you never doubt his genius.

It is curious how very occasional is the anecdote of this Caledonian Grub Street. Here is rather a characteristic straw which the stream of time has carried down regarding a certain drudge called Stewart. One night, homeless and houseless, he staggered into the ash pit of a primitive steam-engine, and lay down to rest. An infernal din aroused him from his drunken slumber; he saw the furnace opened, grimy black figures stoking the fire and raking the bars of the enormous grate, whilst iron rods and chains clanked around him with infernal din. A tardily awakened conscience hinted where he was. "Good God, has it come to this at last?" he growled in abject terror. Another anecdote, though of a later date, is told in Lockhart's *Life of Scott*. Constable, the Napoleon of publishers, called the crafty in the *Chaldean Manuscript*, is reported "a most bountiful and generous patron to the ragged tenants of Grub Street." He gave stated dinners to his "own circle of literary serfs." At one of these David Bridges, "tailor in ordinary to this northern potentate," acted as croupier. According to instructions he brought with him a new pair of breeches, and for these Alister Campbell and another ran a race, and yet this same Campbell was editor of *Albyn's Anthology*, 1816, to which Scott contributed *Jock o' Hazeldean*, *Pibroch of Donald Dhu*, and better than any, that brilliant piece of extravagance, *Donald Caird's come again*. Perhaps the story isn't true, but it is at least significant that Lockhart should tell it.

One glittering Bohemian figure, though he was much greater and much else, lights up for us those Edinburgh taverns, Johnnie Dowie's and the rest, those Edinburgh clubs, the Crochallan Fencibles and the others, that figure is Robert Burns. His winter of 1786–1787 in the Scots capital is famous. To us, more than a century after, it still satisfies the imagination, a striking, dramatic, picturesque appearance. On the whole, Edinburgh, not merely her great but common men, received him fitly. One day in that winter Jeffrey was standing in the High Street staring at a man whose appearance struck him, he could scarce tell why. A person standing at a shop door tapped him on the shoulder and said : " Ay, laddie, ye may weel look at that man ; that's Robert Burns." He never saw him again. His experience in this was like that of Scott ; but you are glad at any rate that Burns and Scott did meet, else had that Edinburgh visit wanted its crowning glory. Scott was then fifteen. He saw Robin in Professor Fergusson's house at Sciennes. It was a distinguished company, and Scott, always modest, held his tongue. There was a picture in the room of a soldier lying dead in the snow, by him his dog and his widow with his child in her arms. Burns was so affected at the idea suggested by the picture that "he

actually shed tears," like the men of the heroic age,
says Andrew Lang; he asked who wrote the lines
which were printed underneath, and Scott alone remembered that they were from the obscure Lang-
horne. "Burns rewarded me with a look and a word
which, though a mere civility, I then received, and still
recollect, with very great pleasure." Scott goes on to
describe Burns as like the "douce guid man who held
his own plough." Most striking was his eye: "It was
large and of a dark cast and glowed (I say literally
glowed) when he spoke with feeling or interest. I
never saw such another eye in a human head, though
I have seen the most distinguished men in my time."
Whether Scott was right in thinking that Burns talked with "too much humility," I will not discuss. We
know what Robin thought of the "writer chiel." The
most pleasing result of his Edinburgh visit, as it is to-
day still the most tangible, was the monument, taste-
ful and sufficient, which he put over Fergusson's grave .
in the Canongate Churchyard. R.L.S., by the way,
from his distant home in the South Seas, was anxious
that if neglected it should be put in order. I do not
think it has ever been neglected. I have seen it often
and it was always curiously spick and span: these
vates have not lacked pious services at the hands of
their followers. Scott was not so enthusiastic an admirer, but he knew his Fergusson well and quotes him
with reasonable frequency. When Fergusson died
Scott was only three years old. Edinburgh was then
a town of little space, and the unfortunate poet may
have seen the child, but he could not have noticed
him, and we have no record.

Just as the last half of the eighteenth century may be said to group itself round Hume, so the first half of the nineteenth has Scott for its central figure. I have spoken of his birthplace in the College Wynd. In 1825 he pointed out its site to Robert Chambers. "It would have been more profitable to have preserved it," said Chambers in a neat compliment to Scott's rapidly growing fame. "Ay, ay," said Sir Walter, "that is very well, but I am afraid that I should require to be dead first, and that would not have been so comfortable, you know." Thus, with good sense and humour, Scott turned aside the eulogium which perhaps he thought too strong. How modest he was! He frankly, and justly, put himself as a poet below Byron and Burns, and as for Shakespeare, "he was not worthy to loose his brogues." His sense and good-nature helped to make him popular with his fellows. Hogg, the Ettrick Shepherd, was a possible exception. Scott did him good, yet after Scott's death he wrote some nasty things. In truth, he had an unhappy nature, since he was somewhat rough to others and yet abnormally sensitive. Lockhart tells a story of Hogg's visit to Scott's house in Castle Street, where he was asked to dinner. Mrs. Scott was not well, and was lying on a sofa. The Shepherd seized another sofa, wheeled it towards her, and stretched himself at full length on it. "I thought I could never do wrong to copy the lady of the house." His hands, we are told, had marks of recent sheep-shearing, of which the chintz bore legible traces; but the guest noted not this; he ate freely, and drank freely, and talked freely; he became gradually more and more familiar; from "Mr. Scott" he

MEN OF LETTERS IN EDINBURGH

advanced to " Shirra " and thence to " Scott," " Walter," " Wattie," until at supper he fairly convulsed the
whole party by addressing Mrs. Scott as "Charlotte."
I think, however, that Scott was too much of a gentleman ever to have told this story. " The Scorpion," as
the *Chaldean Manuscript* named Lockhart, had many
good qualities, but was, after all, a bit of a " superior
person."

Scott's connection with John Leyden was altogether pleasant, and no one mourned more sincerely
over the early death in the East of that indefatigable
poet and scholar. Leyden was of great assistance to
Scott in collecting material for his *Border Minstrelsy.*
Once there was a hiatus in an interesting old ballad,
when Leyden heard of an ancient reported able to re-
cite the whole thing complete. He walked between
forty and fifty miles and back again, turning the recovered verses over in his mind, and as Scott was
sitting after dinner with some company "a sound was
heard at a distance like that of the whistling of a tempest through the torn rigging of a vessel which scuds
before it." It was Leyden who presently burst into
the room, chanting the whole of the recovered ballad. Leyden and Thomas Campbell had a very pretty quarrel about something or other. When Scott repeated to Leyden the poem of *Hohenlinden,* the latter burst out, " Dash it, man, tell the fellow that I hate
him ; but, dash him, he has written the finest verses
that have been published these fifty years." Scott,
thinking to patch up a peace, repeated this to Campbell. He only said, " Tell Leyden that I detest him, but
I know the value of his critical approbation." Well

159

he might! Leyden once repeated to Alexander Murray, the philologist, the most striking lines in Campbell's *Lochiel*, adding, " That fellow, after all, we may say, is King of us all, and has the genuine root of the matter in him." Campbell's verse still lives, but our day would not place it so high. I have spoken of Scott's modesty, also he was quiet under hostile criticism. Jeffrey had some hard things to say of *Marmion* in the *Edinburgh Review*, and immediately after dined in Castle Street. There was no change in Scott's demeanour, but Mrs. Scott could not altogether restrain herself. "Well, good-night, Mr. Jeffrey. They tell me you have abused Scott in the *Review*, and I hope Mr. Constable has paid you very well for writing it," which was rather an odd remark. As that Highland blue-stocking, Mrs. Grant of Laggan, observed, " Mr. Scott always seems to me like a glass through which the rays of admiration pass without sensibly affecting it, but the bit of paper that lies beside it will presently be in a blaze—and no wonder." Scott was " truest friend and noblest foe." In June 1821, as he stood by John Ballantyne's open grave in the Canongate Churchyard, the day, which had been dark, brightened up, and the sun shone forth, he looked up and said with deep feeling to Lockhart, " I feel as if there will be less sunshine for me from this time forth." And yet through the Ballantynes Scott was involved in those reckless speculations which led to the catastrophe of his life. His very generosity and nobleness led him into difficulties. " I like Scott's ain bairns, but Heaven preserve me from those of his fathering," says Constable. As for those " ain bairns," especially

those Waverley Novels, which are a dear possession to each of us, there are anecdotes enough. We know the speed and ease, in truth Shakespearean, with which he threw off the best of them, yet to the outsider he seemed hard at work. In June 1814 a party of young bloods were dining in a house in George Street, at right angles with North Castle Street. A shade over-spread the face of the host. "Why?" said the narrator. "There is a confounded hand in sight of me here which has often bothered me before, and now it won't let me fill my glass with a good will. Since we sat down I have been watching it—it fascinates my eye—it never stops; page after page is finished and thrown on that heap of MS., and still it goes on un-wearied, and so it will be till candles are brought in, and God knows how long after that; it is the same every night." It was the hand of Walter Scott, and in the evenings of three weeks in summer it wrote the last two volumes of Waverley (there were three in all). Whatever impression the novels make upon us has been discounted before we have read them, but when they were appearing, when to the attraction of the volumes themselves was added the romance of mys-tery, when the Wizard of the North was still "The Great Unknown," *then* was the time to enjoy a Wav-erley. James Ballantyne lived in St. John Street, then a good class place off the Canongate. He was wont to give a gorgeous feast whenever a new Wav-erley was about to appear. Scott was there, but he and the staider members of the company left in good time, and then there were broiled bones and a mighty bowl of punch, and James Ballantyne was persuaded to produce the proof-sheets, and, with a word of preface, give the company the liver wing of the forthcoming literary banquet. Long before the end the secret was an open secret, but it was only formally divulged, as we all know, at the Theatrical Fund dinner, on Friday the 23rd February 1827. Among the company was jovial Patrick Robertson, "a mighty incarnate joke." When *Peveril of the Peak* appeared he applied the name to Scott from the shape of his head as he stood chatting in the Parliament House, "better that than Peter o' the Painch," was the not particularly elegant but very palpable retort at Peter's rotundity. At the banquet Scott sent him a note urging him to confess something too. "Why not the murder of Begbie?" (the porter of the British Linen Company Bank, murdered under mysterious circumstances in November 1806, in Tweeddale Close, in the High Street). Immediately after, the farce of *High Life Below Stairs* was played in the theatre. A lady's lady asked who wrote Shakespeare? One says Ben Jonson, another Finis. "No," said an actor, with a most ingenious "gag," "it is Sir Walter Scott; he confessed it at a public meeting the other day."

Most of the literary men of the time were in two camps. Either they wrote for the *Edinburgh Review*, or for *Blackwood's Magazine*, occasionally for both. The opponents knew each other, and were more or less excellent friends, though they used the most violent language. Jeffrey was the great light on the *Edinburgh*; he was described by Professor Wilson's wife as "a horrid little man, but held in as high estimation here as the Bible." Her husband, with Lockhart and

MEN OF LETTERS IN EDINBURGH

Hogg, were the chief writers for the Magazine. The first number of that last, as we now know it, contained the famous *Chaldean Manuscript*, in which uproarious fun was made of friends and foes, under the guise of a scriptural parable. They began with their own publisher and real editor. "And his name was as it had been the colour of ebony, and his number was the number of a maiden when the days of the year of her virginity have expired." In other words, Mr. Blackwood of 17 Princes Street. Constable, the publisher, was the "crafty in council," and he had a notable horn in his forehead that "cast down the truth to the ground." This was the *Review*. Professor Wilson was "the beautiful leopard from the valley of the plane trees," referring to the *Isle of Palms*, the poem of which Christopher North was the author. Lockhart was the 'scorpion which delighteth to sting the faces of men." Hogg was "the great wild boar from the forests of Lebanon whetting his dreadful tusks for the battle." It was the composition of these last three spirits, and is described by Aytoun as "a mirror in which we behold literary Edinburgh of 1817, translated into mythology." It was chiefly put together one night at 53 Queen Street, amidst uproarious laughter that shook the walls of the house, and made the ladies in the room above send to inquire in wonder what the gentlemen below were about. Even the grave Sir William Hamilton was of the party; he contributed a verse, and was so amused at his own performance that he tumbled off his chair in a fit of laughter. Perhaps the personalities by which it gained part of its success were not in the best taste, but never was squib so successful. It shook the town with rage and mirth. After well-nigh a century, though some sort of a key is essential, you read it with a grin; it has a permanent, if small, place in the history of letters. Yet Wilson contributed to the *Edinburgh*! "John," said his mother when she heard it, "if you turn Whig, this house is no longer big enough for us both." There was no fear of of *that*, however.

The most engaging stories of Christopher North tell of his feats of endurance. After he was a grave professor he would throw off his coat and tackle successfully with his fists an obstreperous bully. He would walk seventy miles in the waking part of twenty-four hours. Once, in the braes of Glenorchy, he called at a farmhouse at eleven at night for refreshment. They brought him a bottle of whisky and a can of milk, which he mixed and consumed in two draughts from a huge bowl. He was called to the Scots bar in 1815, and from influence, or favour, agents at first sent him cases. He afterwards confessed that when he saw the papers on his table, he did not know what to do with them. But he speedily drifted into literature, wherein he made a permanent mark. We have all dipped into that huge mine of wit and wisdom, the *Noctes Ambrosianæ*. You would say of him, and you would of Scott, they were splendid men, their very faults and excesses lovable. What a strange power both had over animals! As in the case of Queen Mary, their servants were ever their faithful and devoted friends. Wilson kept a great number of dogs. Rover was a special favourite. As the animal was dying, Wilson bent over it, "Rover, my poor fellow, give me your paw," as if he had been taking leave of a man. When Camp died, Scott reverently buried him in the back garden of his Castle Street house; his daughter noted the deep cloud of sorrow on her father's face. Maida is with him on his monument as in life. Wilson kept sixty-two gamebirds all at once; they made a fearful noise. "Did they never fight?" queried his doctor. "No," was the answer; "but put a hen amongst them, and I will not answer for the peace being long observed. And so it hath been since the beginning of the world." These gifted men played each other tricks of the most impish nature. Lockhart once made a formal announcement of Christopher North's sudden death, with a panegyric upon his character in the *Weekly Journal*; true, he confined it to a few copies, but it was rather a desperate method of jesting. Patrick Robertson, as Lord Robertson, a Senator of the College of Justice, published a volume of poems. This was duly reviewed in the *Quarterly*, which Lockhart edited, and a copy sent to the author; it finished off with this mad couplet:

"Here lies the peerless paper lord, Lord Peter,
  Who broke the laws of God and man and metre."

The feelings of "Peter," as his friends always called Robertson, may be imagined. True, it was the only copy of the *Review* that contained the couplet: it must have been some time before the disturbed poet found out. Yet "Peter" was a "jokist" of a scarcely less desperate character. At a dinner-party an Oxford don was parading his Greek erudition, to the boredom of the whole company. Robertson gravely replied to some proposition, "I rather think, sir, Dionysius of Halicarnassus is against you there." "I beg your par-

don," said the don quickly, " Dionysius did not flour-
ish for ninety years after that period." " Oh," rejoined
Patrick, with an expression of face that must be imagined, " I made a mistake; I meant Thaddeus of War-
saw." There was no more Greek erudition that night.
This fondness for a jest followed those men into every
concern of life. One of Wilson's daughters came to
her father in his study and asked, with appropriate
blushes, his consent to her engagement to Professor
Aytoun. He pinned a sheet of paper to her back, and
packed her off to the next room, where her lover was.
They were both a little mystified till he read the inscription : " With the author's compliments."

De Quincey spent the last thirty years of his life
mainly in Edinburgh. His grave is in St. Cuthbert's
Churchyard. He seems a strange, exotic figure, for
his literary interests, at any rate, were not at all Scots.
Once he paid a casual visit to Gloucester Place, where
Wilson lived. It was a stormy night, and he stayed
on—for about a year. His hours and dietary were
peculiar, but he was allowed to do exactly as he liked.
"Thomas de Sawdust," as W. E. Henley rather cruelly nicknamed him, excited the astonishment of the
Scots cook by the magnificent way in which he ordered a simple meal. " Weel, I never heard the like o'
that in a' my days ; the bodie has an awfu' sicht o'
words. If it had been my ain maister that was wanting his denner he would ha' ordered a hale tablefu'
in little mair than a waff o' his han', and here's a' this
claver aboot a bit mutton no bigger than a preen. Mr.
De Quinshay would mak' a gran' preacher, though
I'm thinking a hantle o' the folk wouldna ken what

he was driving at." During most of the day De Quincey lay in a stupor; the early hours of the next morning were his time for talk. The Edinburgh of that time was still a town of strong individualities, brilliant wits, and clever talkers, but when that weird voice began, the listeners, though they were the very flower of the intellect of the place, were content to hold their peace: all tradition lies, or this strange figure was here the first of them all.

In some ways it was a curious and primitive time, certainly none of these men was a drunkard, but they all wrote as if they quaffed liquor like the gods of the Norse mythology, and with some of them practice conformed to theory, whilst fists and sticks were quite orthodox modes of settling disputes. Even the grave Ebony was not immune. A writer in Glasgow, one Douglas, was aggrieved at some real or fancied reference in the Magazine. He hied him to Edinburgh, and as Mr. Blackwood was entering his shop, he laid a horsewhip in rather a half-hearted fashion, it would seem, about his shoulders. Then he made off. The editor publisher forthwith procured a cudgel, and luckily discovered his aggressor on the point of entering the Glasgow coach; he gave him a sound beating. As nothing more is heard of the incident, probably both sides considered honour as satisfied. How difficult to imagine people of position in incidents like this in Edinburgh of to-day; but I will not dwell longer on them and their likes, but move on to another era.

"*Virgilium vidi tantum*," very happily quoted Scott, the only time he ever saw (save for a casual street view) and spoke with Burns. One wishes that there was more to be said of Scott and Carlyle. Carlyle was a student at Edinburgh, and passed the early years of his literary working life there. He saw Scott on the street many a time and earnestly desired a more intimate knowledge. This meeting would have been as interesting as that, but it was not to be. Never was fate more ironical, nay, perverse. Goethe was the friend and correspondent of both, and it seemed to him at Weimar an odd thing that these men, both students of German literature, both citizens of Edinburgh, should not be personal friends. He did everything he could. Through Carlyle he sent messages and gifts to Scott, and these Carlyle transmitted in a modest and courteous note (13th April 1828). Alas! it was after the deluge. Scott, with the bravest of hearts, yet with lessening physical and mental power, was fighting that desperate and heroic battle we know so well. The letter went unanswered, and they never met. Less important people were kinder. Jeffrey told Carlyle he must give him a lift, and they were great friends afterwards. In 1815 for the first time he met Edward Irving in a room off Rose Street. The latter asked a number of local questions about Annan, which subject did not interest the youthful sage at all; finally, he professed total ignorance and indifference as to the history and condition of some one's baby. "You seem to know nothing," said Irving very crossly. The answer was characteristic. "Sir, by what right do you try my knowledge in this way? I have no interest to inform myself about the births in Annan, and care not if the process of birth and generation there should cease and determine altogether." Carlyle studied for the Scots kirk, but he was soon very doubtful as to his vocation. In 1817 he came from Kirkcaldy to put down his name for the theological hall. "Old Dr. Ritchie was 'not at home' when I called to enter myself. 'Good,' said I, 'let the omen be fulfilled,'" and he shook the dust of the hall from his feet for evermore. Possibly he muttered something about, "Hebrew old Clo"; if he did, his genius for cutting nicknames carried him away. Through it all no one had greater reverence for the written Word. Carlyle, for good or for ill, was a Calvinist at heart. In the winter of 1823 he was sore beset with the "fiend dyspepsia." He rode from his father's house all the way to Edinburgh to consult a specialist. The oracle was not dubious. "It was all tobacco, sir; give up tobacco." But could he give it up? "Give it up, sir?" he testily replied. "I can cut off my hand with an axe if that should be necessary." Carlyle let it alone for months, but was not a whit the better; at length, swearing he would endure the "diabolical farce and delusion" no longer, he laid almost violent hands on a long clay and tobacco pouch and was as happy as it was possible for him to be. Perhaps the doctor was right after all.

Up to the middle of the last century a strange personage called Peter Nimmo, or more often Sir Peter Nimmo, moved about the classes of Edinburgh University, and had done so for years. Professor Masson in *Edinburgh Sketches and Memories* has told with his wonted care and accuracy what it is possible to know of the subject. He was most probably a "stickit minister" who hung about the classes year after year, half-witted no doubt, but with a method in his mad-ness. He pretended or believed or not unwillingly was hoaxed into the belief that he was continually being asked to the houses of professors and others, where not seldom he was received and got some sort of entertainment. Using Professor Wilson's name as a passport he achieved an interview with Wordsworth, who described him as "a Scotch baronet, eccentric in appearance, but fundamentally one of the most sensible men he had ever met with." It was shrewdly suspected that he simply held his tongue, and allowed Wordsworth to do all the talking; a good listener is usually found a highly agreeable person. He tickled Carlyle's sense of humour, and was made the subject of a poem by the latter in *Fraser's Magazine.* It was one of the earliest and one of the very worst things that Carlyle ever did.

I note in passing that Peter Nimmo had a predecessor or contemporary, John Sheriff by name, who died in August 1844 in his seventieth year. He was widely known as Doctor Syntax, from some fancied resemblance to the stock portrait of that celebrity. He devoted all his time to University class-rooms and City churches, through which he roamed at will as by prescriptive right. He boasted that he had attended more than a hundred courses of lectures; but his great joy was when any chance enabled him to occupy the seat of the Lord High Commissioner in St. Giles'.

One of Carlyle's best passages is the account in *Sartor Resartus* of his perambulation of the Rue St. Thomas de L'Enfer, the spiritual conflict that he waged then with himself, the victory that he won in which the everlasting "Yes" answered the everlasting "No." Under the somewhat melodramatic French

name Leith Walk is signified, the most commonplace
thoroughfare in a town where the ways are rarely commonplace. Perhaps the name was suggested by a
quaint incident that befell him there. He was walking along it when a drunken sailor coming from Leith
and "tacking" freely as he walked ran into a countryman going the other way. "Go to hell," said the sailor,
wildly and unreasonably enraged. "Od, man, I'm going
to Leith," said the other, "as if merely pleading a previous engagement, and proceeded calmly on his way."

I have said the fates were kind in linking together
though but for a moment the lives of Burns and Scott,
and they were unkind in refusing this to the lives of
Scott and Carlyle. You wish that in some way or
other they had allowed Carlyle and Robert Louis
Stevenson to meet, if but for a moment, so that the
last great writer whom Edinburgh has produced
might have had the kindly touch of personal inter-
course with his predecessors; but it was not to be, nor
are there many R.L.S. Edinburgh anecdotes worth
the telling. This which he narrates of his grandfather,
Robert of Bell Rock fame, is better than any about
himself. The elder Stevenson's wife was a pious lady
with a circle of pious if humble friends. One of those,
"an unwieldy old woman," had fallen down one of
those steep outside stairs abundant in old Edinburgh,
but she crashed on a passing baker and escaped un-
hurt by what seemed to Mrs. Stevenson a special in-
terposition of Providence. "I would like to know what
kind of Providence the baker thought it," exclaimed
her husband.

R.L.S. had certain flirtations with the Edinburgh

underworld of his time, for the dreary respectability
and precise formalism which has settled like a cloud
on the once jovial Auld Reekie was abhorrent to the
soul of the bright youth. No doubt he had his adventures, but if they are still known they are not recorded.
There is some tradition of a novel, *Maggie Arnot*, I
think it was called, wherein he told strange tales of
dark Edinburgh closes, but pious hands consigned it,
no doubt wisely and properly, to the flames; and
though certain Corinthians were scornful and wrath-
ful, yet you feel his true function was that of the wise
and kindly, sympathetic and humane essayist and
moralist that we have learned to love and admire, the
almost Covenanting writer whom of a surety the men
of the Covenant would have thrust out and perhaps
violently ended in holy indignation. I gather a few
scraps. Of the stories of his childhood this seems admirably characteristic. He was busy once with pencil
and paper, and then addressed his mother: "Mamma, I
have drawed a man. Shall I draw his soul now?" The
makers of the New Town when they planned those
wide, long, exposed streets, forgot one thing, and that
was the Edinburgh weather, against which, if you
think of it, the sheltered ways of the ancient city were
an admirable protection. In many a passage R.L.S.
has told us how the east wind, and the easterly "haar,"
and the lack of sun assailed him like cruel and im-
placable foes. He would lean over the great bridge
that spans what was once the Nor' Loch, and watch
the trains as they sped southward on their way, as it
seemed, to lands of sunshine and romance. It was but
the pathetic inconsistency of human nature that in the

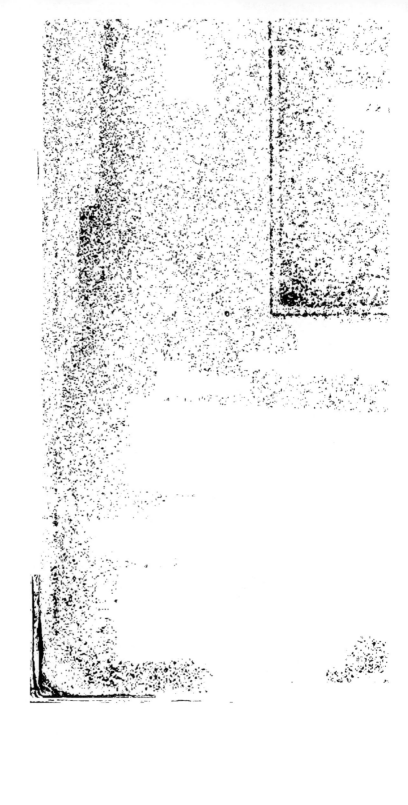

lands of perpetual sunshine made him think no stars
were so splendid as the Edinburgh street lamps, and
so the whole romance of his life was bound up with
" the huddle of cold grey hills from which we came,"
and most of all with that city of the hills, and the winds
and the tempest where he had his origin. He was called to the Scots bar ; his family were powerful in Edinburgh and so he got a little work—four briefs in all
we are told. Even when he was far distant the brass
plate on the door of 17 Heriot Row bore the legend·
"Mr. R. L. Stevenson, Advocate" for many a long day.
Probably the time of the practical joker is passed in
Edinburgh, or an agent might have been tempted
to shove some papers in at the letter-box ; but what
about the cheque with which it used to be, and still is
in theory at any rate, the laudable habit in the north
of enclosing as companion to all such documents ?
Ah ! that would indeed have been carrying the joke
to an unreasonable length. I will not tell here of the
memorable occasion when plain Leslie Stephen, as
he then was, took him to the old Infirmary to introduce him to W. E. Henley, then a patient within those
grimy walls. It was the beginning of a long story of
literary and personal friendship, with strange ups and
downs. Writing about Edinburgh as I do, I would fain
brighten my page and conclude my chapter with one
of his most striking notes on his birthplace. " I was
born likewise within the bounds of an earthly city illustrious for her beauty, her tragic and picturesque as-
sociations, and for the credit of some of her brave sons.
Writing as I do in a strange quarter of the world, and
a late day of my age, I can still behold the profile of

her towers and chimneys, and the long trail of her smoke against the sunset; I can still hear those strains of martial music that she goes to bed with, ending each day like an act of an opera to the notes of bugles; still recall with a grateful effort of memory, any one of a thousand beautiful and spacious circumstances that pleased me and that must have pleased any one in my half-remembered past. It is the beautiful that I thus actively recall, the august airs of the castle on its rock, nocturnal passages of lights and trees, the sudden song of the blackbird in a suburban lane, rosy and dusky winter sunsets, the uninhabited splendours of the early dawn, the building up of the city on a misty day, house above house, spire above spire, until it was received into a sky of softly glowing clouds, and seemed to pass on and upwards by fresh grades and rises, city beyond city, a New Jerusalem bodily scaling heaven."

CHAPTER EIGHT

THE ARTISTS

CHAPTER EIGHT   THE ARTISTS

ST. MARGARET, QUEEN OF MALCOLM
Canmore, has been ingeniously if fancifully claimed
as the earliest of Scots artists. At the end of her life
she prophesied that Edinburgh Castle would be taken
by the English. On the wall of her chapel she pictured a castle with a ladder against the rampart, and on
the ladder a man in the act of climbing. In this fashion
she intimated the castle would fall ; *Gardez vous de
Français*, she wrote underneath. Probably by the
French she meant the Normans from whom she herself had fled. They had taken England and would try,
she thought, to take Scotland. Thus you read the riddle, if it be worth your while. The years after are blank;
the art was ecclesiastical and not properly native. In
the century before the Reformation there is reason to
believe that Edinburgh was crowded with fair shrines
and churches beautifully adorned, but the Reformers
speedily changed all that. The first important native
name is that of George Jamesone (1586–1644), the
Scots Van Dyck, as he is often called, who, though he
was born in Aberdeen, finally settled in Edinburgh,
and, like everybody else, you might say, was buried
in Greyfriars.

In 1729 a fine art association, called the Edinburgh
Academy of St. Luke, was formed, but it speedily
went to pieces. This is not the place to trace the art
history of that or of the Edinburgh Select Society.
In 1760 classes were opened at what was called the
Trustees Academy ; it was supported by an annual
grant of £2000, which was part compensation for the
increased burdens imposed on Scotland by the union
with England. This was successively under the charge

BOOK OF EDINBURGH ANECDOTE

of Alexander Runciman, David Allan, called the "Scots Hogarth," John Graham, and Andrew Wilson. It still exists as a department of the great government art institution at South Kensington. In 1808 a Society of Incorporated Artists was formed, and it began an annual exhibition of pictures which at first were very successful. Then came the institution for the encouragement of fine arts in Scotland, formed in 1819. In 1826 the foundations, so to speak, of the Scottish Academy were laid. In 1837 it received its charter, and was henceforth known as the Royal Scottish Academy; its annual exhibition was the chief art event of the year in Scotland, and since 1855 this exhibition has been held in the Grecian temple on the Mound, which is one of the most prominent architectural effects in Edinburgh. It is a mere commonplace to say there is no art without wealth, and, as far as Edinburgh is concerned, it is only after a new town began that she had painters worth the naming. It is a period of (roughly) 150 years. It is possible that in the future Glasgow may be more important than Edinburgh, but with this I have nothing to do. I have only to tell a few anecdotes of the chief figures, and first of all there is Jamesone.

Whatever be his merits, we ought to be grateful to this artist because he has preserved for us so many contemporary figures. Pictures in those days were often made to tell a story. After the battle of Langside Lord Seton escaped to Flanders, where he was forced to drive a waggon for his daily bread. He returned in happier times for his party, and entered again into possession of his estates. He had himself painted by Jamesone, represented or dressed as a waggoner driving a wain with four horses attached, and the picture was hung at Seton Palace. When Charles I. came to Scotland in 1633 he dined with my Lord. He was much struck with the painting, could not, in fact, keep his eyes off it. The admiration of an art critic of such rank was fatal. What could a loyal courtier do but beg His Majesty's acceptance thereof? "Oh," said the King, " he could not rob the family of so inestimable a jewel." Royally spoken, and, you may be sure, gratefully heard. It is said the magistrates of Edinburgh employed Jamesone to trick up the Netherbow Port with portraits of the century of ancient Kings of the line of Fergus. Hence possibly the legend that he limned those same mythical royalties we see to-day at Holyrood Palace, though it is certain enough they are not his, but Flemish De Witt's. Jamesone was in favour with Charles, assuredly a discriminating patron of art and artists. The King stopped his horse at the Bow and gazed long at the grim phantoms in whose reality he, like everybody else, devoutly believed. He gave Jamesone a diamond ring from his own finger, and he afterwards sat for his portrait. He allowed the painter to work with his hat on to protect him from the cold, which so puffed up our artist that he would hardly ever take it off again, no matter what company he frequented. We don't know his reward, but it seems his ordinary fee was £1 sterling for a portrait. No doubt it was described as £20 Scots, which made it look better but not go farther. You do not wonder that there was a lack of eminent painters when the leader of them all was thus rewarded.

BOOK OF EDINBURGH ANECDOTE

Artists work from various motives. Witness Sir Robert Strange the engraver. He fell ardently in love with Isabella Lumsden, whose brother acted as secretary to Prince Charles Edward Stuart. The lady was an extreme Jacobite, and insisted that Strange should throw in his lot with the old stock. He was present in the great battles of the '45, and at Inverness engraved a plate for bank-notes for the Stuart Government. He had soon other things to think of. When the cause collapsed at Culloden, he was in hiding in Edinburgh for some time, and existed by selling portraits of the exiled family at small cost. Once when visiting his Isabella the Government soldiers nearly caught him; probably they had a shrewd suspicion he was like to be in the house, which they unexpectedly entered. The lady was equal to this or any other occasion. She wore one of the enormous hoops of the period, and under this her lover lay hid, she the while defiantly carolling a Jacobite air whilst the soldiers were looking up the chimney, and under the table, and searching all other orthodox places of refuge. The pair were shortly afterwards married. Strange had various and, finally, prosperous fortunes, and in 1787 was knighted. "If," as George III. said with a grin, for he knew his history, "he would accept that honour from an Elector of Hanover." But the King's great favourite among Scots artists was Allan Ramsay, the son of the poet and possibly of like Jacobite proclivities, although about that we hear nothing. He had studied "at the seat of the Beast," as his father said, in jest you may be sure, for our old friend was no highflyer. Young Ramsay became an accomplished man of the world, and had more

ALLAN RAMSAY, PAINTER

From a Mezzotint after Artist's own painting

than a double share, like his father before him, of the pawkiness attributed, though not always truthfully, to his countrymen. He was soon in London and painting Lord Bute most diligently. He did it so well that he made Reynolds, in emulation, carefully elaborate a full-length that he was doing at the time. "I wish to show legs with Ramsay's Lord Bute," quoth he. The King preferred Ramsay; he talked German, an accomplishment rare with Englishmen at the period, and he fell in, so to say, with the King's homely ways. When His Majesty had dined plentifully on his favourite boiled mutton and turnips he would say : " Now, Ramsay, sit down in my place and take your dinner." He was a curled darling of great folk and was appointed Court painter in 1767. A universal favourite, even Johnson had a good word for him. All this has nothing to do with art, and nobody puts him beside Reynolds, but he was highly prosperous. The King was wont to present the portrait of himself and his consort to all sorts of great people, so Ramsay and his assistants were kept busy. Once he went on a long visit to Rome, partly on account of his health. He left directions with his most able assistant, Philip Reinagle, to get ready fifty pairs of Kings and Queens at ten guineas apiece. Now Reinagle had learned to paint so like Ramsay that no mortal man could tell the difference, but as he painted over and over again the commonplace features of their Majesties, he got heartily sick of the business. He struck for more pay and got thirty instead of ten guineas, so after the end of six years he managed to get through with it, somehow or other, but ever afterwards he looked back upon the period as a horrid nightmare. Ramsay was a scholar, a wit, and a gentleman. In a coarse age he was delicate and choice. He was fond of tea, but wine was too much for his queasy stomach. Art was certainly not the all in all for him, and his pictures are feeble. Possibly he did not much care; he had his reward. Some critics have thought that he might have been a great painter if his heart had been entirely in his work.

It has been said of a greater than he, of the incomparable Sir Henry Raeburn, that the one thing wanting to raise his genius into the highest possible sphere was the chastening of a great sorrow or the excitement of a great passion. I cannot myself conceive anything better than his *Braxfield* among men or his *Mrs. James Campbell* among women, but I have no right to speak. At least his prosperity enabled him to paint a whole generation, though from that generation as we have it on his canvas, a strange malice of fate makes the figure of Robert Burns, the greatest of them all, most conspicuous by its absence. His prosperity and contentment were the result of the simple life and plain living of old Edinburgh. He was a great friend of John Clerk, afterwards Lord Eldin. In very early days Clerk asked him to dinner. The landlady uncovered two dishes, one held three herrings and the other three potatoes. "Did I not tell you, wuman," said John with that accent which was to make "a' the Fifteen" tremble, "that a gentleman was to dine wi' me, and that ye were to get *sax* herrings and *sax* potatoes?"

These were his salad days, and ere they were fled

a wealthy young widow saw and loved Raeburn. She was not personally known to him, but her wit easily devised a method. She asked to have her portrait painted, and the rest was plain sailing. It was then the fixed tradition of all the northern painters that you must study at Rome if you would be an artist. Raeburn set off for Italy. The story is that he had an introduction to Sir Joshua Reynolds, whom he visited as he passed through London. Reynolds was much impressed with the youth from the north, and at the end took him aside, and in the most delicate manner suggested that if money was necessary for his studies abroad he was prepared to advance it. Raeburn gratefully declined. When he returned from Rome he settled in Edinburgh, from which he scarcely stirred. His old master, Martin, jealously declared that the lad in George Street painted better before he went to Rome, but the rest of Scotland did not agree. It became a matter of course that everybody who was anybody should get himself painted by Raeburn. He seemed to see at once into the character of the face he had before him, and so his pictures have that remarkable characteristic of great artists, they tell us more of the man than the actual sight of the man himself does; but again I go beyond my province.

The early life of many Scots artists (and doctors) is connected with Edinburgh, but the most important part is given to London. Thus Sir David Wilkie belongs first of all to Fife, for he was born at Cults, where his father was parish minister. His mother saw him drawing something with chalk on the floor. The child said he was making " bonnie Lady Gonie," referring to Lady Balgonie, who lived near. Obviously this same story might have been told of many people, not afterwards eminent. In fact, Wilkie's development was not rapid. In 1799, when he was fourteen, he went to the Trustees Academy at Edinburgh. George Thomson, the Secretary, after examining his drawings declared that they had not sufficient merit to procure his admission. The Earl of Leven, however, insisted he must be admitted, and admitted he was. He proceeded to draw from the antique, not at first triumphantly. His father showed one of his studies to one of his elders. "What was it?" queried the douce man. "A foot," was the answer. "A fute! a fute! it's mair like a fluke than a fute." In 1804 he returned to Cults where he employed himself painting Pitlessie Fair. At church he saw an ideal character study nodding in one of the pews. He soon had it transferred to the flyleaf of the Bible. He had not escaped attention, and was promptly taken to task. He stoutly asserted that in the sketch the eye and the hand alone were engaged, he could hear the sermon all the time. The ingenuity or matchless impudence of this assertion fairly astounded his accusers, and the matter dropped. I do not tell here how he went to London and became famous. How famous let this anecdote show. In 1817 he was at Abbotsford making a group of the Scott family : he went with William Laidlaw to Altrive to see Hogg. "Laidlaw," said the shepherd, "this is not the great Mr. Wilkie?" "It's just the great Mr. Wilkie, Hogg." The poet turned to the painter : "I cannot tell you how pleased I am to see you in my house and how glad I am to see you are

so young a man." This curious greeting is explained thus: Hogg had taken Wilkie for a horse-couper. What Wilkie would have taken Hogg for we are not told, possibly for something of the same.

Wilkie, as everybody knows, painted subjects of ordinary life in Scotland and England, such as *The Village Festival, Rent Day, The Penny Wedding,* and so forth. In the prime of life he went to Spain, and was much impressed with the genius of Velasquez, then little known in this country. He noticed a similarity to Raeburn, perhaps that peculiar directness in going straight to the heart of the subject, that putting on the canvas the very soul of the man, common to both painters. The story goes that when in Madrid he went daily to the Museo del Prado, set himself down before the picture *Los Borrachos*, spent three hours gazing at it in a sort of ecstasy, and then, when fatigue and admiration had worn him out, he would take up his hat and with a deep sigh leave the place for the time.

Another son of the manse is more connected with Edinburgh than ever Wilkie was, and this is the Rev. John Thomson, known as Thomson of Duddingston, from the fact that he was parish minister there from 1801 till his death in 1840. His father was incumbent of Dailly in Ayrshire, and here he spent his early years. He received the elements of art from the village carpenter—at least, so that worthy averred. He was wont to introduce the subject to a stranger. "Ye'll ken ane John Thomson, a minister?" "Why, Thomson of Duddingston, the celebrated painter? Do you know him?" "*Me* ken him? It was *me* that first taught him to pent." As in the case of Wilkie, his art leanings got him into difficulty. At a half-yearly communion he noted a picturesque old hillman, and needs must forthwith transfer him to paper. The fathers and brethren were not unnaturally annoyed and disgusted, and they deputed one of their number to deal faithfully with the offender. Thomson listened in solemn silence, nay, took what appeared to be some pencil notes of the grave words of censure, at length he suddenly showed the other a hastily drawn sketch of himself. "What auld cankered carl do ye think this is?" The censor could not choose but laugh, and the incident ended. Thomson was twice married. His second wife was Miss Dalrymple of Fordel. She saw his picture of *The Falls of Foyers*, and conceived a passion to know the artist, and the moment he saw her he determined " that woman must be my wife." As he afterwards said, "We just drew together." The manse at Duddingston became for a time a very muses' bower; the choicest of Edinburgh wits, chief among them Scott himself, were constant visitors. Of illustrious strangers perhaps the greatest was Turner, though his remarks were not altogether amiable. "Ah, Thomson, you beat me hollow—in *frames*!" He was more eulogistic of certain pictures. "The man who did *that* could paint." When he took his leave he said, as he got into the carriage, "By God, though, Thomson, I envy you that loch." To-day the prospect is a little spoilt by encroaching houses and too many people, but Scotland has few choicer views than that placid water, the old church at the edge, the quaint village, and the mighty Lion Hill that broods over all. Thomson is said to have

THE ARTISTS OF EDINBURGH

diligently attended to his clerical duties, but he was hard put to it sometimes, for you believe he was more artist than theologian. He built himself a studio in the manse garden down by the loch. This he called Edinburgh, so that too importunate callers might be warded off with the remark that he was at Edinburgh. "Gone to Edinburgh," you must know, is the traditional excuse of everybody in Duddingston who shuts his door. One Sunday John, the minister's man, "jowed" the bell long and earnestly in vain—the well-known figure would not emerge from the manse. John rushed off to the studio by the loch and found, as he expected, the minister hard at work with a canvas before him. He admonished him that it was past the time, that the people were assembled, and the bells 'rung in." "Oh, John," said his master, in perplexed entreaty, "just go and ring the bell for another five minutes till I get in this bonnie wee bit o' sky." An old woman of his congregation was in sore trouble, and went to the minister and asked for a bit prayer. Thomson gave her two half-crowns. "Take that, Betty, my good woman, it's likely to do you more good than any prayer I'm likely to make," a kindly but amusingly cynical remark, in the true vein of the moderates of the eighteenth century. "Here, J. F.," he said to an eminent friend who visited him on a Sunday afternoon, "*you* don't care about breaking the Sabbath, gie these pictures a touch of varnish." These were the days before the Disruption and the evangelical revival. You may set off against him the name of Sir George Harvey, who was made president of the northern Academy in 1864. He was much in sympathy with Scots

187

religious tradition, witness his *Quitting the Manse*, his *Covenanting Preaching*, and other deservedly famous pictures. As Mr. W. D. M'Kay points out, the Disruption produced in a milder form a recrudescence of the strain of thought and sentiment of Covenanting times, and this influenced the choice of subjects. In his early days when Harvey talked of painting, a friend advised him to look at Wilkie; he looked and seemed to see nothing that was worth the looking, but he examined again and again, even as Wilkie himself had gazed on Velasquez, and so saw in him "the very finest of the wheat." In painting the picture *The Wise and Foolish Builders*, he made a child construct a house on the sand, so that he might see exactly how the thing was done, not, however, that he fell into the stupid error of believing that work and care were everything. He would neither persuade a man nor dissuade him from an artistic career. "If it is in him," he was wont to say, "it is sure to come out, whether I advise him or not."

Of the truth of this saying the life of David Roberts is an example. He was the son of a shoemaker and was born at Stockbridge, Edinburgh, at the end of the eighteenth century. Like most town boys of the period he haunted the Mound, then a favourite stand for wild beast caravans. This was before the era of Grecian temples and statues and trim-kept gardens, and "Geordie Boyd's mud brig" (to recall a long-vanished popular name) was an unkempt wilderness. He drew pictures of the shows on the wall of the white-washed kitchen with the end of a burnt stick and a bit of keel, in order that his mother might see what they were like. When she had satisfied her curiosity, why—a dash of white-wash and the wall was as good as ever! His more ambitious after-attempts were exhibited by the honest cobbler to his customers. "Hoo has the callant learnt it?" was the perplexed inquiry. With some friends of like inclination he turned a disused cellar into a life academy: they tried their prentice hands on a donkey, and then they sat for one another; but this is not the place to follow his upward struggles. In 1858 he received the freedom of the city of Edinburgh.

Where there's a will there's a way, but ways are manifold and some of them are negative. Horatio Maculloch, the landscape-painter, in his *Edinburgh from Dalmeny Park*, had introduced into the foreground the figure of a woodman lopping the branches of a fallen tree. This figure gave him much trouble, so he told his friend, Alexander Smith, the poet. One day he said cheerfully, "Well, Smith, I have done that figure at last." "Indeed, and how?" "I have painted it out!" Even genius and hard work do not always ensure success. If ever there was a painter of genius that man was David Scott, most pathetic figure among Edinburgh artists. You scarce know why his fame was not greater, or his work not more sought after. His life was a short one (1806–1849) and his genius did not appeal to the mass, for he did not and perhaps could not produce a great body of highly impressive work. Yet, take the best of his illustrations to Coleridge's *Ancient Mariner*. You read the poem with deeper meaning, with far deeper insight, after you have looked on them; to me at least they seem greater than William Blake's illustrations to *Blair's Grave*, a work of like nature. Still more wonderful is the a-mazing *Puck Fleeing Before the Dawn*. The artist rises to the height of his great argument; his genius is for the moment equal to Shakespeare's; the spirit of un-earthly drollery and mischief and impish humour tak-es bodily form before your astonished gaze. "His soul was like a star and dwelt apart;" the few anecdotes of him have a strange, weird touch. When a boy, he was handed over to a gardener to be taken to the coun-try. He took a fancy he would never be brought back; the gardener swore he would bring him back himself; the child, only half convinced, treated the astonished rustic to a discourse on the commandments, and war-ned him if he broke his word he would be guilty of a lie. The gardener, more irritated than amused, wish-ed to have nothing whatever to do with him. Going into a room once where there was company, he was much struck with the appearance of a young lady there; he went up to her, laid his hand on her knees, "You are very beautiful," he said. As a childish prank he thought he would make a ghost and frighten some other children. With a bolster and a sheet he succeed-ed only too well; he became frantic with terror, and fairly yelled the house down in his calls for help.

A different man altogether was Sir Daniel Macnee, who was R.S.A. in 1876. He was born the same year as David Scott, and lived long after him. The famous portrait painter, kindly, polished, accomplished, was a man of the world, widely known and universally pop-ular, except that his universal suavity of itself now and again excited enmity. "I dinna like Macnee a bit," said a sour-grained old Scots dame; "he's aye everybody's freend!" The old lady might have found Sam Bough more to her taste. Though born in Carlisle he settled in Edinburgh in 1855, and belongs to the northern capital. In dress and much else he delighted to run tilt at conventions, and was rather an *enfant terrible* at decorous functions. At some dinner or other he noted a superbly got up picture-dealer, whom he pretended to mistake for a waiter. " John— John, I say, John, bring me a pint of wine, and let it be of the choicest vintage." His pranks at last provoked Professor Blackie, who was present, to declare roundly and audibly," I am astonished that a man who can paint like an angel should come here and conduct himself like a fool." He delighted in the Lothian and Fife coasts. The Bass he considered in some sort his own property, so he jocularly told its owner, Sir Hew Dalrymple," You get £20 a year or so out of it; I make two or three hundred." Bough was the very picture of a genial Bohemian, perhaps he was rather fitted to shine, a light of the Savage Club than of the northern capital, where, if tradition was followed, there was always something grim and fell even about the merry-making. One or two of his genial maxims are worth quoting. There had been some row about a disputed succession. "It's an awful warning," he philosophised, " to all who try to save money in this world. You had far better spend your tin on a little sound liquor, wherewith to comfort your perishable corps, than have such cursed rows about it after you have gone." And again his golden rule of the *Ars Bibendi*, " I like as much as I can get honestly and carry decently," on which profound maxim let us make an end of our chapter.

CHAPTER NINE

THE WOMEN OF EDINBURGH

N

CHAPTER NINE
THE WOMEN OF EDINBURGH

ANECDOTES OF THE WOMEN OF EDIN-
burgh are mainly of the eighteenth century. The
events of an earlier period are too tragic for a trivial
story or they come under other heads. Is it an anecdote to tell how, on the night of Rizzio's murder (9th
March 1566), the conspirators upset the supper table,
and unless Jane, Countess of Argyll, had caught at a
falling candle the rest of the tragedy had been played
in total darkness? And it is only an unusual fact about
this same countess that when she came to die she was
enclosed in the richest coffin ever seen in Scotland;
the compartments and inscriptions being all set in
solid gold. The chroniclers ought to have some curious anecdotes as to the subsequent fate of that coffin,
but they have not, it vanishes unaccountably from
history. The tragedies of the Covenant have stories
of female heroism; the women were not less constant
than the men, nay, that learned but malicious gossip,
Charles Kirkpatrick Sharpe, insinuates that the husband might have given in at the last minute, ay, when
the rope was round his neck at the Cross or the Grassmarket, but the wife urged him to be true to the death.
The wives of the persecutors had not seldom a strong
sympathy with the persecuted. The Duchess of Rothes, as Lady Ann Lindsay became, sheltered the
Covenanters. Her husband dropped a friendly hint,
"My hawks will be out to-night, my Lady, so you had
better take care of your blackbirds."

It was natural that a sorely tried and oppressed
nation should paint the oppressor in the blackest of

colours. You are pleased with an anecdote like the above, showing that a gleam of pity sometimes crossed those truculent faces. The Duke of York (afterwards James VII.) at Holyrood had his playful and humane hour. There was a sort of informal theatre at the palace. In one of the pieces the Princess Anne lay dead upon the stage—such was her part. Mumper, her own and her father's favourite dog, was not persuaded, he jumped and fawned on her; she laughed, the audience loyally obeyed and the tragedy became a farce. "Her Majesty had *sticked* the part," said Morrison of Prestongrange gruffly. The Duke was shipwrecked on the return voyage to Scotland and Mumper was drowned. A courtier uttered some suavely sympathetic words about the dog. "How, sir, can you speak of *him*, when so many fine fellows went to the bottom?" rejoined His Royal Highness.

Here is a story from the other side. In 1681 the Earl of Argyll was committed to the Castle for declining the oath required by the Test Act. On the 12th December he was condemned to death and on the 20th he learned that his execution was imminent. Lady Sophia Lindsay of Balcarres, his daughter-in-law, comes, it was given out, to bid him a last farewell; there is a hurried change of garments in the prison, and presently Argyll emerges as lacquey bearing her long train. At the critical moment the sentinel roughly grasped him by the arm. Those Scots dames had the nerve of iron and resource without parallel. The lady pulled the train out of his hand into the mud, slashed him across the face with it till he was all smudged over, and rated him soundly for stupidity.

THE WOMEN OF EDINBURGH

The soldier laughed, the lady entered the coach, the fugitive jumped on the footboard behind, and so away into the darkness and liberty of a December night. Ere long he was safe in Holland, and she was just as safe in the Tolbooth, for even that age would give her no other punishment than a brief confinement. Perhaps more stoical fortitude was required in the Lady Graden's case. She was sister-in-law to Baillie of Jerviswood. At his trial in 1684 for treason she kept up his strength from time to time with cordials, for he was struck with mortal sickness; she walked with him, as he was carried along the High Street, to the place of execution at the Cross. He pointed out to her Warriston's window (long since removed from the totally altered close of that name), and told of the high talk he had engaged in with her father, who had himself gone that same dread way some twenty years before. She "saw him all quartered, and took away every piece and wrapped it up in some linen cloth with more than masculine courage." So says Lauder of Fountainhall, who had been one of the Crown counsel at the trial.

Even as children the women of that time were brave and devoted. Grizel Hume, daughter of Sir Patrick Hume of Polwarth, when a child of twelve was sent by her father from the country to Edinburgh to take important messages to Baillie as he lay in prison. A hard task for a child of those years, but she went through it safely; perhaps it was no harder than conveying food at the dead of night to the family vault in Polwarth Churchyard where her father was concealed. When visiting the prison she became acquainted with the son and namesake of Jerviswood: they were afterwards

BOOK OF EDINBURGH ANECDOTE

married. The memories of the Hon. George Baillie of
Jerviswood and of his wife the Lady Grizel Baillie are
preserved for us in an exquisite monograph by their
daughter, Lady Grizel Murray of Stanhope. The name
of a distinguished statesman is often for his own age
merely, but the authoress of a popular song has a
surer title to fame. In one of his last years in Dumfries,
Burns quoted Lady Grizel Baillie's "And werena my
heart licht I wad dee" to a young friend who noted the
coldness with which the townsfolk then regarded him.

It is matter of history that Argyll did not escape
in the long run. In 1685, three years before the dawn
of the Revolution, he made that unfortunate expedition to Scotland which ended in failure, capture and
death on the old charge. One of his associates was
Sir John Cochrane of Ochiltree; he also was captured
and as a "forefaulted traitor" was led by the hangman through the streets of Edinburgh bound and
bareheaded. A line from London and all was over,
so his friends thought, but that line never arrived. On
the 7th of July in that year the English mail was
twice stopped and robbed near Alnwick. The daring
highwayman turned out to be a girl! She was Grizel,
Sir John's daughter, disguised in men's clothes and
(of course) armed to the teeth. In the end Sir John
obtained his pardon, and lived to be Earl of Dundonald.

In the middle of the next century we have this on the
Jacobite side. When the Highlanders were in Carlisle
in the '45 a lady called Dacre, daughter of a gentleman in Cumberland, lay at Rose Castle in the pangs
of childbirth and very ill indeed. A party of High-

THE WOMEN OF EDINBURGH

landers under Macdonald of Kinloch Moidart entered her dwelling to occupy it as their own. When the
leader learned what had taken place, the presumed
Highland savage showed himself a considerate and
chivalrous gentleman. With courteous words he drew
off his men, took the white cockade from his bonnet
and pinned it on the child's breast. Thus it served to
guard not merely the child but the whole household.
The infant became in after years the wife of Clerk of
Pennicuick, her house was at 100 Princes Street, she
lived far into the last century, known by her erect
walk, which she preserved till over her eightieth year,
and by her quaint dress. Once she was sitting in Constable's shop when Sir Walter Scott went by. "Oh, Sir
Walter, are you really going to pass me?" she called
out in a dudgeon that was only half feigned. But she
was easily pacified. "Sure, my Lady," said the Wizard
in comic apology, "by this time I might know your
back as well as your face." She was called the "White
Rose of Scotland" from the really beautiful legend of
the white cockade, which she wore on every important
occasion. And what of the Highland Bayard? His
estates were forfeited, his home was burned to the
ground, and himself on the Gallows Hill at Carlisle
on the 18th October 1746 suffered the cruel and igno-
minious death of a traitor—*aequitate deum erga bona
malaque documenta !*

The women were on the side of the Jacobites even
to the end. " Old maiden ladies were the last leal Jacobites in Edinburgh. Spinsterhood in its loneliness
remained ever true to Prince Charlie and the vanished dreams of its youth." Thus Dame Margaret Sin-

199

clair of Dunbeath; and she adds that in the old Episcopal chapel in the Cowgate the last of those Jacobite
ladies never failed to close her prayer book and stand
erect in silent protest, when the prayer for King George
III. and the reigning family was read in the Church
service. Alison Rutherford, born 1712 and the wife of
Patrick Cockburn of Ormiston, was not of this way
of thinking. She lived in the house of, and (it seems)
under the rule of, her father-in-law. She said she
was married to a man of seventy-five. He was Lord
Justice-Clerk, and unpopular for his severity to the
unfortunate rebels of the '15. The nine of diamonds,
for some occult reason, was called the curse of Scotland, and when it turned up at cards a favourite Jacobite joke was to greet it as the Lord Justice-Clerk.
Mrs. Cockburn is best known as the authoress of one,
and not the best, version of the *Flowers of the Forest.*
But this is not her only piece. When the Prince occupied Edinburgh in the '45, she wrote a skit on the
specious language of the proclamations which did
their utmost to satisfy every party. It began—

> " Have you any laws to mend?
> Or have you any grievance?
> I'm a hero to my trade
> And truly a most leal prince."

With this in her pocket she set off to visit the Keiths
at Ravelston. They were a strong Jacobite family,
which was perhaps an inducement to the lady to wave
it in their faces. She was driven back in their coach,
but at the West Port was stopped by the rough Highland Guard who threatened to search after treason-
able papers. Probably the lady then thought the squib

MRS ALISON COCKBURN

From a Photograph

had not at all a humorous aspect, and she quaked and feared its discovery. But the coach was recognised as loyal by its emblazonry and it franked its freight, so to speak. Mrs. Cockburn was a brilliant letter-writer, strong, shrewd, sensible, sometimes pathetic, sometimes almost sublime, she gives you the very marrow of old Edinburgh. Thus she declines an invitation: " Mrs. Cockburn's compliments to Mr. and Mrs. Chalmers. Would wait on them with a great deal of pleasure, but finds herself at a loss, as Mrs. Chalmers sets her an example of never coming from home, and as there is nobody she admires more, she wishes to imitate her in everything." A woman loses her young child. These are Mrs. Cockburn's truly Spartan comments: " Should she lose her husband or another child she would recover: we need sorrowes often. In the meantime, if she could accept personal severity it would be well,—a ride in rain, wind and storm until she is fatigued to death, and spin on a great wheel and never allowed to sit down till weariness of nature makes her. I do assure you I have gone through all these exercises, and have reason to bless God my reason was preserved and health now more than belongs to my age." And again: "As for me, I sit in my black chair, weak, old, and contented. Though my body is not portable, I visit you in my prayers and in my cups." She tells us that one of her occasional servants, to wit, the waterwife, so called because she brought the daily supply of water up those interminable stairs, was frequently tipsy and of no good repute. She discharged her, yet she reappeared and was evidently favoured by the other servants; this was because she had adopted a foundling called Christie Fletcher, as she was first discovered on a stair in Fletcher's Land. The child had fine eyes, and was otherwise so attractive that Mrs. Cockburn got her into the Orphan Hospital. "By the account," she grimly remarks, " of that house, I think if our young ladies were educated there, it would make a general reform of manners."

She heard Colonel Reid (afterwards General Reid and the founder of the chair of Music in the University, where the annual Reid concerts perpetuate his name) play on the flute. "It thrills to your very heart, it speaks all languages, it comes from the heart to the heart. I never could have conceived, it had a dying fall. I can think of nothing but that flute." Mrs. Cockburn saw Sir Walter Scott when he was six, and was astonished at his precocity. He described her as " a virtuoso like myself," and defined a virtuoso as " one who wishes and will know everything."

The other and superior set of *The Flowers of the Forest* was written by Miss Jean Elliot, who lived from 1727 till 1805. The story is that she was the last Edinburgh lady who kept a private sedan chair in her "lobby." In this she was borne through the town by the last of the caddies. The honour of the last sedan chair is likewise claimed for Lady Don who lived in George Square; probably there were two "lasts." Those Edinburgh aristocratic lady writers had many points in common; they mainly got fame by one song, they made a dead secret of authorship, half because they were shy, half because they were proud. Caroline Baroness Nairne was more prolific than the others, for *The Land of the Leal, Caller Herrin'* (the refrain to which was caught from the chimes of St. Giles'), *The Auld Hoose*, and *John Tod* almost reach the high level of masterpieces, but she was as determined as the others to keep it dark. Her very husband did not know she was an authoress; she wrote as Mrs. Bogan of Bogan. In another direction she was rather too daring. She was one of a committee of ladies who proposed to inflict a bowdlerised Burns on the Scots nation. An emasculated *Jolly Beggars* had made strange reading, but the project fell through.

Lady Anne Barnard, one of the Lindsays of Balcarres, was another Edinburgh poetess. She is known by her one song, indeed only by a fragment of it, for the continuation or second part of *Auld Robin Gray* is anti-climax, fortunately so bad, that it has well-nigh dropped from memory. The song had its origin at Balcarres. There was an old Scots ditty beginning, " The bridegroom grat when the sun gaed doon." It was lewd and witty, but the air inspired the words to the gifted authoress. She heard the song from Sophy Johnstone—commonly called "Suff" or "the Suff," in the words of Mrs. Cockburn—surely the oddest figure among the ladies of old Edinburgh. Part nature, part training, or rather the want of it, exaggerated in her the bluntness and roughness of those old dames. She was daughter of the coarse, drunken Laird of Hilton. One day after dinner he maintained, in his cups, that education was rubbish, and that his daughter should be brought up without any. He stuck to this: she was called in jest the "natural" child of Hilton, and came to pass as such in the less proper sense of the word. She learned to read and write from the but-

BOOK OF EDINBURGH ANECDOTE

ler, and she taught herself to shoe a horse and do an artisan's work. She played the fiddle, fought the stable boys, swore like a trooper, dressed in a jockey coat, walked like a man, sang in a voice that seemed a man's, and was believed by half Edinburgh to be a man in disguise. She had strong affections and strong hates, she had great talent for mimicry, which made her many enemies, was inclined to be sceptical though not without misgivings and fears. She came to pay a visit to Balcarres, and stayed there for thirteen years. She had a choice collection of old Scots songs. One lingered in Sir Walter Scott's memory:

"Eh," quo' the Tod, "it's a braw, bricht nicht,
The wind's i' the wast and the mune shines bricht."

She gave her opinion freely. When ill-pleased her dark wrinkled face looked darker, and the hard lines about her mouth grew harder, as she planted her two big feet well out, and murmured in a deep bass voice, "Surely that's great nonsense." One evening at Mrs. Cockburn's in Crichton Street, the feet of Ann Scott, Sir Walter's sister, touched by accident the toes of the irascible Suff, who retorted with a good kick. "What is the lassie wabster, wabster, wabstering that gait for?" she growled. When she was an old woman, Dr. Gregory said she must abstain from animal food unless she wished to die. "Dee, Doctor! odd, I'm thinking they've forgotten an auld wife like me up yonder." But all her gaiety vanished near the end. From poverty or avarice she half starved herself. The younger generation of the Balcarres children brought tit-bits to her garret every Sunday. "What hae ye brocht? What hae ye brocht?" she would snap out greedily.

MISS JEAN ELLIOT

From a Sepi. Drawing

THE WOMEN OF EDINBURGH

And so the curtain falls on this strange figure of old Edinburgh.

I cannot leave those sweet singers without a passing word on the old ballad, surely of local origin:

> "Now Arthur's Seat shall be my bed,
> The sheets shall ne'er be pressed by me.
> St. Anton's Well shall be my drink
> Since my true love's forsaken me!
>
> Martinmas wind, when wilt thou blaw
> An' shake the green leaves aff the tree?
> O! gentle death, when wilt thou come?
> For o' my life I am wearie."

Is this a woman's voice? You cannot tell. It is supposed to commemorate the misfortunes of Lady Barbara Erskine, daughter of the Earl of Mar and wife of the second Marquis of Douglas. A rejected and malignant suitor is rumoured to have poisoned her husband's mind against her, till he drove her from his company.

Edinburgh has many records of high aristocratic, but very unconventional or otherwise remarkable, dames. Lady Rosslyn sat in the company of her friends one day when a woman whose character had been blown upon was announced. Many of her guests rose in a hurry to be gone. "Sit still, sit still," said the old lady, "it's na catchin'." Dr. Johnson, on his visit to Scotland, met Margaret, Duchess of Douglas, at James's Court. He describes her as "talking broad Scots with a paralytic voice scarcely understood by her own countrymen." It was enviously noted that he devoted his attention to her exclusively for the whole evening. The innuendo was that Duchesses in England had not paid much attention to Samuel, and that he was inclined to make as much of a Scots specimen as he could. An accusation of snobbery was a good stick wherewith to beat the sage. The lady was a daughter of Douglas of Maines, and the widow of Archibald, Duke of Douglas, who died in 1761. A more interesting figure was the Duchess of Queensberry, daughter of the Earl of Clarendon. The Act of the eleventh Parliament of James II., providing that "no Scotsman should marry an Englishwoman without the King's license under the Great Seal, under pain of death and escheat of moveables," was long out of date. She detested Scots manners, and did everything to render them absurd. She dressed herself as a peasant girl, to ridicule the stiff costumes of the day. The Scots made an excessive and almost exclusive use of the knife at table, whereat she screamed out as if about to faint. It is to her credit, however, that she was a friend and patron of Gay the poet, entertained him in Queensberry House, Canongate. Perhaps his praises of her beauty ought thus to suffer some discount; but Prior was as warm; and Pope's couplet is classic:

"If Queensberry to strip there's no compelling,
'Tis from a handmaid we must take a Helen."

A little coarse, perhaps, but it was "the tune o' the time." "Wild as colt untamed," no doubt; and she got herself into some more or less laughable scrapes; but what would not be pardoned to a beautiful Duchess? Her pranks were nothing to those of Lady Maxwell of Monreith's daughters. They lived in Hyndford's Close, just above the Netherbow. One of them, a future Duchess of Gordon, too, chased, captured, and bestrode a lusty sow, which roamed the streets at will, whilst

THE WOMEN OF EDINBURGH

her sister, afterwards Lady Wallace, thumped it behind with a stick. In the mid-eighteenth century, you perceive, swine were free of the High Street of Edinburgh. In after years Lady Wallace had, like other Edinburgh ladies, a sharp tongue. The son of Kincaid, the King's printer, was a well-dressed dandy—"a great macaroni," as the current phrase went. From his father's lucrative patent, he was nicknamed "young Bibles." "Who is that extraordinary-looking young man?" asked some one at a ball. "Only young Bibles," quoth Lady Wallace, "bound in calf and gilt, but not lettered." Not that she had always the best of the argument. Once she complained to David Hume that when people asked her age she did not know what to say. "Tell them you have not yet come to the years of discretion," said the amiable philosopher. It was quite in his manner. He talked to Lady Anne Lindsay (afterwards Barnard) as if they were contemporaries. She looked surprised. "Have not you and I grown up together; you have grown tall, and I have grown broad."

Lady Anne Dick of Corstorphine, granddaughter of "Bluidy" Mackenzie, was another wild romp. She loved to roam about the town at night in man's dress. Every dark close held the possibility of an exciting adventure. Once she was caught by the heels, and passed the night in the guard-house which, as Scott tells us, "like a huge snail stretched along the High Street near the Tron Kirk for many a long day." She wrote society verses, light or otherwise. She fancied herself or pretended to be in love with Sir Peter Murray—at least he was a favourite subject for her muse. Your Edinburgh fine lady could be high and mighty when she

207

chose, witness Susanna Countess of Eglinton, wife of Alexander the ninth Earl, and a Kennedy of the house of Colzean. When she was a girl, a stray hawk alighted on her shoulder as she walked in the garden at Colzean ; the Eglinton crest or name was on its bells, and she was entitled to hail the omen as significant. Perhaps the prophecy helped to bring its own fulfilment : at least she refused Sir John Clerk of Eldin for my Lord, though he was much her senior. "Susanna and the elder," said the wits of the time. She was six feet in height, very handsome and very stately, and she had seven daughters like unto herself. One of the great sights of old Edinburgh were the eight gilded sedan chairs that conveyed those ladies, moving in stately procession from the old Post Office Close to the Assembly Rooms.

Their mansion house, by the way, afterwards served as Fortune's tavern, far the most fashionable of its kind in Edinburgh. The Countess has her connection with letters: Allan Ramsay dedicated his *Gentle Shepherd* to her, William Hamilton of Bangour chanted her in melodious verse, and Dr. Johnson and she said some nice things to one another when he was in Scotland. She was a devoted Jacobite, had a portrait of Charles Edward so placed in her bedroom as to be the first thing she saw when she wakened in the morning. Her last place in Edinburgh was in Jack's Land in the Canongate. We have ceased to think it remarkable, that noble ladies dwelt in those now grimy ways. She had a long innings of fashion and power, for it was not till 1780, at the ripe age of ninety-one, that she passed away. She kept her looks even in age. "What would

SUSANNAH, COUNTESS OF EGLINTON

From the Painting by Gavin Hamilton

you give to be as pretty as I ? " she asked her eldest daughter, Lady Betty. "Not half so much as you would give to be as young as I," was the pert rejoinder.

Another high and mighty dame was Catharine, daughter of John, Earl of Dundonald, and wife of Alexander, sixth Earl of Galloway. She lived in the Horse Wynd in the Cowgate, and, it is averred, always went visiting in a coach and six. It is said—and you quite believe it—that whilst she was being handed into her coach the leaders were already pawing in front of the destined door. In youth her beauty, in age her pride and piety, were the talk of the town. Are they not commemorated in the *Holyrood Ridotto*? A more pleasing figure is that of Primrose Campbell of Mamore, widow of that crafty Lord Lovat whose head fell on Tower Hill in 1747. She dwelt at the top of Blackfriar's Wynd, where Walter Chepman the old Edinburgh printer had lived 240 years before. She passed a pious, peaceable, and altogether beautiful widowhood; perhaps her happiest years, for old Simon Fraser had given her a bad time. She looked forward to the end with steady, untroubled eyes, got her grave-clothes ready, and the turnpike stair washed. Was this latter, you wonder, so unusual a measure? She professed indifference as to her place of sepulchre "You may lay me beneath that hearthstane." And so, in 1796, in her eighty-sixth year, she went to her rest.

Some of those ladies were not too well off. Two of the house of Traquair lived close by St. Mary's Wynd. The servant, Jenny, had been out marketing. "But, Jenny, what's this in the bottom of the basket?" "Oo, mem, just a dozen o' taties that Lucky, the green-wife, wad hae me to tak'; they wad eat sae fine wi' the mutton." "Na, na, Jenny, tak' back the taties—we need nae provocatives in this house."

A curious story is narrated of Lady Elibank, the daughter of an eminent surgeon in Edinburgh. She told a would-be suitor, " I do not believe that you would part with a 'leith' of your little finger for my whole body." Next day the young man handed her a joint from one of his fingers; she declined to have anything to do with him. " The man who has no mercy on his own flesh will not spare mine," which served *him* right. She was called up in church, as the use was, to be examined in the Assembly's catechism, as Betty Stirling. " Filthy fellow," she said ; " he might have called me Mrs. Betty or Miss Betty; but to be called bare Betty is insufferable." She was called bare Betty as long as she lived, which served *her* right.

The servants of some of those aristocratic ladies were as old-fashioned, as poor, and as devoted as themselves. Mrs. Erskine of Cardross lived in a small house at the foot of Merlin's Wynd, which once stood near the Tron Kirk. George Mason, her servant, allowed himself much liberty of speech. On a young gentleman calling for wine a second time at dinner, George in a whisper, reproachful and audible, admonished him, " Sir, you have had a glass already." This strikes a modern as mere impudence, yet passed as proper enough.

The fashionable life of old Edinburgh had its headquarters in the Assembly Rooms, first in the West Bow and then after 1720 south of the High Street in the Assembly Close. The formalities of the meetings and dances are beyond our scope. The "famed Miss Nicky Murray," as Sir Alexander Boswell called her, presided here for many years; she was sister of the Earl of Mansfield, and a mighty fine lady. "Miss of What?" she would ask when a lady was presented. If of nowhere she had short shrift: a tradesman, however decked, was turned out at once. Her fan was her sceptre or enchanted wand, with a wave of which she stopped the music, put out the lights, and brought the day of stately and decorous proceedings to a close.

Another lady directress was the Countess of Panmure. A brewer's daughter had come very well dressed, but here fine feathers did not make a fine bird. Her Ladyship sent her a message not to come again, as she was not entitled to attend the assemblies. Her justice was even-handed. She noted her nephew, the Earl of Cassillis, did not seem altogether right one evening. "You have sat too late after dinner to be proper company for ladies," quoth she; she then led him to the door, and calling out, "My Lord Cassillis's chair!" wished him "good-night." Perhaps my Lord betook himself to the neighbouring Covenant Close, where there was a famed oyster-seller commemorated by Scott, who knew its merits. Was it on this account or because the Covenant had lain for signature there that Sir Walter made it the abode of Nanty Ewart when he studied divinity at Edinburgh with disastrous results? Unfortunate Covenant Close! The last time I peered through a locked gate on its grimy ways I found it used for the brooms and barrows of the city scavengers. But to resume.

The dancing in the Assembly Room was hedged about with various rites that made it a solemn function. When a lady was assigned to a gallant he needs must present her with an orange. To "lift the lady" meant to ask her to dance. The word was not altogether fortunate; it is the technical term still used in the north to signify that the corpse has begun its procession from the house to the grave. "It's lifted," whispers the undertaker's man to the mourners, as he beckons them to follow. Another quaint custom was to "save the ladies" by drinking vast quantities of hot punch to their health or in their honour. If they were not thus "saved" they were said to be "damned."

There are as racy stories of folk not so well known, and not so exalted. Mrs. Dundas lived on Bunker's Hill (hard by where the Register House now stands). One of her daughters read from a newspaper to her as to some lady whose reputation was damaged by the indiscreet talk of the Prince of Wales. "Oh," said old fourscore with an indignant shake of her shrivelled fist and a tone of cutting contempt, "the dawmed villain! Does he kiss and tell?"

This is quaint enough. Miss Mamie Trotter, of the Mortonhall family, dreamt she was in heaven, and describes her far from edifying experience. "And what d'ye think I saw there? De'il ha'it but thousands upon thousands, and ten thousands upon ten thousands o' stark naked weans! That wad be a dreadfu' thing, for ye ken I ne'er could bide bairns a' my days!"

"Come away, Bailie, and take a trick at the cairds," Mrs. Telfer of St. John Street, Canongate, and sister of Smollett, would exclaim to a worthy magistrate and tallow chandler who paid her an evening visit. "Troth,

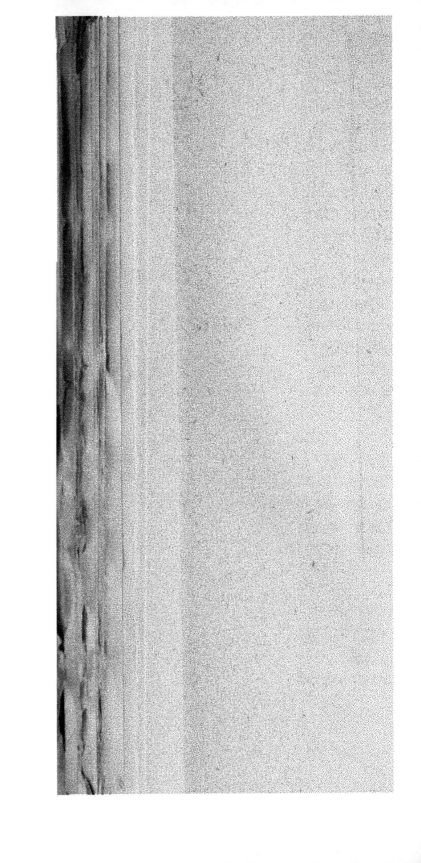

madam, I hae naesiller." "Then let us play for a p'und of can'le," rejoined the gamesome Telfer.

On the other side of the Canongate, in New Street, there lived Christina Ramsay, a daughter of Allan Ramsay. She was eighty-eight before she died. If she wrote no songs she inherited, at any rate, her father's kindly nature; she was the friend of all animals, she used to remonstrate with the carters when they ill-treated their horses, and send out rolls to be given to the poor overburdened beasts that toiled up the steep street. But she specially favoured cats. She kept a huge number cosily stowed away in band-boxes, and put out food for others round about her house; she would not even permit them to be spoken against, any alleged bad deed of a cat she avowed must have been done under provocation.

Here are two marriage stories. Dugald Stewart's second wife was Ellen D'Arcy Cranstoun, daughter of the Hon. George Cranstoun, and sister of Lord Corehouse. She had written a poem, which her cousin, the Earl of Lothian, had shown to the philosopher who was then his tutor. The criticism was of a highly flattering nature. The professor fell in love with the poetess, and she loved him for his eulogy; they were married, and no union ever turned out better. The other is earlier and baser. In November 1731 William Crawford, the elderly janitor of the High School, proposed to marry a lady very much his junior. He and his friends arrived at the church. She did not turn up, but there was a letter from her. "William you must know I am pre-engaged I never could like a burnt cuttie I have now by the hand my sensie menseful strapper, with whom I intend to pass my youthful days. You know old age, and youth cannot agree together. I must then be excused if I tell you I am not your humble servant." Crawford took his rebuff quite coolly. "Let us at least," said he to his friends, "keep the feast as a feast-day. Let us go drink and drive care away. May never a greater misfortune attend any man." An assemblage numerous, if not choice, graced the banquet; they got up a subscription among themselves of one hundred marks and presented it to Crawford, "with which he was as well satisfied as he who got madam."

From all those clever and witty people it is almost a relief to turn to some anecdotes of sheer stupidity. Why John Home the poet married Miss Logan, who was not clever or handsome or rich, was a problem to his friends. Hume asked him point-blank. "Ah, David, if I had not who else would have taken her?" was his comic defence. Sir Adam Fergusson told the aged couple of the Peace of Amiens. "Will it mak' ony difference in the price o' nitmugs?" said Mrs. Home, who meant nutmegs, if indeed she meant anything at all.

Jean, sister-in-law to Archibald Constable the publisher, had been educated in France and hesitated to admit that she had forgotten the language, and would translate coals "collier" and table napkin "table napkune," to the amazement and amusement of her hearers. Her ideas towards the close got a little mixed. "If I should be spared to be taken away," she remarked, "I hope my nephew will get the doctor to open my head and see if anything can be done for my hearing." This is a masterpiece of its kind, and perhaps too good to be perfectly true. She played well; "gars the instrument speak," it was said. There was one touch of romance in her life. A French admirer had given her a box of bonbons, wherein she found " a puzzle ring of gold, divided yet united," and with their joint initials. She never saw or heard from her lover, yet she called for it many times in her last illness. It was a better way of showing her constancy than that taken by Lady Betty Charteris, of the Wemyss family. Disappointed in love, she took to her bed, where she lay for twenty-six years, to the time of her death, in fact. This was in St. John Street in the latter half of the eighteenth century.

The stage was without much influence in Edinburgh save on rare occasions. One of them was when Sarah Siddons was in Edinburgh in 1784. Her first appearance was on the 22nd May of that year, when she scored a success as Belvedere in *Venice Preserved*. The audience listened in profound silence, and the lady, used to more enthusiasm, got a little nervous, till a canny citizen was moved audibly to admit, "That's no bad." A roar of applause followed that almost literally brought down the galleries. She played Lady Randolph in *Douglas* twice; "there was not a dry eye in the whole house," observed the contemporary *Courant*. Shakespeare was not acted during her visit; the folk of the time were daring enough to consider him just so-so after Home! Everybody was mad to hear her. At any rate, the General Assembly of the Church was deserted until its meetings were arranged not to clash with her appearance. There were applications for 2550 places where there were only 630 of that description on hand. The gallery doors were guarded by detachments of soldiers with drawn bayonets, which they are said to have used to some purpose on an all too insistent crowd. Her tragedy manner was more than skin deep, she could never shake it off; she talked in blank verse. Scott used to tell how, during a dinner at Ashestiel, she made an attendant shake with—

"You've brought me water, boy—I asked for beer."

Once in Edinburgh she dined with the Homes, and in her most tragic tones asked for a "little porter." John, the old servant-man, took her only too literally; he reappeared, lugging in a diminutive though stout Highland caddie, remarking, "I've found ane, mem ; he's the least I could get." Even Sarah needs must laugh, though Mrs. Home, we are assured, on the authority of Robert Chambers, never saw the joke.

Another time Mrs. Siddons dined with the Lord Provost, who apologised for the seasoning.

"Beef cannot be too salt for me, my Lord,"
was the solemn response of the tragic muse.

Such tones once heard were not to be forgotten. A servant-lass, by patience or audacity, had got into the theatre and was much affected by the performance. Next day, as she went about the High Street, intent on domestic business, the deep notes of the inimitable Siddons rang in her ears; she dropped her basket in uncontrollable agitation and burst forth, "Eh, sirs, weel do I ken the sweet voice ("vice," she would say, in the dulcet dialect of the capital) that garred me greet sae sair yestre'n."

After all, Mrs. Siddons does not belong to Edinburgh, though I take her on the wing, as it were, and here also I take leave both of her and the subject.

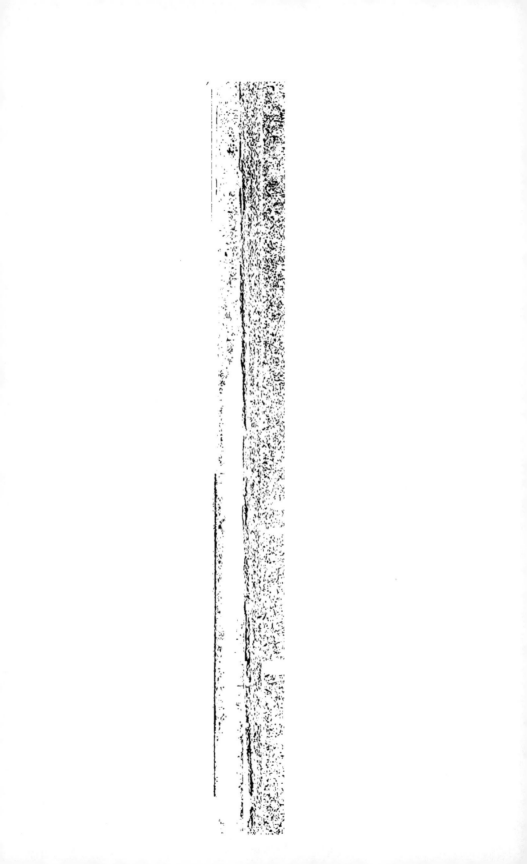

CHAPTER TEN

THE SUPERNATURAL

CHAP. TEN THE SUPERNATURAL

PERHAPS THE SHARPEST CONTRAST BE-
tween old Scotland and the Scotland of to-day is the
decline of belief in the supernatural. Superstitions of
lucky and unlucky things and days and seasons still
linger in the south, nay, the byways of London are
rich in a peculiar kind of folklore which no one thinks
it worth while to harvest. A certain dry scepticism
prevails in Scotland, even in the remote country dis-
tricts; perhaps it is the spread of education or the hard
practical nature of the folk which is, for the time, upper-
most; or is it the result of a violent reaction? In former
days it was far other. Before the Reformation the Scot
accepted the Catholic faith as did the other nations of
Europe. And there was the usual monastic legend, to
which, as far as it concerns Edinburgh, I make elsewhere sufficient reference. Between the Reformation
and the end of the eighteenth century, or even later,
the supernatural had a stronger grip on the Scots than
on any other race in Europe. The unseen world beck-
oned and made its presence known by continual signs;
portents and omens were of daily occurrence; men like
Peden, the prophet, read the book of the future, every
Covenanter lived a spiritual life whose interest far ex-
ceeded that of the material life present to his senses.
As a natural result of hard conditions of existence,
a sombre temperament, and a gloomy creed, the portents were ever of disaster. The unseen was full of hostile forces. The striking mottoes, that still remain on
some of the Edinburgh houses, were meant to ward off
evil. The law reports are full of the trials and cruel
punishment of wizards and witches, malevolent spir-

219

its bent on man's destruction were ever on the alert, ghostly appearances hinted at crime and suffering; more than all, there was the active personality of Satan himself, one, yet omnipresent, fighting a continual and, for the time, successful war against the saints. Burns, whose genius preserves for us in many a graphic touch that old Scotland which even in his time was fast fading away, pictures, half mirthful, yet not altogether sceptical, the enemy of mankind:

> "Great is thy pow'r an' great thy fame;
> Far ken'd an' noted is thy name;
> An' tho' yon lowin' heuch's thy hame,
> Thou travels far.
> An' faith! thou's neither lag nor lame,
> Nor blate nor scaur."

And now for some illustrations. After the monkish legends, one of the earliest, as it is the most famous, story of all is the appearance of the ghostly heralds in the dead of night at the Cross in Edinburgh, before the battle of Flodden, and the summons by them of the most eminent Scotsmen of the day, including King James himself, to appear before Pluto, Lord of the netherworld. A certain gentleman, Mr. Richard Lawson, lay that night in his house in the High Street. He was to follow the King southward, but his heart was heavy with the thought of impending evil; he could not sleep, and roamed up and down the open wooden gallery, which was then so marked a feature on the first floor of Edinburgh houses. It was just in front of the Cross. He saw the dread apparition, he heard his own name amongst the list of those summoned. Loudly, he refused obedience, and protested, and appealed to God and Christ. Lindsay of Pitscottie, whose chronicles

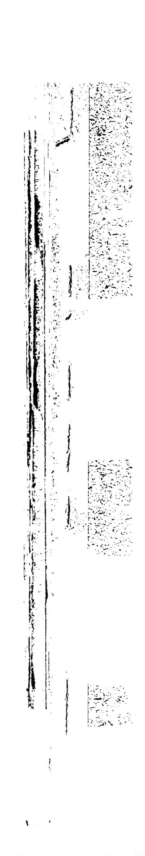

preserve many a picturesque tale of old Scotland, had this story at first hand from Lawson himself, who assured him that of all those mentioned he alone had escaped. It is scarce necessary to remind the reader how admirably Scott has told this story in the fifth canto of *Marmion*. The Cross was the chief place from which a summons must issue to the absent, and the heralds were the persons to make it. The appeal and protest by Mr. Richard Lawson were also quite in order. And there is the figure of St. John the Apostle which appeared in St. Michael's Church at Linlithgow to warn James IV. from his projected expedition. Again Scott has told this in the fourth canto of *Marmion*. It has been suggested that neither legend is mere fancy, that both were elaborate devices got up by the peace party to frighten James. This may be true of the Linlithgow apparition, but it does not reasonably account for the other.

It strikes you at first as odd that there are no ghost stories about Holyrood, but there is a substantial reason. These would mar the effect, the illustrious dead with their profoundly tragic histories leave no room for other interest. The annals of the Castle are not quite barren. Here be samples at any rate. It was the reign of Robert III., and the dawn of the fifteenth century. The Duke of Albany, the King's brother, was pacing, with some adherents, the ramparts of the Castle when a bright meteor flared across the sky. Albany seemed much impressed, and announced that this portended some calamity as the end of a mighty Prince in the near future. Albany was already engaged in plots which resulted, in March 1402, in the imprisonment and death by famine of his nephew, David, Duke of Rothesay, so it may be said that he only prophesied because he knew. However, the age believed in astrology; held as indisputable that the stars influenced man's life, and that every sign in the firmament had a meaning for those who watched. Not seldom were battles seen in the skies portending disasters to come. As you con over the troubled centuries of old Scots history, it seems that disaster always did come, there was nothing but wars and sieges, and red ruin and wasting.

Before the death of James V. dread warnings from the other world were conveyed to him. Sir James Hamilton, who had been beheaded, appeared with a drawn sword in his hand, and struck both the King's arms off. Certain portents preceded the murder of Darnley. Some of his friends dreamed he was in mortal danger, and received ghostly admonition to carry help to him. It is easy to rationalise those stories. Many were concerned in the murder, and it is not to be supposed that they all kept quite discreet tongues.

Again, the following picturesque legend is exactly such as a troubled time would evolve. After the coronation of Charles II. at Scone, Cromwell marched towards Scotland. The Castle was put in order under Colonel Walter Dundas. As the sentinel paced his rounds one gloomy night he heard the beat of a drum from the esplanade, and the steady tramp of a great host; he fired his musket to give the alarm, and the Governor hurried to the scene, but there was nothing. The sentinel was punished and replaced, but the same thing happened, till in the end Dundas mounted guard himself. He hears the phantom drummer beating a weird measure, then there is the tramp of innumerable feet and the clank of armour. A mighty host, audible yet invisible, passes by, and the sound of their motion dies gradually away. What could these things mean but wars and rumours of wars? And there followed in quick succession Dunbar and Worcester, commemorated with the victor in a high passage of English literature:

> "While Derwen stream, with blood of Scots imbued,
>   And Dunbar field resounds thy praises loud
>   And Worcester's laureat wreath,"

but then Milton was the laureate of the other side, and his view was not that of the Scots.

Time passes on, and brings not merely the Restoration, but the Revolution; the Castle is true to the old cause under the Duke of Gordon, yet it gives in finally and becomes a hold for Jacobite prisoners, among whom was Lord Balcarres. On the night of the 27th of July 1689, a hand drew aside the curtains of the bed, and there was Graham of Claverhouse, Viscount Dundee, gazing at his startled friend. Balcarres addressed the vision, but received no answer. The figure looked steadfastly upon the captive, moved towards the mantelpiece, and finally disappeared from the room. At that very hour, Dundee was lying dead at Killiecrankie, the most splendid and most useless of victories. The silver bullet had found its billet. The Covenanters were absolutely convinced that the persecutors were in direct league with Satan, who protected them to the utmost of his power. How else to explain their charmed lives, when so many hungered and thirsted after their death? How else to account for that reckless courage that provoked whilst it avoided the mortal stroke? What the object of those legends thought of them, we cannot tell, perhaps they were flattered. Dundee could turn his horse on the slope of a hill like a precipice, and his courage—but then courage was so cheap a commodity in old Scotland that only when it failed was there cause for wonder and contemptuous comment. However, the silver bullet was proof against enchantment, and Dundee ended as surely himself had wished. Legends gathered about a much grimmer figure, the very grimmest figure of all, Sir Thomas Dalzell of Binns. The long beard, the truculent, cruel visage, the martial figure, trained in the Muscovite service, well made up the man who never knew pity. Is it not told that he bent forward from his seat in the Privy Council, at a meeting in 1681, to strike with clenched fist the accused that was there for examination? "Is there none other hangman in the toun but yourself?" retorted the undaunted prisoner. Dalzell had the gift of devoted loyalty, no razor had touched his face since the death of Charles I. The legends about him are in character. At Rullion Green the Covenanters feeling their cause lost ere the battle was fought, noted with dismay that Dalzell was proof against all their shot. The bullets hopped back from his huge boots as hail from an iron wall. Ah, those terrible boots! if you filled them with water it seethed and boiled on the instant. Certain sceptics declare, by the way, he never wore boots at all! Did he spit on the ground, a hole was forthwith burnt in the earth. And yet, strange malice of fate, Sir Thomas

SUPERNATURAL IN EDINBURGH

died peaceably in his bed, even though his last hours were rumoured as anguished.

I pick up one or two memories of the supernatural from the closes and ways of old Edinburgh. The "sanctified bends" of the Bow are long vanished, and to-day nothing is more commonplace than the steps and the street that bears that memorable name. Its most famous inhabitant was no saint, except in appearance, for here abode Major Weir. From here he was hauled to prison in 1670, and thence to his doom at the Gallow Lee. "The warlock that was burned," says "Wandering Willie" of him. The legend is too well known for detailed description. Here he lived long in the odour of sanctity, and finally, struck by conscience, revealed unmentionable crimes. This story had a peculiar fascination, both for Sir Walter Scott and R.L.S., both Edinburgh men, both masters of Scots romance, and they have dwelt lovingly on the strange details. The staff which used to run the Major's errands, which acted as a link-boy to him o' dark nights, which answered the door for him, on which he leaned when he prayed, and yet whereon were carved the grinning heads of Satyrs, only visible, however, on close inspection, and after the downfall of its master, was sure the strangest magic property ever wizard possessed. Its "rare turnings" in the fire wherein it was consumed, along with its master, were carefully noted. Long after strange sights were seen around his house. At midnight the Major would issue from the door, mount a fiery steed, which only wanted the head, and vanish in a whirlwind. His sister, Grizel Weir, who ended as a witch, span miraculous quantities of yarn. Perhaps this accounted for the sound as of a spinning-wheel that echoed through the deserted house for more than a century afterwards; but how to explain the sound as of dancing, and again as of wailing and howling, and that unearthly light wherewith the eerie place was flooded? How to explain, indeed! The populace had no difficulty, it was the Devil!

It would seem that Satan had an unaccountable and, one might say, a perverse fancy for the West Bow, a-bode of the righteous as it was. There are distinct traces of him there in the early part of November 1707. At that time a certain Mr. John Strahan, W.S., was owner of Craigcrook on Corstorphine Hill, the house that was to become a literary centre under Lord Jeffrey. He had left his town mansion under the care of a young servant-girl called Ellen Bell. On Halloween night, still a popular festival in Scotland, she had entertained two sweethearts of hers called Thomson and Robertson. She told them she was going to Craigcrook on the second morning thereafter, so they arranged to meet her and convoy her part of the way. At five o'clock on the Monday morning, behold the three together in the silent streets of the capital. The two youths politely relieved the girl of the key of the house and some other things she was carrying, and then, at the three steps at the foot of the Castle rock, they suddenly threw themselves upon her and beat the life out. They then returned to rob the house; probably they had gone further than they intended in committing murder. They were panic-stricken at what they had done, and each swore that if he informed against the other he was to be devoted, body and soul, to the Devil. It were better, quoth one, to put the matter in writing in a bond. "Surely," echoed a suave voice, and by their side they found an agreeable smiling gentleman of most obliging disposition, who offered to write out the bond for them, and suggested as the most suitable fluid for signature their own blood. The story does not tell whether the two noticed anything remarkable about their courteous friend, something not quite normal about the foot, possibly a gentle hint of a tail. At any rate, they received the advances of the stranger in anything but an affable spirit, so presently found themselves alone. Mr. Strahan seems to have been a wealthy gentleman, for there was £1000 in his abode (sterling, be it observed, not Scots), with which the robbers made off. Robertson suggested the firing of the house, but this Thomson would not allow. Mr. Strahan advertised a substantial reward for the discovery of the criminals, but nothing was heard for a long time. If we are to believe Wodrow in his agreeable *Analecta* it required the supernatural intervention of Providence to unravel the mystery. Twelve months after, Lady Craigcrook (so Mrs. Strahan was known, by the courtesy of the time) had a strange dream. She saw Robertson, who had once been in her service, murder Ellen Bell, rob the house, and conceal the money in two old barrels under some rubbish. A search followed, unmistakable evidences of the robbery were found in Thomson's possession. He confessed his guilt, and after the usual formalities made what might almost be called the conventional exit at the Grassmarket. We are not told whether he was favoured with another visit from his courteous old friend of the West

Bow. The Scots criminal, like all his countrymen, had abundant courage; he was ready to "dree his weird," or, in the popular language of our day, "face the music" with a certain stoical philosophy, but he almost invariably did so in a pious and orthodox frame of mind. Nothing could show more strongly the depth and strength of the popular belief than the frequency with which both persecutor and criminal turned at the end with whole-hearted conviction to the creed of the people. There is nothing in Scotland of those jovial exits which highwaymen like Duval and Sixteen-String Jack made at Tyburn tree, unless we count M'Pherson an exception. He was hanged at Banff in 1700. For the last time he played the tune called M'Pherson's Rant on his fiddle, and we know how excellently Burns has written his epitaph; but he was only a wild Hielandman, so the contemporary Lowlander would have observed.

The West Bow runs off southward just where the Castle Hill joins the Lawnmarket. On the north side of the Lawnmarket a little way down there still stands Lady Stair's Close and in it Lady Stair's house, and about the same time, that is, the early years of the eighteenth century, there happened to Lady Stair, or Lady Primrose, as she then was, certain miraculous events which constitute the most romantic tradition of the Old Town. Scott has written a charming novelette, *My Aunt Margaret's Mirror*, on the theme, and I can only present it here in the briefest possible fashion. Lord Primrose, the lady's first husband, was, it would appear, mad, at any rate, he tried to kill his wife, in the which failing he left Auld Reekie and went abroad. As she wondered and speculated what had become of him, she heard a gossiping rumour of an Italian sorcerer possessed of strange power then in Edinburgh. He had a magic mirror wherein he could show what any absent person was doing at that precise moment. Lady Stair and her friend presently procured what we should call a séance. The magician dwelt in a dark recess of some obscure Canongate close, at least we must suppose so in order to get sufficient perspective, for all those localities in Edinburgh were so terribly near to one another. From Lady Stair's Close to the Canongate is but a few minutes' leisurely promenade. After certain preliminary rites the lady gazed in the magic mirror: it showed forth a bridal, and the bridegroom was her own husband; the service went on some way, and then it was interrupted by a person whom she recognised as her own brother. Presently the figures vanished, and the curtain fell. The lady took an exact note of the time and circumstances, and when her brother returned from abroad she eagerly questioned him. It was all true: the church was in Rotterdam, and her husband was about to commit the unromantic offence of bigamy with the daughter of a rich merchant when "the long arm of coincidence" led the brother to the church just in time. "Excursions and alarums" of an exciting nature at once ensued, but neither these nor the rest of the lady's life, though that was remarkable enough, concern us here.

A little way farther down the street, as it nears the western wall of the Municipal Buildings, otherwise the Royal Exchange, there stood Mary King's Close. I cannot, nor can anybody, it seems, tell who Mary King was. We have a picture of the close, or what remain- ed of it in 1845; then the houses were vacant and roof- less, the walls ruined, mere crumbling heaps of stones —weeds, wallflowers rankly flourishing in every cre- vice, for as yet the improver was only fitfully in the land. As far back as 1750 a fire had damaged the south or upper part of the close, which disappeared in the Royal Exchange. The place had been one of the spots peculiarly affected by the great plague of 1645; the houses were then shut up, and it was feared that if they were opened the pest would stalk forth again, but popular fancy soon peopled the close. If you lusted after a tremor of delicious horror you had but to step down its gloomy ways any night after dark and gaze through one of the windows. You saw a whole family dressed in the garb of a hundred years earlier and of undeniable ghost-like appearance quiet- ly engaged in their ordinary avocations; then all of a. sudden these vanished, and you spied a company "linking" it through the mazes of the dance, but not a mother's son or daughter of them but wanted his or her head. In the close itself you might see in the air above you a raw head or an arm dripping blood. Such and other strange sights are preserved for us in *Sa- tan's Invisible World Displayed* which was published in 1685 by Professor George Sinclair of Glasgow, af- terwards minister of Eastwood. He tells us wondrous tales of the adventures in this close of Thomas Colt- heart and his spouse. After their entry on the premises there appeared a human head with a grey floating beard suspended in mid air, to this was added the phantom of a child, and then an arm, naked from the elbow and totally unattached, which made desperate but unsuccessful efforts to shake Mrs. Coltheart by the hand. Mr. Coltheart, in the most orthodox fashion, begged from the ghosts an account of their wrongs, that he might speedily procure justice for them; but in defiance of all precedent they were obstinately silent, yet they grew in number—there came a dog and a cat, and a number of strange and grotesque beings, for whom natural history has no names. The flesh-and-blood inhabitants of the room were driven to kneel on the bed as being the only place left unoccupied. Finally, with a heart-moving groan, the appearances vanished, and Mr. Coltheart was permitted to enjoy his house in peace till the day of his death, but then he must himself begin to play spectre. He appeared to a friend at Tranent, ten miles off, and when the trembling friend demanded, "Are you dead? and if so, why come you?" the ghost, who was unmistakably umquhile Coltheart, shook its head twice and vanished without remark. The friend proceeded at once to Edinburgh and (of course) discovered that Mr. Coltheart had just expired. The fact of the apparition was never doubted, but the why and the wherefore no man could discover, only the house was again left vacant. In truth, the ghost must have been rather a trouble to Edinburgh landlords; it was easy for a story to arise, and immediately it arose the house was deserted. An old soldier and his wife were persuaded to take up their abode there, but the very first night the candle burned blue, and the head, without the body, though with wicked, selfish eyes, was present, suspended in mid air, and the inmates fled and Mary King's Close was given over as an entirely bad business. After all, the old soldier was not very venturesome, no more so than another veteran, William Patullo by name, who was induced to take Major Weir's mansion. He was effectually frightened by a beast somewhat like a calf which came and looked at him and his spouse as they lay in bed and then vanished, as did the prospective tenants forthwith. It was not the age of insurance companies, else had there been a special clause against spooks!

One is able to smile at some of those stories because there is a distinctly comic touch about them. No one was the better or the worse for those quaint visions of the other world, except the landlords who mourned for the empty houses, against the which we must put the delight of the "groundlings" whose ears were delicately "tickled"; but the witches are quite another matter. Old Scots life was ugly in many respects, in none more so than in the hideous cruelties practised on hundreds of helpless old women, and sometimes on men, but to a much less extent. Some half-century ago the scientific world looked on tales of witchcraft as mere delusion, even though then the chief facts of mesmerism were known and noted. But phenomena which we now call "hypnotism" and "suggestion" are accepted to-day as facts of life, they are thought worthy of scientific treatment, and we now see that they explain many phenomena of witchcraft. Three hundred years ago everything was ascribed to Satan, and fiendish tortures were considered the due of his supposed children. A detailed examination is undesirable. What are we to learn, for instance, from the story of the Broughton witches who were burned alive, who, in the extremity of torture, renounced their Maker and cursed their fellow-men? Some escaped half burned from the flames and rushed away screaming in their agony, but they were pursued, seized, and thrown back into the fire, which, more merciful than their kind, at length terminated their life and suffering together. The leading case in Scotland was that of the North Berwick witches; it properly comes within our province, insomuch as James VI. personally investigated the whole matter at Holyrood. James was the author of a treatise on witchcraft, and was vastly proud of his gift as a witch-finder. The story begins with a certain Jeillie Duncan, a servant-girl at Tranent; she made so many cures that she was presently suspected of witchcraft. She was treated to orthodox modes of torture; her fingers were pinched with the pilliwinks, her forehead was wrenched with a rope, but she would say nothing until the Devil's mark was found on her throat, when she gave in and confessed herself a servant of Satan. Presently there was no end to her confessions! She accused all the old women in the neighbourhood, especially Agnes Sampson "the eldest witch of them all resident in Haddington," and one man, "Dr. Fian alias John Cunningham, Master of the Schoole at Saltpans in Lowthian." Agnes Sampson was taken to Holyrood for personal examination by the King. At first she was obdurate, but after the usual tortures she developed a story of the most extraordinary description. She told how she was one of two hundred witches who sailed over the sea in riddles or sieves, with flagons of wine, to the old kirk of North Berwick. Jeillie

Duncan preceded them to the kirk dancing and playing on the jews' harp, chanting the while a mad rhyme.
Nothing would serve the King but to have Jeillie brought before him. She played a solo accompaniment
the while Agnes Sampson went on with her story. She
described how the Devil appeared in the kirk, and
preached a wretched sermon, mixed with obscene
rites and loaded with much abuse of the King of
Scotland, "at which time the witches demanded of
the Devill why he did beare such hatred to the King?"
who answered, " by reason the King is the greatest
enemie hee hath in the world." Solomon listened with
mouth and ears agape, and eyes sticking out of his
head in delighted horror, yet even for him the flattery
was a little too gross or the wonders were too as-
tounding. "They were all extreame lyears," he roundly declared. But Agnes was equal to the occasion. She
took His Highness aside, and told him the " verie
wordes which passed betweene the Kinges majestie
and his queene at Upslo in Norway, the first night
of mariage, with there answere ech to other, wherat
the Kinges majestie wondered greatly and swore by
the living God that he believed that all the devils in
hell could not have discovered the same, acknowledg-
ing her words to be most true, and therefore gave the
more credit to the rest that is before declared."

Thus encouraged she proceeded to stuff James with
a choice assortment of ridiculous details; sometimes
fear had the better of her and she flattered him, then
possibly rage filled her heart and she terrorised him.
For her and her " kommers " there was presently the
same end. The King then moved on to Dr. Fian's

case, and he, after a certain amount of torture, began his extraordinary confessions, which, like his sisters in misfortune, he embroidered with fantastic details. Here is one incident. The doctor was enamoured of a young lady, a sister of a pupil. To obtain her affection he persuaded the boy to bring him three of his sister's hairs. The boy's mother was herself a witch, and thus trumped *his* cards. She "went to a young heyfer which never had borne calfe," took three hairs from it, and sent them to Fian. He practised his incantations with surprising result. "The heyfer presently appeared leaping and dancing," following the doctor about and lavishing upon him the most grotesque marks of affection.

There is a curious little story of Balzac's *Une passion dans le desert* which recalls in an odd way this strange Scots episode, whereof it is highly improbable Balzac ever heard. Fian, it seems, had acted as registrar to the Devil in the North Berwick kirk proceedings. With it all he might possibly have escaped, but having stolen the key of his prison he fled away by night to the Saltpans. The King felt himself defrauded, and he soon had the doctor again in safe keeping. He felt himself still more defrauded when Fian not merely refused to continue his revelations, but denied those he had already made, and then "a most straunge torment" was ordered him. All his nails were torn off, one after another, with a pair of pincers, then under every nail there was thrust in, two needles up to the heads. He remained obdurate. He was then subjected to the torture of the "bootes," "wherein hee continued a long time and did abide so many blowes in them that his legges were crusht and beaten together as small as might bee, and the bones and flesh so bruised that the blood and marrow spouted forth in great abundance, whereby they were made unserviceable forever." He still continued stubborn, and finally was put into a cart, taken to the Castle Hill, strangled and thrown into a great fire. This was in January 1591. In trying to bring up the past before us it is necessary to face such facts, and to remember that James VI. was, with it all, not a cruel or unkindly man.

I gladly turn to a lighter page. The grimy ways of Leith do not suggest Fairyland, but two quaint legends of other days are associated therewith. In front of the old battery, where are now the new docks, there stood a half-submerged rock which was removed in the course of harbour operations. This was the abode of a demon named Shellycoat, from the make of his garments, which you gather were of the most approved Persian attire. He was a malevolent spirit of great power, a terror to the urchins of old Leith, and perhaps even to their elders, but like "the dreaded name of Demogorgon" his reputation was the worst of him. If he wrought any definite evil, time has obliterated the memory. When his rock was blasted, poor Shellycoat was routed out, and fled to return no more.

The other legend is of the fairy boy of Leith who o' Thursday nights beat the drum to the fairies in the Calton Hill. Admission thereto was obtained by a pair of great gates, which opened to them, though they were invisible to others. The fairies, said the boy, "are entertained with many sorts of music besides my drum; they have besides plenty of variety of meats and wine, and many times we are carried into France or Holland in a night and return again, and whilst we are there we enjoy all the pleasures the country doth afford." The fairy boy must at least be credited with a very vivid imagination. His questioner trysted him for next Thursday night: the youth duly turned up, apparently got what money he could, but towards midnight unaccountably disappeared and was seen no more. When people were so eager to discover the supernatural, one cannot wonder that they succeeded. In 1702, Mr. David Williamson was preaching in his own church in Edinburgh when a "rottan" (rat) appeared and sat down on his Bible. This made him stop, and after a little pause he told the congregation that this was a message of God to him. He broke off his sermon and took a formal farewell of his people and went home and continued sick. This was the time of the Union of the Kingdoms, and two years later, that is, in 1707, a mighty shoal of whales invaded the Firth of Forth, "roaring, plunging, and threshing upon one another to the great terror of all who heard the same." Thirty-five of them foundered on the sands of Kirkcaldy, where they made a yet "more dreadful roaring and tossing, when they found themselves aground so much that the earth trembled. What the unusual appearance of so great a number of them at this juncture may portend, shall not be our business to inquire." The chronicler is convinced that there must be some deep connection between such portentous events as the Union of the Crowns and the appearance of the whales, though with true scientific caution he does not think it proper to further riddle out the matter!

CHAPTER ELEVEN

THE STREETS

A BEDESMAN, OR BLUEGOWN

From a Sketch by Monro S. Orr

CHAPTER ELEVEN THE STREETS

I COLLECT HERE A FEW ANECDOTES OF
life on the streets, and among the people of old Edinburgh. The ancient Scots lived very sparely, yet sump-
tuary laws were passed, not to enable them to fare
better, but to keep them down to a low standard. The
English were judged mere gluttons; "pock puddings"
the frugal Caledonian deemed them. It was thought
the Southern gentlemen whom James I. and his Queen
brought into Scotland introduced a sumptuous mode
of living. In 1533, the Bishop of St. Andrews raged
in the pulpit against the wasteful luxury of later years.
A law was presently passed, fixing how each order
should live, and prohibiting the use of pies and other
baked meats to all below the rank of baron. In fashionable circles there were four meals a day, breakfast,
dinner, supper, and livery, which last was a kind of
collation taken in the bedchamber, before retiring to
rest. A century ago it was usual to furnish the bedroom
with liquor, which, perhaps, was a reminiscence of this
old-world meal. The time for breakfast was seven, then
came dinner at ten, supper at four, and livery between
eight and nine. This detail is only of the well-off minority. Legislators need not have alarmed themselves,
grinding poverty was the predominant note of old
Scots life. Pestilence swept the land from time to time
—one cause was imperfect sanitation; a stronger was
sheer lack of food.

Here is James Melville's account of plague-torn
Edinburgh in November 1585 :—"On the morn we
made haste and coming to Losterrick (Restalrig) dis-
joined, and about eleven hours came riding in at the

Water-gate up through the Canongate, and rode in at the Nether Bow through the great street of Edinburgh, *in all whilk way we saw not three persons*, sae that I miskenned Edinburgh, and almost forgot that I had ever seen sic a town."

One effect of poverty was innumerable beggars. Naturally they thronged Edinburgh, where they made themselves a well-nigh intolerable nuisance. The Privy Council formulated edicts against "the strang and idle vagabonds" who lay all day on the causeway of the Canongate, and bullied the passers-by into giving them alms. Perhaps it was to regulate an abuse which could not be entirely checked, that the King's bedesmen, or Bluegowns, as they were called, from their dress, were established or re-formed as licensed beggars. These assembled yearly on the King's birthday to receive an annual dole of bread and ale and blue gown, and to hear service in St. Giles'. More welcome than all was the gift of a penny for every year of the King's reign, which was given in a leather purse. The place was the north side of the Tolbooth, hence called "The Puir Folks' Purses," or more briefly, "The Purses." The scene was afterwards transferred to the Canongate Church, and then it was done away with altogether. The analogous Maundy money is still distributed annually at Westminster Abbey. The classic example of this picturesque figure of old Scots life is Edie Ochiltree in *The Antiquary*, but in Scott's time Bluegowns still adorned Edinburgh streets; hence the following anecdote. Scott, as he went to and fro from college, was in the habit of giving alms to one of those gentlemen. It turned out that he kept a son Willy, as a divinity student at college, and he made bold to ask Scott to share a humble meal with them in their cottage at St. Leonards, at the base of Arthur's Seat. "Please God I may live to see my bairn wag his head in a pulpit yet." At the time appointed Scott partook of the meal with father and son, the latter at first not unnaturally a little shamefaced. The fare was simple, but of the very best; there was a "gigot" of mutton, potatoes, and whisky. "Dinna speak to your father about it," said Mrs. Scott to Walter; "if it had been a shoulder he might have thought less, but he will say that gigot was a sin." The old Edinburgh beggars were no doubt a droll lot, though particulars of their pranks are sadly lacking. When Sir Richard Steele, known to his familiars as Dickie Steele, was in Edinburgh in 1718, he collected the oldest and oddest of them to some obscure "howf" in Lady Stair's Close; he feasted them to their heart's content and avowed "he found enough native drollery to compose a comedy." Well, he didn't, but the same century was to give us a greater than Steele and—*The Jolly Beggars!*

The folk of old Edinburgh were used to scenes of bloodshed—I tell elsewhere the story of "Cleanse the Causey," as the historic street fight between the Douglases and the Hamiltons was called. It was almost a matter of necessity that men should go armed. Wild dissipation was a common incident, passions were high, and people did not hold either their own lives or those of others at any great rate. Here is a story from 1650, when the English were in occupation of Edinburgh, and so for the time the predominant party. An English officer had a squabble with some natives; he mounted his horse and said to them disdainfully, "With my own hands I killed that Scot which ought this horse and this case of pistols and who dare say that in this I wronged him?" He paid bitterly for his rashness. "I dare say it," said one of his audience, "and thus shall avenge it." He stabbed him with a sword right through the body so that he fell dead. The Scot threw himself into the vacant saddle, dashed over the stones to the nearest Port, and was lost for ever to pursuit.

The measures against those acts of violence were ludicrously ineffectual. In the houses the firearms were chained down lest they should be used in accidental affrays; but the streets were not policed at all, and gentlemen did much as they liked. It is told of Hugh Somerville of Drum, who died in 1640, that he went one day to St. Giles' with Lady Ross, his sister-in-law. A gentleman happened by chance, it would seem, to push against him, there was a scuffle and Somerville had his dagger out on the instant, and would have stuck it into the intruder had not Lady Ross seized and held him; the while she begged the stranger to go away. A duel was like to ensue, but in cold blood the affair no doubt seemed ridiculous, and was made up. Quarrels about equally small matters often led to duels. In January 1708, two friends, young Baird of Saughtonhall and Robert Oswald, were drinking in a tavern at Leith, when they had a dispute; they accommodated it, and drove to Edinburgh together, they leave the coach at the Netherbow, when Baird revives the quarrel, and in a few minutes, or perhaps seconds, kills his friend with his sword. A reaction followed, and the assassin

IN THE STREETS OF EDINBURGH

expressed his deep regret, which did not bring the dead man to life again; the other fled, but finally escaped without punishment as the act was not premeditated. One of the last incidents of this class was a duel between Captain Macrae of Marionville and Sir George Ramsay of Bamff in 1790. It arose out of a quarrel caused by the misconduct of a servant. Macrae shot his opponent dead, and then fled to France, and he never thought it safe to return to Scotland. Duelling was considered proper for gentlemen, but only for gentlemen, and not to be permitted to all and sundry. Towards the end of the sixteenth century a barber challenged a chimney sweep, and they had a very pretty " set to " with swords at which neither was hurt. The King presently ordered the barber to summary execution because he presumed to take the revenge of a gentleman. The upper classes did not set a good example to their inferiors. One need not discuss whether the Porteous mob was really a riot of the common people. The *Heart of Midlothian*, if nothing else, has made it a very famous affair. The Edinburgh mob, which was very fierce and determined according to Scott, had one or two remarkable maxims. At an Irish fair the proper course is to bring down your shillelagh on any very prominent head. Here the rule was to throw a stone at every face that looked out of a window. Daniel Defoe was in Edinburgh in 1705, on a special mission from Government, to do all he could to bring about the Union. From his window in the High Street he was gazing upon the angry populace and only just dodged a large stone. He afterwards discovered not merely the rule but the reason thereof, that there might be no recognition of faces. As the old cock crows the young cock learns, even the children were fighters. I have already told how the boys of the High School killed Bailie Macmorran in a barring out business. There is a legend of the famous Earl of Haddington, "Tam of the Coogate," that when a fight was on between the lads of the High School and the students of the College, he took strenuously the side of the former. Nay, he drove the students out of the West Port, locked the gate in their faces, that they might cool themselves by a night in the fields, and placidly retired to his studies. The fighting tradition lasted through the centuries. Scott tells us of the incessant bickers between the High School and street callants, which, however lawless, had yet their own laws. During one of those fights a youth known from his dress as Greenbreeks, a leader of the town, was stuck with a knife, and somewhat seriously wounded. He was tended in the Infirmary and in due time recovered, but nothing would prevail upon him to give any hint whereby his assailant might be discovered. The High School boys took means to reward him, but the fights were continued with unabated vigour.

Student riots are a chapter by themselves, and in Edinburgh were almost to be looked upon as a matter of course, and to a mild extent still are, on such occasions as Rectorial elections. In past times no occasion was lost for burning the Pope in effigy, that was always a safe card to play. Even the piety of old Edinburgh served to stimulate its brawls. The famous commotion at the reading of the service book in St. Giles' on 23rd July 1637 is a case in point. Jenny

IN THE STREETS OF EDINBURGH

Geddes is to-day commemorated within the Cathedral itself, and she lives in history by her classic pleasantry, on the Dean announcing the collect for the day: "Deil colic the wame o'thee fause thief, wilt thou say mass at my lug?" There is one other story about Jenny to be told. On 19th June 1660 there were great rejoicings in Edinburgh upon the Restoration. There was service at the Church, banquet of sweetmeats and wine at the Cross, which ran claret for the benefit of the populace; at night there were fireworks at the Castle, effigies of Cromwell and the Devil were paraded through the streets, bonfires blazed everywhere, and as fuel for these last Jenny is reported to have contributed her stool. No doubt much water had run under the bridge since 1637; Jenny may or may not have changed her views, but she was nothing if not enthusiastic, and there was really no inconsistency in her conduct. Other folk than Jenny had a difficulty to reconcile their various devotions!

The people of Edinburgh had a strong aversion from bishops. On 4th June 1674, as the members of the Council were going to their meeting-place in the Parliament Close, fifteen ladies appeared with a petition for a free ministry. Archbishop Sharp was pointedly described as Judas, and Traitor. Indeed one of the ladies struck him on the neck, screaming that he should yet pay for it ere all was done. Any scandal against a bishop was readily circulated. Bishop Patterson of Edinburgh was lampooned as a profligate and loose liver. In the midst of a seemingly impassioned discourse he is said to have kissed, in the pulpit, his band-strings, that being the signal agreed upon between

247

him and his lady-love to prove that he could think upon her even in the midst of solemn duties. He was nicknamed "Bishop Bandstrings." The bishops of the persecuting Church disappear from history in a rather undignified manner. Patrick Walker tells with great glee how at the Revolution, as the convention grew more and more enthusiastic for the new order, they, fourteen in number, "were expelled at once and stood in a crowd with pale faces in the Parliament Close." Some daring members of the crowd knocked the heads of the poor prelates "hard upon each other," the bishops slunk off, and presently were seen no more in the streets. "But some of us," continues Patrick, "would have rejoiced still more to have seen the whole cabalsie sent closally down the Bow that they might have found the weight of their tails in a tow to dry their stocking soles, and let them know what hanging was."

Villon had long before sung on a near prospect of the gallows—

> " Or d'une corde d'une toise
>   Saura mon col que mon cul poise."

But you are sure Patrick had never heard of François, and the same dismally ludicrous idea had occurred independently.

Certain picturesque figures or rather classes of men lent a quaint or comic touch to the streets of old Edinburgh, but all are long swept into Time's dustbin. One of these consisted of the chairmen. The Old Town was not the place for carriages; cabs were not yet, and even to-day they do not suit its steep and narrow ways; but the sedan chair was the very thing, you could trundle

1

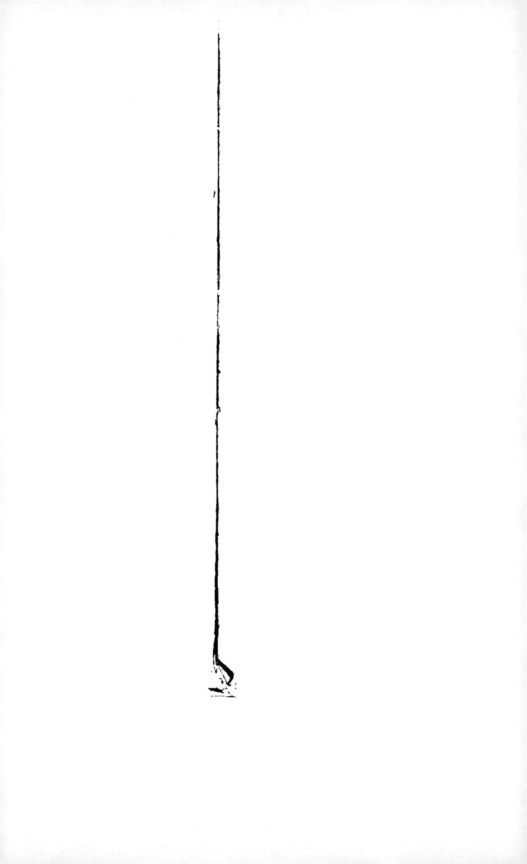

ALLAN RAMSAY, POET

IN THE STREETS OF EDINBURGH

it commodiously up and down hill, and narrow must have been the close through which it could not pass. The chairmen who bore the burden of the chair were mainly Highlanders, who flocked to Edinburgh as the Irish did afterwards, and in early days formed a distinct element in city life. They are reported as of insatiable greed, but their earnings probably were but small and uncertain. Still such was their reputation, and it was once put to the test to decide a wager. Lord Panmure hired a chair and proceeded a short way down the Canongate. When he got out he handed the chairman a guinea. Millionaires were not yet in the land, possibly the chairman imagined he had found a benevolent lunatic, or he may even have smelt a wager. "But could her honour no' shuist gie the ither sixpence to get a gill?" The coin was duly handed over, then Donald thought he might do something for his companion and preferred a modest request for "three bawbees of odd change to puy snuff." But even the chairmen had another side. Among them was Edmund Burke, who died in 1751. He had been an attendant on Prince Charlie, and had as easily as you like netted £30,000 by treachery, for such was the handsome price fixed for the young chevalier, "dead or alive"; but it never crossed his mind to earn it!

Of much the same class were the caddies, whose name still lingers as the attendants on golf-players; the caddie was the man-of-all-work of old Edinburgh, for various indeed were his functions. Even to-day, if you look at some of the high houses, you remember how much time inhabitants must have spent in going up and down stairs; load the climber with burdens and life were scarce worth living. The chief burden was water, and the caddies were the class who bore the stoups containing it up and down. These water-carriers soon acquired a pronounced and characteristic stoop; they were dressed in the cast-off red jackets of the City Guard, the women among them had thick felt greatcoats and hats like the men, their fee was a penny a barrel. The same name was applied to a division that worked with their brains rather than their hands; they knew every man in the town, and the name, residence, and condition of every stranger to whom they acted as guides and even companions. You sought your caddie at the Cross, where he would lounge of a morning on a wooden bench till some one was good enough to employ him. You remember the interesting account Scott gives of the caddies in the part of *Guy Mannering* which treats of the visit to Edinburgh of the Colonel.

Still more characteristic of old Edinburgh was the Town Guard, who for many a long day acted most inefficiently as police and guardians of the peace to the city. They are, so to speak, embalmed in the pages of Scott and Fergusson. The first treats them with a touch of comic contempt, the other calls them " the black banditti," and deprecates their brutal violence. He had some cause, personal or otherwise. One of their number, Corporal John Dhu, a gigantic Highlander, as short of temper as he was long of body, during a city row with one fell stroke stretched a member of the mob lifeless on the pavement. The populace told wondrous legends of this corps. They existed, it was averred, before the Christian era, nay, some of them were present

IN THE STREETS OF EDINBURGH

at the Crucifixion as Pilate's guard! In truth they only dated from the seventeenth century, at any rate as a regularly constituted corps, and they came to an end early in the nineteenth. They attended all civic ceremonies and civic functions, their drums beat every night at eight o'clock in the High Street. Their guard house long stood opposite the Tron Church. There was always a collision between them and the populace on occasion of rejoicing, as witness Fergusson's *Hallow Fair*:

> "Jock Bell gaed forth to play his freaks,
>   Great cause he had to rue it,
> For frae a stark Lochaber aix
>   He gat a *clamihewit*
>   Fu' sair that night."

The unfortunate wretch received a still worse blow, nor even then were his troubles ended:

> "He, peching on the causey, lay
>   O' kicks an' cuffs well sair'd.
> A highland aith the serjeant gae
>   She maun pe see our guard.
> Out spak the warlike corporal,
>   'Pring in ta drunken sot!'
> They trail'd him ben, an' by my saul
>   He paid his drucken groat
>   For that neist day."

Once in the year, at any rate, the populace got their own back again—that was the King's birthday, when the authorities assembled in the Parliament House to honour the occasion. Thereafter the mob went with one accord for the Guard, and always routed them after a desperate resistance. Scott jocosely laments the disappearance of those picturesque figures, with their uniform of rusty red, their Lochaber axes, their huge

251

cocked hats. But two survived to be present at the inauguration of his monument on 15th August 1846. Their pay was sixpence a day. The Gaelic poet, Duncan Macintyre, was once asked if anything could be done to improve his worldly prospects. He confessed a modest ambition to be enrolled in the Edinburgh Town Guard! After this Burns's post as a Dumfries exciseman might seem princely. All competent critics agree that Macintyre was the sweetest of singers, a poet of true genius, and that his laudatory epitaph in old Greyfriars was justly earned. Captain James Burnet, who died on the 24th August 1814, was the last commander of this ancient corps. If not so famous as some of his predecessors, Major Weir or Captain Porteous, for instance, he was still a prominent Edinburgh character. He weighed nineteen stones, yet, for a wager, climbed Arthur's Seat in a quarter of an hour. You do not wonder that he lay panting on the earth " like an expiring porpoise." He was one of the "Turners," as those were scornfully called who assembled on Sunday afternoons, *not* to go to church, but to take a walk or turn. At an earlier day he and his fellows had been promptly pounced upon by the seizers, who were officials appointed to promenade the streets during the hours of divine service. These would apprehend the ungodly wanderer and even joints of mutton frizzling and turning with indecent levity on the roasting-jacks. In or about 1735 the blackbird of a Jacobite barber, in horrid defiance of the powers that were, civil and ecclesiastical, and to the utter subversion of Kirk and State, touched "the trembling ears" of the seizers with " The King shall enjoy his own again," most audaciously whistled. The songster was forthwith taken into custody and transported to the guard house.

Once the " seizers " got emphatically the worst of it. Dr. Archibald Pitcairne, poet, scholar, Jacobite, latitudinarian, was not in sympathy in many points with the Edinburgh of Queen Anne's day, but he loved his glass as well as any of them. He had sent for some claret one Sunday forenoon, which the seizers had confiscated ere it reached his thirsty palate. The wit was furious, but he had his revenge. He doctored a few bottles of the wine with some strong drug of disagreeable operation, and then he procured its capture by the seizers. As he expected, the stuff went speedily down their throats ; the result was all he could have wished. But Burnet came too late for all this, and a nickname was the only punishment for him and his fellows. He was also a prominent member of the Lawnmarket Club—the popular name for certain residents who met every morning about seven to discuss the news of the day, and to take their morning draught of brandy together. Nothing was done in old Edinburgh without the accompaniment of a dram; the "meridian" followed the "morning" (the very bells of St. Giles that chime the hour were known as the " gill " bells), as a matter of course, and both only sustained the citizen for the serious business of the evening. True, a great deal of the drinking was claret, indeed, huge pewter jugs or stoups of that wine were to be seen moving up and down the streets of Edinburgh in all directions, as ale jugs in London. When a ship arrived from Bordeaux the claret hogsheads were carted through the streets, and vessels were filled from the spigot at a very cheap rate. There was always a native-brewed " tippeny." The curtain was already falling on old Edinburgh ere whisky was introduced as a regular article of consumption. A thin veil of decency was thrown over the dissipation; it was made a matter of aggravation in the charge against a gentleman of rank that he had allowed his company to get drunk in his house before it was dark in the month of July. The peculiar little separate boxes wherein the guests revelled in the Edinburgh taverns threw an air of secrecy and mystery over the proceedings. One of the most famous taverns was Johnny Dowie's, in Libberton's Wynd, where George IV. Bridge now stands. Its memories of Burns and Fergusson and a hundred other still famous names make it the *Mermaid* of Edinburgh. It had many baser clients. A visitor opens a door and finds a room, the floor covered with snoring lads. "Oh," explains mine host with a tolerant grin, "just twa-three o' Sir Wullie's drucken clerks!" (Sir William Forbes the banker is meant). "The clartier the cosier," says a wicked old Scots apothegm. Wolfe, the hero of Quebec, says that it was not till after Christmas, when the better folk had come into it from the country, that Edinburgh was "in all its perfection of dirt and gaiety." There could not have been anything like sufficient water wherewith to wash, and all sorts of filth were hurled from the lofty houses into the street. "*Gardy loo*" was the conventional word of warning, uttered not seldom *after* and not *before* the event. Whether it was from the French "*Gare à l'eau*" may or may not be true. The delightful Mrs.

254

IN THE STREETS OF EDINBURGH

Winifred Jenkins aptly translates it as: "May the Lord have mercy on your souls."

Until imprisonment for debt was abolished the precincts of Holyrood were inhabited by fugitive debtors, for there these had the privilege of sanctuary. They were called Abbey lairds, and many were the stories told of the dodges to get them out of the bounds or to remain after Sunday was finished, for that was a free day for them. Two anecdotes may be quoted. On a certain Sunday in July 1709, Patrick Haliburton, one of those Abbey lairds, was induced to visit a creditor, by whom he was received with the utmost geniality. The bottle was produced and Patrick quaffed to his heart's content; as he staggered from the door *after* midnight, a messenger seized him under a Writ of Caption and haled him off to prison. In 1724 Mrs. Dilkes, a debtor, had an invitation to a tavern within the verge, but to enter it she had to go a few paces beyond the Girth Cross. The moment she was outside she was nabbed; but this was too much for the women of the place, who rose in their might and rescued her.

The wit of old Edinburgh was satirical, bitter, scornful, and the practical jokes not in the best of taste. The Union, we know, was intensely unpopular, nowhere more than in the Canongate.

"London and death gar thee look dool,"

sings Allan Ramsay. Holyrood was at an end, save for the election of representative Peers. At the first after the Union it was noted that all elected were loyal to the English government, "a plain evidence of the country's slavery to the English Court." A fruit-woman paraded the courts of the palace bawling most lustily, " Who would buy good pears, old pears, new pears, fresh pears—rotten pears, sixteen of them for a plack." Remember that pears is pronounced "peers" in Scots and the point of the joke is obvious.

In the suburb of the Pleasance a tailor called Hunter had erected a large house which folk named Hunter's Folly, or the Castle of Clouts. Gillespie, the founder of Gillespie's Hospital, was a snuff merchant ; when he started a carriage the incorrigible Harry Erskine suggested as a motto:

> " Wha wad hae thocht it
> That noses had bocht it?"

Harry was usually more good-humoured. A working man complained to him of the low value of a dollar, which he showed him. Now, from the scarcity of silver at the time, a number of Spanish dollars were in circulation, on which the head of George III. had been stamped over the neck of the Spanish King; the real was some sixpence less than the nominal value. Erskine gravely regretted that two such mighty persons had laid their heads together to do a poor man out of a sixpence. Not that the lawyers always had the best of it. Crosby, the original Counsellor Pleydell in *Guy Mannering*, was building a spacious mansion in St. Andrew Square. His home in the country was a thatched cottage. " Ah, Crosby," said Principal Robertson to him one day at dinner, " were your town and country house to meet, how they would stare at one another." Nor did the people always get the laugh. Walter Ross, an Edinburgh character of the eighteenth century, had built a square tower in his property on the north side

ANDREW CROSBIE, "PLEYDELL"

From a Painting in the Advocates' Library, by permission of the
Faculty of Advocates

of the New Town; in this were all the curious old stones he could procure. The people called it Ross's Folly, and notwithstanding his prominently displayed threats of man-traps and spring-guns they roamed at will over his domain. Somehow or other he procured a human leg from the dissecting room, dressed it up with stocking, shoe, and buckle and sent the town-crier with it, announcing that "it had been found that night in Walter Ross's policy at Stockbridge," and offering to restore it to the owner!

A more innocent pleasantry is ascribed to Burns. A lady of title, with whom he had the slightest acquaintance, asked him to a party in what was no doubt a very patronising manner. Burns never lost his head or his independence in Edinburgh. He replied that he would come if the Learned Pig was invited also. The animal in question was then one of the attractions of the Grassmarket. To balance this is a story of a snub by a lady. Dougal Geddie, a successful silversmith, had donned with much pride the red coat of a Town Guard officer. He observed with concern a lady at the door of the Assembly Rooms without an attendant beau. He courteously suggested himself "if the arm of an old soldier could be of any use to her." "Hoot awa', Dougal, an auld tinkler you mean," said the lady.

One constantly recurring street scene in old Edinburgh was the execution of criminals. Not a mere case of decorous hanging, but a man, as like as not, dismembered in sight of the gaping crowd, and that man was often one who had been within the memory of all a great personage in the State, to whom every knee had been bowed, and every cap doffed. Great executions were famous events, and were distinguished by impressive and remarkable incidents; but I shall not attempt to record these. Some little remembered events must serve for illustration.. In 1661 Archibald Cornwall, town officer, was hanged at the Cross. He had "poinded" an honest man's house, wherein was a picture of the King and Queen. These, from carelessness or malice or misplaced sense of humour, he had stuck on the gallows at the Cross from which as noted he presently dangled. In 1667 Patrick Roy Macgregor and some of his following were condemned at Edinburgh for sorning, fire-raising, and murder. Those caterans were almost outside the law, and they were duly hanged, the right hand being previously cut off —a favourite old-time addition to capital punishment. Macgregor was a thick-set, strongly-built man of fierce face, in which gleamed his hawk-like eye, a human wolf the crowd must have thought him. He was "perfectly undaunted" though the hangman bungled the amputation business so badly that he was turned out of office the next day. Executions were at different periods carried out on the Castle Hill, at the Cross, the Gallow Lee, on the road to Leith, and at various places throughout the city, but the ordinary spot was, from about 1660 till 1785, in the Grassmarket, at the foot of the West Bow, after that at the west end of the Tolbooth, till its destruction in 1817, then at the head of Libberton's Wynd, near where George IV. Bridge now is, till 1868, when such public spectacles were abolished. An old Edinburgh rhyme commemorates the old-time progress of the criminal.

IN THE STREETS OF EDINBURGH

"Up the Lawnmarket, And doun the West Bow,
Up the big ladder, And doun the wee tow."

As the clock struck the hour after noon, the City Guard knocked at the door of the Tolbooth. It was flung open and the condemned man marched forth. The correct costume was a waistcoat and breeches of white, edged with black ribbon, wherewith the night-cap on his head was also trimmed. His hands were tied behind him, and a rope was round his neck. On each side was a parson, behind shuffled the hangman, disguised in an overcoat, round were the City Guard, with their arms ready. Among the fierce folk of that violent town a rescue was always a possibility, and so the gruesome figure went to his doom. One other case and I leave the subject. It was a popular belief in Edinburgh that a man could not be hanged later than four o'clock afternoon. A certain John Young had been convicted of forgery, and condemned to death. The time appointed for his execution was the 17th December 1750, between two and four in the afternoon. Under the pretence of private devotion he locked himself in the inner room of the prison, and nothing would persuade him to come out. He was only got at by breaking the floor of the room overhead, and even then there was difficulty. A gun was presented at his head; it happened to be unloaded. On a calculation of probabilities he even then refused to surrender; he was finally seized and dragged headlong downstairs. He anxiously inquired if it were not yet four o'clock, and was assured he would be hanged, however late the hour. As a matter of fact, it was already after four, though not by the clock, which had been stopped by the au-

259

thorities. He refused to move, declined, as he said, to be accessory to his own murder, but was hanged all the same about half-past four. His pranks had only given him another half-hour of life. There were numerous lesser punishments: flogging, mutilation, branding, all done in public, to the disgust or entertainment of the populace. I tell one story, farce rather than tragedy. On the 6th of November 1728, Margaret Gibson, for the crime of theft, was drummed through the town; over her neck was fixed a board provided with bells which chimed at each step she made, a little from her face there was attached a false face adorned with a fox's tail, " In short she was a very odd spectacle." No doubt; but where did the edification come in? I ought to mention that the officials who attended an execution were wont thereafter to regale themselves at what was called the Deid Chack. The cheerful Deacon Brodie, just before his violent exit from life, took leave of a town official in this fashion, "Fare ye weel, Bailie! Ye needna be surprised if ye see me amang ye yet, to tak' my share o' the Deid Chack." Perhaps he meant his ghost would be there, or—but it is not worth speculating. This gruesome feast was abolished through the influence of Provost Creech, who did much for the city.

> "Auld Reekie aye he keepit tight
> And trig an' braw."

The crook in Creech's lot was an old soldier, Lauchlin M'Bain, who pretended to sell roasting-jacks. He had a street call of " R-r-r-roasting toasting-jacks," which was found perfectly unbearable, even by the not too nice ears of the citizens. He blackmailed various parties, and then attached himself like a burr to Creech. He bellowed before his door with such fell intent that the civic dignitary was frantic. He had Lauchlin up before the local courts, but the old soldier, who had fought on the government side at Culloden, produced his discharge which clearly gave him a right to practise his business in Edinburgh. Creech had to submit and buy the intruder off. Creech himself played pranks just as mischievous on a certain drunken Writer to the Signet called William Macpherson, a noted character of the day. He lived in the West Bow with his two sisters, whom he, with quaint barbarity, nicknamed Sodom and Gommorah. He was not above taking fees in kind. Once he thus procured an armful of turnips, with which he proceeded homewards; but he was tipsy, and the West Bow was near the perpendicular, and ere long he was flat on his face, and the turnips flying in every direction. He staggered after them and recovered most. The Governor of the Castle had asked Creech to procure him a cook ; he became so insistent in his demands that the bookseller got angry, and happening to meet Macpherson, he coolly told him that the Governor wished to see him on important business. Macpherson could not understand why everybody treated him in such a cavalier manner, and a comical conversation took place, which was brought to a head by the Governor demanding his character. At last he blurted out in rage that he was a Writer to the Signet. "Why, I wanted a cook," said the Governor. Macpherson retired in wrath to comfort himself with that unfailing remedy, the bottle.

These were not the days of care for the insane, the

"natural" was allowed to run about the streets untouched. Jamie Duff was one of the most famous of those. In old Scotland a funeral was a very pompous and very solemn function. Duff made it a point to be present at as many as possible, with cape, cravat, and weepers of the most orthodox pattern, however shabby the material, even paper not being disdained. He commonly marched at the head of the procession—a hideous burlesque of the whole affair. His pranks met with strange and unexpected tolerance; instead of being driven away, he was feed and encouraged. He appears at the funeral of Miss Bertram in *Guy Mannering*. Scott has gathered many such memories into his works. One adventure of Duff's was not a success. He had got together, or aped the cast-off suit of a bailie, and assumed the title of that mighty functionary. The authorities interfered and stripped him, thus making themselves the butt of many a local witticism. He subsisted on stray gifts of all kinds, but he refused silver money. He thought it was a trick to enlist him. Another feature of the street was the Highland gentleman. The memory of one, Francis M'Nab, Esq. of M'Nab, still lingers. Once a Lowland friend inquired if Mr. M'Nab was at home. "No," was the answer, and the door was shut in his face, not before he had heard the tones of the chieftain in the background. Apprised of his error, he called next day, and asked for "The M'Nab," and was received with open arms. It happened on the way to Leith races that the chieftain's horse dropped down dead under him. "M'Nab, is that the same horse you had last year?" said an acquaintance at the next race-meeting. "No, py Cot," re-

IN THE STREETS OF EDINBURGH

plied the Laird; "but this is the same whip"—the other made off at full speed. When in command of the Breadalbane Fencibles, he allowed his men to smuggle a huge quantity of whisky from the Highlands. A party of excisemen laid hands on the baggage of the corps. M'Nab pretended to believe they were robbers. He was a big man, with a powerful voice; he thundered out to his men "Prime, load"—the gaugers took to their heels, and the whisky was saved.

Smuggling might almost be called the first of Highland virtues. Archibald Campbell, the city officer, had the misfortune to lose his mother. He procured a hearse, and reverently carried away the body to the Highlands for burial. He brought the hearse back again, not empty, but full of smuggled whisky. This fondness for a trick or practical joke was a feature of old Edinburgh. It lived on to later times. In 1803 or 1804, Playfair, Thomas Thomson, and Sydney Smith instigated by Brougham, proceeded one night to George Street, with the intention of filching the Galen's Head, which stood over the door of Gardiner, the apothecary. By one climbing on the top of the others their object was all but attained, when, by the dim light of the oil-lamps, Brougham was descried leading the city watch to the spot, his design being to play a trick within a trick. There was a hasty scramble, and all got off. None save Brougham was very young, and even he was twenty-six, and to-day the people are decorous and the place is decorous. Who can now recall what the Mound was like, when it was the chosen locus of the menageries of the day? Fergusson, Lord Hermand, was proceeding along it just having heard

263

of the fall of the "ministry of all the talents"; he could not contain himself. " They are out—by the Lord, they are all out, every mother's son of them!" A passing lady heard him with absolute horror. "Good Lord, then we shall all be devoured!" she screamed, not doubting but that the wild beasts had broken loose.

A word as to weather. The east coast of Scotland is exposed to the chilling fog or mist called haar, and to bitter blasts of east wind, as well as to the ordinary rain and cloud. Edinburgh, being built on hills, is peculiarly affected by those forces, and the broad streets and open spaces of the New Town worst of all. The peculiar build of the old part was partly, at least, meant as a defence from weather. Fergusson boldly says so.

> " Not Boreas that sae snelly blows
>   Dare here pap in his angry nose,
>   Thanks to our dads, whase biggin stands
>   A shelter to surrounding lands."

But there is no shelter in Princes Street. On the 24th of January 1868 a great storm raged. Chimney-pots and portions of chimney-stacks came down in all directions. Fifty police carts were filled with the rubbish. Cabs were blown over, an instance of the force of the east wind which impressed James Payn the novelist exceedingly. A gentleman had opened Professor Syme's carriage door to get out. The door was completely blown away; a man brought it up presently, with the panel not even scratched and the glass unbroken. Another eminent doctor, Sir Robert Christison, was hurled along Princes Street at such a rate, that when, to prevent an accident, he seized hold of a lamp-post he was dashed violently into the gutter

IN THE STREETS OF EDINBURGH

and seriously hurt his knee. The street was deserted, people were afraid to venture out of doors. Even on a moderately gusty night the noise of the wind a-midst the tall lands and narrow closes of the Old Town, as heard from Princes Street, is a sound never to be forgotten; it has a tragic mournful dignity in its infinite wail, the voice of old Edinburgh touched with pity and terror! Some one has said what a charming place Edinburgh would be if you could only put up a screen against the east wind. As that is impossible it may be held to excuse everything from flight to dissipation!

CHAPTER TWELVE

THE CITY

CHAPTER TWELVE   THE CITY

I CONTINUE THE SUBJECTS OF MY LAST chapter, though this deals rather with things under cover and folk of a better position than the common objects of the street. I pass as briefly as may be the more elaborate legends of Edinburgh, they are rather story than anecdote. I have already dealt with Lady Stair and her close. It is on the north side of the Lawnmarket. If you go down that same street till it becomes the Canongate, on the same side, you have Morocco Land with its romantic legend of young Gray, who showed a clean pair of heels to the hangman, only to turn up a few years after as a bold bad corsair. But he came to bless and not to rob, for by his eastern charms or what not he cured the Provost's daughter, sick well-nigh to death of the plague, and then married her. They lived very happily together in Morocco Land, outside the Netherbow be it noted, and so outside old Edinburgh, for Gray had vowed he would never again enter the city. If you find a difficulty in realising this tale of eastern romance amid the grimy surroundings of the Canongate of to-day, lift up your eyes to Morocco Land, and there is the figure of the Moor carved on it, and how can you doubt the story after that? On the opposite side is Queensberry House, which bears many a legend of the splendour and wicked deeds of more than one Duke of Queensberry. Chief of them was that High Commissioner who presided over the Union debates, he whom the Edinburgh mob hated with all the bitter hatred of their ferocious souls. They loved to tell how when he was strangling the liberties of his country in the Parliament House, his idiot son and heir was strangling the poor boy that turned the spit in Queensberry House, and was roasting him upon his own fire so that when the family returned to their mansion a cannibal orgie was already in progress. You are glad that history enables you to doubt the story just as you are sorry you must doubt the others.

Edinburgh has had a Provost for centuries (since 1667 he has been entitled by Royal command to the designation of Lord Provost), Bailies, Dean of Guild, Town Council, and so forth, but you must not believe for a moment that these were ever quite the same offices. The old municipal constitution of Edinburgh was curious and complicated. I shall not attempt to explain it, or how the various deacons of the trades formed part of it. When it was reformed and the system of self-election abolished, the city officer, Archibald Campbell, is said to have died out of sheer grief, it seemed to him defiling the very Ark of God. The old-time magistrates were puffed up with a sense of their own importance, that of itself invited a "taking down." It was the habit of those dignitaries to pay their respects to every new President of the Court of Session. President Dundas, who died in 1752, was thus honoured. He was walking with his guests in the park at Arniston, when the attention of Bailie M'Ilroy, one of their number, was attracted by a fine ash tree lately blown to the ground. He was a wood merchant, and thought the occasion too good to be lost. He there and then proposed to buy it, and not accepting the curt refusals of the President, finally offered to pay a halfpenny a foot above the ordinary price. "Sir," said Dundas in a burst of rage, "rather than cut up that tree, I would see you and all the magistrates of Edinburgh hanging on it." But the roll of civic dignitaries contains more illustrious names.

Provost Drummond, who may be called the founder of the New Town, had long cherished and developed the scheme in his mind. Dr. Jardine, his son-in-law, lived in part of a house in the north corner of the Royal Exchange from which there was a wide prospect away over the Nor' Loch to the fields beyond. It was plain countryside in those days. The swans used to issue from under the Castle rock, swim across the Nor' Loch, cross the Lang Gate and Bearford's Park, and make sad havoc of the cornfields of Wood's farm. Bearford's Park was called after Bearford in East Lothian, which had the same owner. Perhaps you remember the wish of Richard Moniplies in *The Fortunes of Nigel*, that he had his opponent in Bearford's Park. But to return to Provost Drummond. He was once with Dr. Thomas Somerville, then a young man, in Dr. Jardine's house, above mentioned. They were looking at the prospect, perhaps watching the vagaries of the audacious swans. "You, Mr. Somerville," said the Provost, "are a young man and may probably live, though I will not, to see all these fields covered with houses, forming a splendid and magnificent city," all which in due time was to come about. Dr. Somerville tells us this story in his *My Own Life and Times,* a work still important for the history of the period. All this building has not destroyed the peculiar characteristic of Edinburgh scenery. It is still true that "From the crowded city we behold the undisturbed dwellings of the Hare and the Heath fowl; from amidst the busy hum of men we look on recesses where the sound of the human voice has but rarely penetrated, on mountains surrounding a great metropolis, which rear their mighty heads in solitude and silence. What pleases me more in this scenery is that it is so perfectly characteristic of the country, so purely Scottish . . . No man in Edinburgh can for a moment forget that he is in Scotland." It is almost startling to look up from the grime of the Canongate to the solitary nooks of Arthur's Seat, though the sea of houses spreads miles around. Whatever scenic effects remain, the historical effects of the landscape are vanished. With what various emotions the crowd from every point of vantage must have watched Dundee's progress along the Lang Gate to his interview with the Duke of Gordon on the Castle rock! And the town was not much changed when, rather more than half a century afterwards, the citizens, some of them the same, watched, after the affair at Coltbridge, the dragoons gallop along the same north ridge in headlong flight, a sight which promptly disposed the townsfolk's minds in the direction of surrender. One gloomy tragedy of the year 1717 affords a curious illustration of this command of prospect. A road called Gabriel's Road once ran from the little hamlet of Silvermills on the Water of Leith southward to where the Register House now stands. Formerly you crossed the dam which bounded the east end of the Nor' Loch, and by the port at the bottom of Halkerston's Wynd you entered old Edinburgh just as you might enter it now by the North Bridge, though at a very different level. To-day Gabriel's Road still appears in the street directory, but it is practically a short flight of

REV. THOMAS SOMERVILLE

From a Photograph in the Scottish National Portrait Gallery

steps and a back way to a collection of houses. In the year mentioned a certain Robert Irvine, a probationer of the church, on or near this road, cruelly murdered his two pupils, little boys, and sons of Mr. Gordon of Ellom, whose only offence was some childish gossip about their preceptor. The instrument was a penknife, and the second boy fled shrieking when he saw the fate of his brother, but was pursued and killed by Irvine, whom you might charitably suppose to be at least partially insane were not deeds of ferocious violence too common in old Scots life. The point of the story for us is that the tragedy was clearly seen by a great number from the Old Town, though they were powerless to prevent. The culprit was forthwith seized, and as he was taken red-handed, was executed two days after by the authorities of Broughton, within whose territory the crime had occurred. His hands were previously hacked off with the knife, the instrument of his crime. The reverend sinner made a specially edifying end, not unnaturally a mark of men of his cloth. In 1570, John Kelloe, minister of Spott, near Dunbar, had, for any or no reason, murdered his wife. So well had he managed the affair that no one suspected him, but after six weeks his conscience forced him to make a clean breast of the matter. He was strangled and burned at the Gallow Lee, between Edinburgh and Leith. His behaviour at the end was all that could be desired. It strikes you as overdone, but from the folk of the time it extorted a certain admiration. The authorities were as cruel as the criminals. A boy burns down a house and he is himself burned alive at the Cross as an example. In 1675 two striplings named Clarke and Ram-

say, seventeen and fifteen years old, robbed and poisoned their master, an old man named Anderson. His
nephew, Sir John Clerk of Penicuik, warned by a recurring dream, set off for Edinburgh, and instituted in-
vestigations which led to the discovery of the crime.
The youthful culprits were hanged "both in regard to
the theft clearly proven and for terror that the Italian
trick of sending men to the other world in figs and pos-
sits might not come overseas to our Island." Now and
again there is a redeeming touch in the dark story. In
1528 there was an encounter between the Douglases
and the Hamiltons at Holyrood Palace. A groom of
the Earl of Lennox spied Sir James Hamilton of Fin-
nart, who had slain his master, among the crowd. He
presently attacked Sir James in a narrow gallery, and
wounded him in six places, though none was mortal.
The groom was discovered and dragged off to torture
and mutilation. His right hand was hacked off; whereupon "he observed with a sarcastic smile that it was
punished less than it deserved for having failed to revenge his beloved master." I have mentioned the Gallow Lee between Edinburgh and Leith. It was the
chosen spot for the execution of witches, and for the
hanging in chains of great criminals. The hillock was
composed of very excellent sand. When the New
Town was built it had been long disused as a place of
execution, and the owner of the soil had no difficulty
in disposing of a long succession of cartloads to the
builders. He insisted on immediate payment and immediately spent the money at an adjacent tavern, maintained if not instituted for his special benefit. He drank
to the last grain as well as to the last drop and van-

ishes from history, the most extreme and consistent of countless Edinburgh topers!

I have still something illustrative to say of prisoners. When Deacon Brodie was executed, 1st October 1788, his abnormal fortitude was supposed to ground itself on an expectation that he would only be half hanged, would be resuscitated, and conveyed away a free man. He seems to have devised some plan to this end, but "the best laid schemes o' mice an' men," we are told on good authority, " aft gang agley," and so it was here. Edinburgh has one or two instances of revival. On the 18th February 1594–95, Hercules Stewart was hanged at the Cross for his concern in the crimes of his relative the Earl of Bothwell. He was an object of popular sympathy, as believed to be " ane simple gentleman and not ane enterpriser." The body, after being cut down, was carried to the Tolbooth to be laid out, "but within a little space he began to recover, and moved somewhat, and might by appearance have lived. The ministers being advertised hereof went to the King to procure for his life, but they had already given a new command to strangle him with all speed, so that no man durst speak in the contrary." There was not much encouragement to be got from this story. Yet a woman some generations afterwards had better fortune—the very name of "half-hangit Maggie Dixon" of itself explains the legend. She was strung up for child-murder in the Grassmarket, and her body had a narrow escape from being carried off by a party of medical students to the dissecting room, as it was put in a cart and jolted off landward. Those in charge stopped before a little change-house for refreshment,

however, and when they came forth, Maggie sat up-
right in the cart, very much alive and kicking. Apparently she lived happy ever after. She was married,
had children, and, no doubt, looked upon herself as a
public character. Was it only popular imagination that
perceived a certain twist in the neck of the good lady?
Many famous men perished on Edinburgh scaffolds,
and many more filled the Edinburgh prisons, were
they Castle or Tolbooths, namely, the Heart of Midlothian cheek by jowl with St.Giles', or the quaint smal-
ler one, which still stands in the Canongate. The anecdotes of prisoners are numerous. Here is one lighter
and less grimy than the bulk. When Principal Carstares was warded in the Castle in 1685, a charming
youth of twelve years, son of Erskine of Cambo, came
to his prison daily, and brought him fruit to relieve
the monotony of the fare, and what to a scholar was
just as essential, pen, ink, and paper. He ran his errands and sat by the open grating for hours. After the
revolution "the Cardinal" was all-powerful in Scots
matters; he did not forget his young friend, and procured him the post of Lord Lyon King at Arms, but
the family were out in the '15' and the dignity was
forfeit. You gather from this pleasing story that prison
life in Edinburgh had its alleviations, also escapes were
numerous. In 1607, Lord Maxwell was shut up in the
Castle, and there also was Sir James Macdonald from
the Hebrides. They made the keepers drunk, got their
swords from them by a trick, and locked them safely
away. The porter made a show of resistance. "False
knave," cried Maxwell, "open the yett, or I shall hew
thee in bladds" (pieces), and he would have done it

you believe! They got out of the Castle, climbed over the town wall at the West Port, and hid in the suburbs. Macdonald could not get rid of his fetters, and was ignominiously taken in a dung-hill where he was lurking; Maxwell made for the Border on a swift horse, and remained at large, in spite of the angry proclamations of the King. James Grant of Carron had committed so many outrages on Speyside that the authorities, little as they recked of what went on "benorth the mont," determined to "gar ane devil ding another." Certain men, probably of the same reputation as himself, had undertaken to bring him in dead or alive. He and his fellows were in fact captured. The latter were speedily executed, but he was kept for two years in the Castle, and you cannot now guess wherefor. One day he observed from his prison window a former neighbour, Grant of Tomnavoulen, passing by. "What news from Speyside?" asked the captive. "None very particular," was the reply; "the best is that the country is rid of you." "Perhaps we shall meet again," quoth James cheerfully. Presently his wife conveyed to him what purported to be a cask of butter, in fact it held some very serviceable rope, and so in the night of the 15th October 1632 the prisoner lowered himself over the Castle wall, and was soon again perambulating Speyside, where, you guess, his reception was of a mixed description.

Among the escapes of the eighteenth century I pick out two, both from the Heart of Midlothian. One was that of Catherine Nairn in 1766. She had poisoned her husband, and was the mistress of his brother. She was brought to Leith from the north in an open boat, and shut up in the Tolbooth. The brother, who had been an officer in the army, was executed in the Grassmarket, but judgment was respited in the case of the lady on the plea of pregnancy. She escaped by changing clothes with the midwife, who was supposed to be suffering from severe toothache. She howled so loudly as she went out, that she almost overdid the part. The keeper cursed her for a howling old Jezebel, and wished he might never see her again. Possibly he was in the business himself. The lady had various exciting adventures before she reached a safe hiding-place, almost blundered, in fact, into the house of her enemies. She finally left the town in a postchaise, whose driver had orders, if he were pursued, to drive into the sea and drown his fare as if by accident, and thus make a summary end of one whose high-placed relatives were only assisting her for the sake of the family name. The levity of her conduct all through excited the indignation and alarm of those who had charge of her; perhaps she was hysterical. She got well off to France, where she married a gentleman of good position, and ended " virtuous and fortunate." This seems the usual fate of the lady criminal; either her experience enables her to capture easily the male victim, or her adventures give her an unholy attraction in the eyes of the multitude. She is rarely an inveterate law-breaker, as she learns from bitter experience that honesty and virtue are the more agreeable policies. Other than wealthy and well-connected criminals escaped. In 1783 James Hay lay in the condemned hold for burglary. Hay and his father filled the keeper drunk. Old Hay, by imitating the drawl of the keeper uttering the stereo-

IN THE CITY OF EDINBURGH

typed formula of 'turn your hand,' procured the opening of the outer door, and the lad was off like a hare
into the night. With a fine instinct of the romantic he
hid himself in " Bluidy Mackenzie's " tomb, held as
haunted by all Edinburgh. He was an " auld callant "
of Heriot's Hospital, which rises just by old Greyfriars', and the boys supplied him with food in the night-
time. When the hue and cry had quieted down, he
crawled out, escaped, and in due time, it was whispered,
began a new life under other skies. Probably the ghostly reputation of that stately mausoleum in Greyfriars'
Churchyard was more firmly established than ever.
What could be the cause of those audible midnight
mutterings, if not the restless ghost of the persecuting
Lord Advocate?

As drinking was *the* staple amusement of old Edinburgh, " the Ladies " was naturally the most popular
toast: a stock one was, " All absent friends, all ships at
sea, and the auld pier at Leith." This last was not so
ridiculous as might be supposed, for it was famous in
Scott's song, *teste* the only Robin, to name but him,
and Scots law, for it was one of the stock places at which
fugitives were cited, as witness godly Mr. Alexander
Peden himself. The toastmakers were hard put to it
sometimes for sentiments. A well-known story relates
how one unfortunate gentleman could think of nothing better than "the reflection of the mune on the calm
bosom o' the lake." As absurd is the story of the antiquary who sat at his potations in a tavern in the old
Post Office Close on the night of 8th February 1787.
Suddenly he burst into tears; he had just remembered
on that very day " twa hunner year syne Queen Mary

279

was beheaded." His plight was scarce so bad as that of the shadow or hanger-on of Driver clerk to the famous Andrew Crosbie, otherwise Counsellor Pleydell. The name of this satellite was Patrick Nimmo. He was once mistaken, when found dead drunk in the morning after the King's birthday, for the effigy of Johnnie Wilkes which had been so loyally and thoroughly kicked about by the mob on the previous evening. One of his cronies wrote or rather spoke his epitaph in this fashion : "Lord, is he dead at last! Weel, that's strange indeed. I drank sax half mutchkins wi' him doun at the Hens only three nichts syn! Bring us a biscuit wi' the next gill, mistress. Rab was aye fond o' bakes." Of course the scene was a tavern, and the memory of poor Rob was at least an excuse for another dram.

This is not very genial merrymaking, but geniality is never the characteristic note of Scots humour from the earliest times. In 1575 the Regent Morton kept a fool named Patrick Bonney, who, seeing his master pestered by a crowd of beggars, advised him to throw them all into one fire. Even Morton was horrified. "Oh," said the jester coolly, "if all these poor people were burned you would soon make more poor people out of the rich." No wonder the old-time fools were frequently whipped. The precentor and the beadle were in some ways successors of the old-time fool. Thomas Neil fulfilled the first office in old Greyfriars' in the time of Erskine and Robertson. He could turn out a very passable coffin, and did some small business that way which made him look forward to the decease of friends with a not unmixed sorrow. "Hech,

WILLIAM SMELLIE

From an Engraving after George White

IN THE CITY OF EDINBURGH

man, butye smell sair o'earth," was his cheerful greeting to a sick friend. One forenoon the then Nisbet of Dirleton met him in the High Street rather tipsy. Even the dissipation of old Edinburgh had its laws, and the country gentleman pointed out that the precentor's position made such conduct improper. "I just tak' it when I can get it," said Neil, with a leer.

All the wits of old Edinburgh hit hard. Alexander Douglas, W.S., was known as " dirty Douglas." He spoke about going to a ball, but he did not wish it reported that he attended such assemblies. "Why, Douglas," said Patrick Robertson, "put on a well-brushed coat and a clean shirt and nobody will know you." Andrew Johnson, a teacher of Greek and Hebrew, combined in himself many of the characteristics of Dominie Sampson. He averred that Job never was a schoolmaster, otherwise we should not have heard so much about his patience. He was on principle against the sweeping of rooms. "Cannot you let the dust lie quietly ? " he would say. " Why wear out the boards rubbing them so?" He wished to marry the daughter of rich parents though he had no money himself. The father objected his want of means. "Oh dear, that is nothing," was the confident answer. "You have plenty."

The stage occupied a very small place in the history of old Edinburgh. We know that a company from London were there in the time of James VI. It is just possible that Shakespeare may have been one of its members, and again when the Duke of York, afterwards James VII. and II., was in Edinburgh a company of English actors were at his court. Dryden has various satiric lines on their performances, in which he has some more or less passable gibes at that ancient theme, so sadly out of date in our own day, the poverty of the Scots nation. It is but scraps of stage anecdotes that you pick up. Once when a barber was shaving Henry Erskine he received the news that his wife had presented him with a son. He forthwith decreed that the child should be called Henry Erskine Johnson. The boy afterwards became an actor, and was known as the Scottish Roscius; his favourite part was young Norval—of course from *Douglas.* The audience beheld with sympathy or derision the venerable author blubbering in the boxes, and declaring that only now had his conception of the character been realised.

At the time of the French Revolution one or two of the Edinburgh sympathisers attempted a poor imitation of French methods. A decent shopkeeper rejoicing to be known as "Citizen M." had put up at "The Black Bull." He told the servant girl to call him in time for the Lauder coach. "But mind ye," says he, "when ye chap at the door, at no hand maun ye say 'Mr. M., its time to rise,' but ye maun say, 'Ceetizan, equal rise." The girl had forgotten the name by the morning, and could only call out, "Equal rise." Of one like him it was reported, according to the story of an old lady, that he "erekit a gulliteen in his back court and gulliteen'd a' his hens on't."

The silly conceited fool is not rare anywhere, but only occasionally are his sayings or doings amusing. Harry Erskine's elder brother the Earl of Buchan was as well known in Edinburgh as himself. He certainly had brains, but was very pompous and puffed up.

IN THE CITY OF EDINBURGH

When Sir David Brewster was a young man and only beginning to make his name a paper of his on optics was highly spoken of. "You see, I revised it," said the Earl with sublime conceit. Asked if he had been at the church of St. George's in the forenoon, "No," he said, "but my mits are left on the front pew of the gallery. When the congregation see them they are pleased to think that the Earl of Buchan is there." He believed himself irresistible with the other sex. He thus addressed a handsome young lady: "Good-bye, my dear, but pray remember that Margaret, Countess of Buchan, is not immortal." An article in the *Edinburgh Review* once incurred his displeasure, so he laid the offending number down in the hall, ordered his footmen to open the front door of his house in George Street, and then solemnly kicked out the offending journal. When Scott was ill, Lockhart tells us the Earl composed a discourse to be read at his funeral and brought it down to read to the sick man, but he was denied admittance.

The Scots have always been noted for taking themselves seriously. *Nemo me impune lacessit* is no empty boast. In Charles the Second's time the Bishop of St. Asaph had written a treatise to show that the antiquity of the royal race was but a devout imagination; that the century and more of monarchs of the royal line of Fergus were for the most part mere myth and shadow. Sir George Mackenzie grimly hinted that had my Lord been a Scots subject, it might have been his unpleasant duty to indict him for high treason.

An earlier offender felt the full rigour of the law. In 1618 Thomas Ross had gone from the north to study at Oxford. He wrote a libel on the Scots nation and pinned it to the door of St. Mary's Church. He was good enough to except the King and a few others, but the remaining Caledonians were roundly, not to say scurrilously, rated. Possibly the thing was popular with those about him, but the King presently discovered in it a deep design to stir up the English to massacre the Scots. Ross was seized and packed off to Edinburgh for trial. Too late the unfortunate man saw his error or his danger. His plea of partial temporary insanity availed him not, his right hand was struck off and then he was beheaded and quartered, his head was stuck on the Netherbow Port and his hand at the West Port. To learn him for his tricks, no doubt!

A great feature of old Edinburgh from the days of Allan Ramsay to those of Sir Walter Scott was the Clubs. These, you will understand, were not at all like the clubs of to-day, of which the modern city possesses a good number, political and social—institutions that inhabit large and stately premises with all the usual properties. The old Edinburgh club was a much simpler affair. It was a more or less formal set who met in a favourite tavern, ate, drank, and talked for some hours and then went their respective ways. Various writers have preserved the quaint names of many of these clubs, and given us a good deal of information on the subject. When you think of the famous men that were members, the talk, you believe, was worth hearing, but the memory of it has well-nigh perished, even as the speakers themselves, and bottle wit is as evanescent as that which produced it. The extant jokes seem to us of the thinnest. The Cape Club was named, it is said, from the difficulty one of its members found in reaching home. When he got out at the Netherbow Port he had to make a sharp turn to the left, and so along Leith Wynd. He was confused with talk and liquor, and he found some difficulty in "doubling the cape," as it was called. Perhaps the obstacle lay on the other side of the Netherbow. The keeper had a keen eye for small profits, and was none too hasty in making the way plain either out of or into the city. Allan Ramsay felt the difficulty when he and his fellows lingered too long at Luckie Wood's—

> "Which aften cost us mony a gill
> To Aikenhead."

Of this club Fergusson the poet was a member. Is it not commemorated in his verse? Fergusson was catholic in his tastes. Johnnie Dowie's in Libberton's Wynd has been already mentioned in these pages. Here was to be met Paton the antiquary, and here in later days came Robert Burns, but indeed who did not at some time or other frequent this famous tavern? noted for its Nor' Loch trout and its ale—that justly lauded Edinburgh ale of Archibald Younger, whose brewery was in Croft-an-righ, hard by Holyrood. The Crochallan Fencibles which met in the house of Dawney Douglas in the Anchor Close is chiefly known for its memories of Burns. Here he had his famous wit contest with Smellie, his printer, whose printing office was in the same close, so that neither Burns nor he had far to go after the compounding or correcting of proofs. We picture Smellie to ourselves as a rough old Scot, unshaven and unshorn, with rough old clothes —his " caustic wit was biting rude," and Burns con-

285

fessed its power. The poet praises the warmth and benevolence of his heart, and we need not rake in the ashes to discover his long-forgotten failings. William Smellie was another William Nicol. There was a touch of romance about the name of the club. It meant in Gaelic Colin's cattle; there was a mournful Gaelic air and song and tradition attached to it. Colin's wife had died young, but returned from the spirit world, and was seen on summer evenings, a scarce mortal shape, tending his cattle. Perhaps some antiquarian Scot or learned German will some day delight the curious with a monograph on the word Crochallan, but as yet the legend awaits investigation. Some of the clubs were " going strong " in the early years of the nineteenth century. There was a Friday Club founded in June 1803 which met at various places in the New Town. Brougham made the punch, and it was fearfully and wonderfully made. Lord Cockburn is its historian. He has some caustic sentences, as when he talks of Abercrombie's " contemptible stomach," and says George Cranstoun, Lord Corehouse, " is one of the very few persons who have not been made stupid by being made a Judge." This Friday Club was imitated in the Bonally Friday Club, which met twice a year at Bonally House, where Lord Cockburn lived. It was in its prime about 1842. Candidates for admission were locked up in a dark room well provided with stools and chairs—not to sit on, but to tumble over! The members dressed themselves up in skins of tigers and leopards and what not, and each had a penny trumpet. Among these the candidate was brought in blindfold, had first to listen to a solemn, pompous address," then the bandage was removed and a spongeful of water dashed in his face. In a moment the wild beasts capered about, the masked actors danced around him, and the penny trumpets were lustily blown. The whole scene was calculated to strike awe and amazement into the mind of the new member." It would require a good deal of witty talk to make up for such things. I shall not pursue this tempting but disappointing subject further. I have touched sufficiently on the proceedings of the Edinburgh clubs.

Here let fall the curtain.

INDEX

289

INDEX

INDEX

291

INDEX

INDEX

SONGS & POEMS OF BURNS

With 36 fine Illustrations in Colour by eminent artists. Quarto, 600 pp., buckram, **10s. 6d. net**; printed in fine rag paper, and bound in fine vellum, **21s. net.**

A handsome presentation edition of The Songs and Poems of Burns, *containing an appreciation of the poet by Lord Rosebery. While many eminent artists have painted some of their finest pictures in depicting scenes from Burns, no attempt has previously been made to collect these within the bounds of an edition of his works. This new edition contains most of the finest of these pictures reproduced in colour, and forms a most admirable gift-book. The text is printed in black and red, with ample margins, and no expense has been spared to make the work a finite presentation edition. It may be added that everything in connection with the production of the work is of purely Scottish manufacture.*

SONGS OF THE WORLD

Fcap. 8vo, **2s. 6d. net**; in velvet Persian, **3s. 6d. net.**

In this series, attractively illustrated in colour and produced for presentation purposes, are included such poets and song writers as may not have reached the very first rank, but whose work is worthy of much wider recognition.

1. SONGS OF LADY NAIRNE

With 8 Illustrations in Colour of popular Scottish songs by J. CRAWHALL, K. HALSWELLE, G. OGILVY REID, R.S.A., and eminent Scottish Artists.

2. THE SCOTS POEMS OF ROBERT FERGUSSON

With 8 Illustrations in Colour by MONRO S. ORR.

3. SONGS & POEMS OF THE ETTRICK SHEPHERD

With 8 Illustrations in Colour by JESSIE M. KING.

T. N. FOULIS, PUBLISHER, 91 GREAT RUSSELL STREET LONDON, W.C.; 15 FREDERICK STREET, EDINBURGH

THE LIFE & CHARACTER SERIES

THE KIRK AND ITS WORTHIES

By NICHOLAS DICKSON. Edited by D. MACLEOD MALLOCH. With 16 Illustrations in Colour, depicting old Scottish life, by well-known artists. Extra crown 8vo, 340 pp., buckram, **5s. net**; leather, **7s. 6d. net**; vellum, **10s. 6d. net.**

MANSIE WAUCH

Life in a Scottish Village a hundred years ago. By D. M. MOIR. New Edition. With 16 Illustrations in Colour by C. MARTIN HARDIE, R.S.A. Extra crown 8vo, 360 pages, buckram, **5s. net**; leather, **7s. 6d. net**; vellum, **10s. 6d. net.**

Mansie Wauch stands among the great classics of Scottish life, such as Dean Ramsay and Annals of the Parish. It faithfully portrays the village life of Scotland at the beginning of last century in a humorous and whimsical vein.

ANNALS OF THE PARISH

By JOHN GALT. With 16 Illustrations in Colour by HENRY W. KERR, R.S.A. Extra crown 8vo, 316 pp., buckram, **5s. net**; leather, **7s. 6d. net**; vellum, **10s. 6d. net.**

" Certainly no such picture of the life of Scotland during the closing years of the 18th century has ever been written. He shows us with vivid directness and reality what like were the quiet lives of leal folk, burghers, and ministers, and country lairds a hundred years ago."—S. R. CROCKETT.

SCOTTISH LIFE & CHARACTER

By DEAN RAMSAY. New Edition, entirely reset. Containing 16 Illustrations in Colour by HENRY W. KERR, R.S.A. Extra crown 8vo, 400 pp., buckram, **5s. net**; leather, **7s. 6d. net**; vellum, **10s. 6d. net.**

This great storehouse of Scottish humour is undoubtedly " the best book on Scottish life and character ever written." This edition owes much of its success to the superb illustrations of Mr. H. W. Kerr, R.S.A.

THE BOOK OF EDINBURGH ANECDOTE

By FRANCIS WATT, Joint-Author of "Scotland of To-day," etc. etc. With 32 Portraits in Collotype. Extra crown 8vo, 312 pp., buckram, **5s. net**; leather, **7s. 6d. net**; parchment, **10s. 6d. net.**

THE BOOK OF GLASGOW ANECDOTE

By D. MACLEOD MALLOCH. With a Frontispiece in Colour and 32 Portraits in Collotype. Extra crown 8vo, 400 pp., buckram, **5s. net**; leather, **7s. 6d. net**; parchment, **10s. 6d. net.**

T. N. FOULIS, PUBLISHER, 91 GREAT RUSSELL STREET
LONDON, W.C.; 15 FREDERICK STREET, EDINBURGH

THE LITERARY MEMOIR SERIES

THE R. L. STEVENSON ORIGINALS

By E. B. SIMPSON, Author of "R. L. Stevenson's Early Edinburgh Days," "Sir James Y. Simpson." With 4 Illustrations in Colour, and 26 mounted Illustrations in Collotype. Extra crown 8vo, 260 pp., buckram, **6s. net**; vellum, **10s. 6d. net.**

THE CHARLES DICKENS ORIGINALS

By EDWIN PUGH, Author of "Charles Dickens, the Apostle of the People," "The Enchantress," "Tony Drum," etc. With 30 mounted Illustrations in Collotype. Extra crown 8vo, 340 pp., buckram, **6s. net**; vellum, **10s. 6d. net.**

THE SIR WALTER SCOTT ORIGINALS

Being an Account of Notables and Worthies, the Originals of Characters in the Waverley Novels. By W. S. CROCKETT. Frontispiece in Colour, and 44 Illustrations in Collotype. Extra crown 8vo, 448 pp., buckram, **6s. net**; vellum, **10s. 6d. net.**

THE RIVER OF LONDON

By HILAIRE BELLOC, M.A., Author of "The Path to Rome," "The Historic Thames," "The Old Road," etc. etc. With 16 Illustrations in Colour by JOHN MUIRHEAD. Extra crown 8vo, 200 pp., buckram, **5s. net**; leather, **7s. 6d. net**; vellum, **10s. 6d. net.**

DR. JOHNSON'S MRS. THRALE

Being the Autobiography of Mrs. Thrale, the friend and confidante of Dr. Samuel Johnson. With 27 Portraits in Collotype by Sir JOSHUA REYNOLDS, and other Illustrations. Extra crown 8vo, 368 pp., buckram, **6s. net**; vellum, **10s. 6d. net.**

AUTOBIOGRAPHY OF
DR. ALEXANDER CARLYLE

of INVERESK (1722-1805). Edited by J. HILL BURTON. New Edition, with many additional Notes, Frontispiece in Colour, and 32 Portraits in Photogravure. Extra crown 8vo, 600 pp., buckram, **6s. net**; in vellum, **10s. 6d. net.**

MEMORIALS OF HIS TIME

By LORD COCKBURN. New Edition, with many additional Notes and Preface. With 12 Portraits in Colour by Sir HENRY RAEBURN, and other Illustrations. Extra crown 8vo, 480 pp., buckram, **6s. net**; vellum, **10s. 6d. net.**

T. N. FOULIS, PUBLISHER, 91 GREAT RUSSELL STREET LONDON, W.C.; 15 FREDERICK STREET, EDINBURGH

THE LIFE & CHARACTER SERIES

THE KIRK AND ITS WORTHIES

By NICHOLAS DICKSON. Edited by D. MACLEOD MALLOCH. With 16 Illustrations in Colour, depicting old Scottish life, by well-known artists. Extra crown 8vo, 340 pp., buckram, **5s. net**; leather, **7s. 6d. net**; vellum, **10s. 6d. net.**

MANSIE WAUCH

Life in a Scottish Village a hundred years ago. By D. M. MOIR. New Edition. With 16 Illustrations in Colour by C. MARTIN HARDIE, R.S.A. Extra crown 8vo, 360 pages, buckram, **5s. net**; leather, **7s. 6d. net**; vellum, **10s. 6d. net.**

Mansie Wauch stands among the great classics of Scottish life, such as Dean Ramsay and Annals of the Parish. It faithfully portrays the village life of Scotland at the beginning of last century in a humorous and whimsical vein.

ANNALS OF THE PARISH

By JOHN GALT. With 16 Illustrations in Colour by HENRY W. KERR, R.S.A. Extra crown 8vo, 316 pp., buckram, **5s. net**; leather, **7s. 6d. net**; vellum, **10s. 6d. net.**

" Certainly no such picture of the life of Scotland during the closing years of the 18th century has ever been written. He shows us with vivid directness and reality what like were the quiet lives of leal folk, burghers, and ministers, and country lairds a hundred years ago."—S. R. CROCKETT.

SCOTTISH LIFE & CHARACTER

By DEAN RAMSAY. New Edition, entirely reset. Containing 16 Illustrations in Colour by HENRY W. KERR, R.S.A. Extra crown 8vo, 400 pp., buckram, **5s. net**; leather, **7s. 6d. net**; vellum, **10s. 6d. net.**

This great storehouse of Scottish humour is undoubtedly " the best book on Scottish life and character ever written." This edition owes much of its success to the superb illustrations of Mr. H. W. Kerr, R.S.A.

THE BOOK OF EDINBURGH ANECDOTE

By FRANCIS WATT, Joint-Author of "Scotland of To-day," etc. etc. With 32 Portraits in Collotype. Extra crown 8vo, 312 pp., buckram, **5s. net**; leather, **7s. 6d. net**; parchment, **10s. 6d. net.**

THE BOOK OF GLASGOW ANECDOTE

By D. MACLEOD MALLOCH. With a Frontispiece in Colour and 32 Portraits in Collotype. Extra crown 8vo, 400 pp., buckram, **5s. net**; leather, **7s. 6d. net**; parchment, **10s. 6d. net.**

T. N. FOULIS, PUBLISHER, 91 GREAT RUSSELL STREET LONDON, W.C.; 15 FREDERICK STREET, EDINBURGH

THE LIFE & CHARACTER SERIES

THE ENGLISH CHARACTER

By SPENCER LEIGH HUGHES, M.P., "Sub-Rosa" of the *Daily News and Leader*. With 16 Illustrations in Colour, depicting types of English Character by FREDERICK GARDNER. Extra crown 8vo, 280 pp., buckram, **5s. net**; leather, **7s. 6d. net**; vellum, **10s. 6d. net.**

THE LIGHTER SIDE OF IRISH LIFE

By GEORGE A. BIRMINGHAM, Author of "Spanish Gold," etc. With 16 Illustrations in Colour by HENRY W. KERR, R.S.A. New Edition. Extra crown 8vo, 288 pp., buckram, **5s. net**; velvet Persian, **7s. 6d. net**; vellum, **10s. 6d. net.**

ENGLISH COUNTRY LIFE

By WALTER RAYMOND, Author of "The Book of Simple Delights," etc. With 16 Illustrations in Colour by WILFRED BALL, R.E. Extra crown 8vo, 462 pp., buckram, **5s. net**; velvet Persian, **7s. 6d. net**; vellum, **10s. 6d. net.**

Mr. Raymond, in this book, describes English country life as it still is in the hamlets of to-day, just as a hundred years ago. His well-known touch sympathetically lights up the rustic character, its humour, and its simplicity. Mr. Wilfred Ball's illustrations are a notable feature of this interesting work, which will be one of the best gift-books of the season

ENGLISH LIFE AND CHARACTER

By MARY E. MITFORD, Author of "Our Village." With 16 Pictures in Colour by STANHOPE A. FORBES, R.A., of typical scenes of English rural life. Extra crown 8vo, 350 pages, buckram, **5s. net**; velvet Persian, **7s. 6d. net**; vellum, **10s. 6d. net.**

To every lover of old English life this will prove a most attractive presentation book. The fine colouring of the artist's famous pictures will appeal strongly to all admirers of the real charm of quiet English rural life and character.

IRISH LIFE AND CHARACTER

By Mrs. S. C. HALL. Containing 16 Reproductions in Colour from the famous paintings of ERSKINE NICOL, R.A. Extra crown 8vo, 330 pp., buckram, **5s. net**; velvet Persian, **7s. 6d. net**; vellum, **10s. 6d. net.**

The finest of Erskine Nicol's inimitable and world-famous pictures of Irish life appropriately illustrate Mrs. S. C. Hall's well-known tales, and charmingly depict the full wit and humour of the true Irish character.

T. N. FOULIS, PUBLISHER, 91 GREAT RUSSELL STREET LONDON, W.C.; 15 FREDERICK STREET, EDINBURGH

R O M A N T I C   L I V E S

A series of monographs, handsomely and artistically produced, of the lives of such beautiful and famous women and chivalrous men, whose careers provide to the present-day reader possibly the most fascinating stories in history. Each volume is written by a recognised authority on his subject, and contains illustrations in colour and in imitation photogravure of the best portraits and pictures relating to the period.

With many Illustrations in Colour, in Gravure-tint, and in Collotype. Crown 8vo, buckram, with mounted illustrations, **5s. net** ; bound in velvet Persian and boxed, **7s. 6d. net** ; vellum, **10s. 6d. net.**

NELL GWYN

By CECIL CHESTERTON. With 4 Illustrations in Colour and 16 in Gravure-tint.

The story of Nell Gwyn, who won the heart of King Charles II, is presented in this volume by Mr. Chesterton in a most attractive and readable manner.

LADY HAMILTON

By E. HALLAM MOORHOUSE, Author of " Nelson's Lady Hamilton." With 4 Illustrations in Colour and 19 in Gravure-tint.

Emma Hamilton is one of the most picturesque feminine figures on the stage of history by reason of the great beauty which caused her to play such a conspicuous part in the events of Europe in her day.

MARIE ANTOINETTE

By FRANCIS BICKLEY, Author of "King's Favourites." With 4 Illustrations in Colour and 16 in Gravure-tint.

Marie Antoinette stands out as one of the tragic figures of history. How her brilliant, extravagant court and her light-hearted intrigues culminated in the storm of the French Revolution, and her tragic end on the scaffold, is a most fascinating study.

MARY, QUEEN OF SCOTS

By HILDA T. SKAE, Author of " The Life of Mary, Queen of Scots." With 16 Illustrations in Colour and 8 Portraits in Collotype.

PRINCE CHARLIE

By WILLIAM POWER. With 16 Illustrations in Colour and 8 Portraits in Collotype.

T. N. FOULIS, PUBLISHER, 91 GREAT RUSSELL STREET LONDON, W.C.; 15 FREDERICK STREET, EDINBURGH

Lightning Source UK Ltd.
Milton Keynes UK
UKHW011347220219
337800UK00009B/1658/P